*The History Lesson* (1989)
*Oil on canvas 120 x 120 x 120cm*
*Cold Spring Harbour Laboratory, USA.*

CITIZEN ARTIST

CIARAN CARTY

Zeus Medea

Published in 2010 by Zeus Medea Publishing, Harbour House, Howth, Co. Dublin, Ireland.

www.zeuscreative.ie

Design by Paul Rattigan.

Book printing and production by Castuera, Spain.

ISBN 978-0-9525376-1-8

*Elgin Road, Ballsbridge, 2009.
This leafy suburb has hardly changed
since the 1950s.*

# Preface

*Robert Ballagh: Citizen Artist* is an attempt to portray Robert Ballagh in the manner of one of his paintings. It is a sequel to my book *Robert Ballagh* which was published by Vincent Browne at Magill in 1986, but is now long out of print and something of a collector's item. *Citizen Artist* follows Ballagh's life and art forward to the present but with echoes of what went before: the hope is that the essentials of his early years will be implicit in the narrative.

When I first met Robert in 1978, we found we had so many experiences in common it was as if we'd known each other from childhood. We were both born in the same month – Robert on September 22, 1943 – but six years apart, and we both grew up in Ballsbridge, a residential area developed in the late 19th century to provide the ruling ascendency classes with an environment appropriate to what they might find in England. Its tall, terraced Victorian houses were by the 1940s and 1950s mostly partitioned into flats or offices, and the red post boxes with royal insignia were painted over in patriotic green. Only the street names around where Ballagh lived in a rented flat on Elgin Road remained as reminders of the colonial past: Lansdowne Road, Prince of Wales Terrace, Serpentine Avenue, Churchill Terrace, Waterloo Road, Clyde Road, Wellington Road.

*Top: The High School Rugby team 1928-29.
Robert Ballagh senior sitting on ground, left.*

*Above: St. Michael's School Rugby team 1954-55.
Robert Ballagh junior standing, extreme right.*

We attended the same private schools, first Miss Meredith's 'School For Young Ladies' on Pembroke Road, and later Blackrock College, established in 1860 by the French Holy Ghost Fathers to meet the need for Catholic secondary schooling following Catholic Emancipation: before that Catholic schools were precluded from public funding on the grounds that they were denominational, and the state refused to recognise their courses. Blackrock set out to show that given the same opportunities, Catholic students could compete as equals in exams. It was soon fielding rugby teams capable of beating the English elite at their own game, but Professor Mahaffy of Trinity College dismissed the new Catholic schools as "institutions calculated to produce saints perhaps, but not scholars". Blackrock, which numbered among its teachers Eamonn De Valera and

the future Archbishop of Dublin, John Charles McQuaid, saw its role as shaping the new sovereign Ireland, an ambition that failed to impress Ballagh. He was frequently in trouble for breaches in conduct and deportment. "I had an impulse from an early age to take the opposite view to the established position on anything. I suppose I've always been a natural dissident."

Cinema was a dominant cultural influence of his childhood and mine: reality perceived in terms of photographic images. It offered glimpses of worlds excitingly different to our own. Every Saturday he queued for the four-penny rush at the local Ritz Cinema, popularly known as 'The Shack'. He'd watch for hours the man doing the hand-lettering on the billboard advertising the week's programme, fascinated by his craftsman-like skill. Films would shape his way of seeing as a painter: some of his early paintings were unconsciously shaped in the format of the academy scale of the screen on which he saw his first pictures.

Ballagh has always made things. He used put on puppet shows for his school friends. "It was the making of the thing that really appealed to me. The actual performance didn't matter that much." At art classes in Blackrock, taught by the figurative painter John Coyle, he conceived the idea of portraying motion by constructing from soldered tin a running figure which he called *The Rapid Man*. "I soldered on little spikes which I called arcs of motion. The whole thing looked like those multiple-image photographs of a golfer's swing."

His parents – his mother came from a well-to-do Catholic family, his father was Presbyterian but converted to Catholicism, part of an easy-going tolerance that was to make a success of their marriage – were, like mine, members of the

*Self Portrait* (1959)
Oil on board. 38 x 26cm.
Private Collection.

nearby Royal Dublin Society (it dates back to 1731) where he was free to roam through its ancient oak-floored library, lined to the ceiling with shelves of art books: from an early age he was familiar with reproductions of many of the great paintings and sculptures of Western civilisation. He would try to imitate his favourites and showed a talent for pastiche. He remembers doing a Louis le Brocquy, which his mother showed proudly to friends. At 16 he painted a self-portrait which anticipated elements of the stylised realism he later adopted. Nearly all his reading was visual: he collected Marvel and DC comics, attracted by their American feel, which reinforced the cultural conditioning he was getting from movies. He never missed an issue of the *Eagle* with its dramatic airbrushed drawings: years later the same flat finish was to show in his paintings.

*The Ritz Cinema was converted into the Oscar Theatre in the 1980s. It is now a Sikh Temple.*

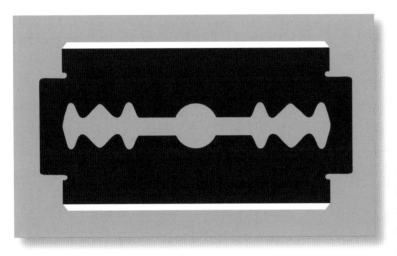

*Blade* (1967)
*Acrylic on canvas. 92 x 183cm.*
*Collection: The Arts Council.*

*Torso* (1967)
*Aluminium construction. 65 x 46cm.*

*Robert Ballagh playing bass guitar
with The Chessmen.*

Although he dropped out of architecture at Bolton Street College of Technology to join a rock band – his mother had ruled out Coyle's suggestion that he might take up art – the influence of his lecturer Robin Walker, who had worked with Le Corbusier in France and Mies van der Rohe in Chicago, stuck with him. He picked up the Bauhaus message first-hand: form follows function. There had to be logic and a reason behind everything you did: the principle came first. He was attracted to the clean look of things, the neatness of the hand-painted movie posters or the tidy finish of his model aeroplanes. "I'm not a person for the primitive gesture. The precise way of doing things has always been a constant in my life. It is much easier to dash something off. But my nature has never let me do that." All his work as a painter has been designed according to scaled architectural plans. Everything is calculated and worked out using tracing paper and T-square on a drawing board. Nothing is left to chance.

His brief but glorious career as bass-guitarist with The Chessmen, a popular show-band managed by budding impresario Noel Pearson, took him touring all over Ireland and England. "In Cricklewood or Hammersmith you could tell the year someone had left Ireland by the tune requested. The GAA results were read out at the break. They were an abandoned generation of emigrants." Up North the band was booked at both Protestant and Catholic halls – "always careful to check beforehand whether to play the Queen or the Soldier's Song". By 20 he was already earning £100 a week and driving a flashy Ford Corsair. "But I could tell that I hadn't the makings of a true musician. If you're going to give your life to music you have to be able to grow into other forms of music. I'd a pretty shrewd idea I didn't have anything like that in me."

Rock music was all about attitude. You had to know what you were doing and you had to know where and what it related to. A painter friend Micheal Farrell, back from New York preaching the gospel of hard-edge abstraction, hired him ("because I could draw a straight line") to assist on two huge acrylic murals commissioned for the National Bank in Suffolk Street. He quickly picked up the technique of blending paint with badger brushes and using masking tape and realised modern art was just a matter of attitude, too. He made small aluminium constructions of an erotic female torso and a pinball machine, sprayed with cellulose paint, which were promptly accepted by the Irish Exhibition of Living Art. An acrylic razor blade, a clever response to New York critic Clement Greenberg's theory of painting as simply a flat two-dimensional surface, was bought by the Arts Council.

Through these early attempts at pop art and his reading of Che Guevara's essay 'Man and Socialism in Cuba' he arrived at the idea of merging social realism with the brash techniques of American advertising layout. Combining acrylic paint on canvas

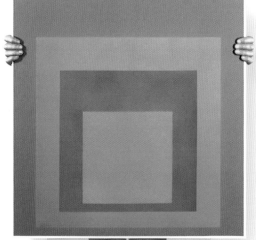

*Gordon Lambert* (1971)
Acrylic and silkscreen on canvas. 180 x 92cm.
Collection: The Irish Museum of Modern Art.

and plywood with a silkscreen treatment of photographs taken from newspapers and magazines, he produced a series of multiple images of Civil Rights marches, refugees, firing squads and a burning monk that gave stunningly direct expression to the radical concerns of the late 1960s.

The marrying of abstract hard-edge techniques to simple figurative ideas led him to a style of painting that was an honest response to his own experience – "an artist can only be of his own time, he has to play with the cards he's dealt" – but also prompted him to look more closely at the tradition of political art. He found in Goya's *Third of May*, Delacroix's *Liberty at the Barricades* and David's *Rape of the Sabines* inspiration for a series of large-scale versions reflecting the burgeoning conflict in the North: his forceful replication of the originals in hard-edge, black-outline pop language gave startling contemporary immediacy to their historical content.

While Ballagh clearly had the attitude to win recognition as "an exceptionally gifted, thoughtful young artist" (to quote Conor Cruise O'Brien opening his first exhibition), he was only too aware that he was a beginner in terms of the craft of painting. He had to do his learning in public, turning his limitations to advantage. When he accepted a commission to paint a portrait of businessman Gordon Lambert, a leading collector of contemporary Irish art, he found he hadn't yet developed the figurative skills to capture a satisfactory likeness. He decided to silkscreen a photograph of Lambert's face, a pop device which in fact enhanced the impact of the image. Lambert was depicted in a businessman's suit but holding a large Josef Albers abstract. The figure was cut out rather than framed and the hands, gripping the edge of the canvas, were modelled in three-dimensional form: which got around the fact that Ballagh hadn't yet mastered a technique for painting hands.

The concept of the Lambert portrait led to a series of pictures of people looking at paintings – their backs to the viewer, to get around the difficulty with faces – which over the next four years established his international reputation with sell-out exhibitions in Switzerland and Belgium. The series gradually developed into his own personal exploration of modernism that left him disillusioned by the sterility of its dogma of art-for-art's sake.

Having grown up in a neighbourhood and a city richly pervaded by literary awareness, he was itching to say more than purely formal things with the

*View of Robert Ballagh's exhibition in the David Hendriks Gallery in 1972.*

visual vocabulary he had acquired. Among his neighbours were Brendan Behan on Anglesea Road and Patrick Kavanagh on Pembroke Road. WB Yeats was born a few streets away. He used play on Sandymount Strand where James Joyce once strolled. Modernist painting had become an aesthetic cul-de-sac where neither literary, nor social and historical references were admitted, and the classical art that preceded it was deemed to be irrelevant to its concerns.

He painted a massive mural dealing with the concepts of time and memory in Lawrence Sterne's novel *The Life and Opinions of Tristram Shandy, Gentleman*, and a series of paintings celebrating characters from Flann O'Brien's *The Third Policeman*. Inspired by Sterne he adopted an approach to portraiture – now working in oils rather that acrylics, and using photographs as a tool – that was readily accessible, yet multi-layered, placing his subjects in the context of their life and work as icons of their time. He engaged in dialogue with Vermeer in *The Conversation* and Velazquez in *Winter in Ronda*, the latter work part of a series of autobiographical paintings featuring himself and his family.

My 1986 book *Robert Ballagh* was a portrait of the artist mid-career. After the death of his dealer and mentor David Hendriks in 1981, he decided not to work with another gallery but to go out on his own – a courageous decision at a time of economic recession, high unemployment and emigration. It didn't endear him to the small coterie of dealers, curators and civil servants who pulled the strings in Irish art: they apparently distrusted the popularity of his work among the general public. "The visual arts are a means of communication and if you want to communicate, surely you want to communicate with as many people as possible," he argued. "You use a language that is universally accessible."

Michael Colgan had approached him to design the set for Barry McGovern's one-man Beckett show *I'll Go On* at the Gate Theatre, his first experience of working in theatre. His portrait of Noël Browne was on the cover of the controversial politician's best-selling autobiography *Against The Tide*, which I had edited. As Minister for Health from 1948 to 1951 Browne had successfully spearheaded a programme to eradicate tuberculosis – a disease which killed his mother, a brother and a sister and also afflicted him – but he resigned

*'The Life and Opinions of Tristram Shandy, Gentleman' in the restaurant in Clonmel, Co. Tipperary for which it was comissioned. The large painting was subsequently donated to the South Tipperary County Museum.*

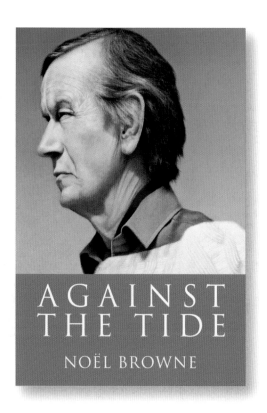

AGAINST
THE TIDE

NOËL BROWNE

after his controversial Mother and Child Health Scheme was vetoed by the Catholic Church and abandoned by the Inter-Party cabinet. Ballagh empathised with his social concerns and with his defining outsider role in modern Irish history. Nobody had commissioned him to paint Browne: it was his own choice. Although Browne had represented the Dublin South-East constituency of which Ballsbridge was a part – "I remember my parents going out to vote for him" – they had never met.

Ballagh depicts Browne in a cruciform format, standing in an Aran sweater in front of his Connemara cottage. His gaze is as unflinching as the bleak landscape around him: here is a man who has stood his ground. The emotive shape of the portrait has obvious spiritual connotations, but was originally chosen for practical reasons: it was the most effective way to evoke Browne's affection for the west of Ireland while avoiding having to paint a vast backdrop. "Landscape has been such a significant part of Irish art, yet it is something that living in the city I've always felt unable to deal with adequately."

*Robert Ballagh: Citizen Artist* is a companion piece to *Robert Ballagh* and mirrors its structure: the evolution of a portrait of James D Watson, the genetic scientist whose Nobel Prize-winning discovery of the Double Helix in 1953 led to the decoding of DNA, provides a framework for the narrative of Ballagh's career since 1986.

The two texts were published together as an exclusive two-volume monograph in January 2010 and presented in a specially designed, hand-made solander case in an edition of 350 with each copy signed, numbered and dated by the artist. The design and production of the monograph was directed by Ballagh's long-time collaborator Paul Rattigan. Each copy of the edition contained 24 original gyclée prints which were hand-produced by Bernard Ruijgrok at Piezografie Studio in Amsterdam, using archival inks on acid-free, museum-quality paper with each print individually embossed with the artist's own monogram. The volumes were hand-bound by Wim Karnsteeg of Boekbinderij De Distelkamp in Arnhem, and the solander case hand-made by Judith van Daal and Pau Groenendijk of Mooie Boeken, Amsterdam. Photography for the project was by Davison and Associates, Dublin.

This present edition of *Robert Ballagh: Citizen Artist*, is the first available in bookshops, and includes a new preface and an afterword dealing with Ballagh's latest project, a set of eight self-portraits. It is illustrated with hundreds of archival photographs and colour reproductions not in the monograph. It could not have been written without the generous cooperation over many years of Ballagh and his wife Betty. It draws on personal meetings with James D Watson and Gerry Adams and various interviews with Louis le Brocquy, JP Donleavy, Michael Colgan, Patrick Mason and others.

"Robert Ballagh isn't a political artist but his art is made by an intensely political person," says the New York-based critic and artist Brian O'Doherty. *Robert Ballagh: Citizen Artist* explores this intriguing creative dichotomy to reveal an engagingly articulate but surprisingly private man who through his life and art has become a witness to history.

*" Anyone who disowns any of their experience is foolish. Everything you do is of benefit to your development as a painter. "*

"Can you tell me who bought my painting?" "Sorry, we are unable to give out that information." "Isn't there anything you can tell me?" "I'm afraid all we can say is that it may be a New York collector."

So here's what happened. One September afternoon in 2005 Robert Ballagh was walking past the James Adam's Salerooms at the corner of Kildare Street and St Stephen's Green. On looking in the window he was surprised to see his painting *The History Lesson* prominently displayed. He had no idea it was coming up for auction.

This was at a time when sales of contemporary art were reaching record levels, their prices fuelled by a property and financial boom that transformed Ireland into one of the wealthiest countries per capita in the European Union, a phenomenon famously labelled 'the Celtic Tiger' by a 1994 Morgan Stanley report. Next to none of this sudden affluence was finding its way into the pockets of artists whose work went under the hammer, although fetching high prices did their reputations no harm.

The EU had issued a directive in 2000 entitling artists to resale rights whenever their work came on the market. This followed a long campaign going back to the early 1980s in which Ballagh played a forceful role, but so far the Irish Government had failed to implement it.

Earlier in 2005 another of Ballagh's paintings, a cruciform portrait of the socialist leader and revolutionary James Connolly – originally purchased by the architect Sam Stephenson in 1972 at the David Hendriks Gallery, but later sold on at auction in 1985 – realised €14,000 at auction at Whytes in Molesworth Street. A study for *The Life and Opinions of Tristram Shandy, gentleman,* which Ballagh painted in 1976, sold for €20,000. The previous year *My Studio 1969* – expected to reach €20,000-30,000 – was knocked down for €96,000.

*The History Lesson* was listed as Lot 65 at the Adam's auction. It portrays Ballagh at a table in conversation with two of the 1916 Easter Rising leaders, Patrick Pearse and James Connolly, who sit on either side of him. His head swivels from one to another – much as at a tennis match – trying to decide which of their visions of Ireland to follow. The format of the painting is a triangle with a black frame. Ballagh painted it in 1989 in response to knee-jerk historical revisionism, prompted partly by bombings and killings in the North, that sought to rewrite Ireland's revolutionary past as a shameful mistake.

Under the provisions of Section 31 of the Broadcasting Act, introduced by Fianna Fáil's Gerry Collins in 1971 and broadened substantially by Labour's Conor Cruise-O'Brien in 1977, no member of any proscribed organisation including Sinn Féin – the political wing of the Provisional IRA – could be interviewed or quoted on radio or television. The intent was to deny the IRA what Margaret Thatcher described as "the oxygen of publicity", but in Ireland this censorship was pushed to ludicrous extremes, outlawing even the broadcasting of Paul Robeson's rendition of the ballad 'Kevin Barry'. "I thought if we're not allowed to talk about people like Pearse and Connolly on radio, I'd talk to them in my art," Ballagh recalls.

Although *The History Lesson* won the Douglas Hyde Gold Medal at the Oireachtas Exhibition – as did the Connolly

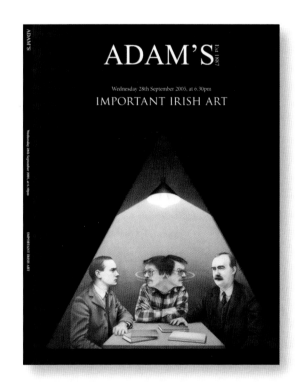

portrait in 1971 – he was unable to sell it. Pat Cooke, who was in charge of Kilmainham Jail and St Enda's School which houses the Pearse Museum, sought to buy it, but was overruled by the Office of Public Works advisory art committee. "Over my dead body," snorted one influential member.

The History Lesson remained in Ballagh's studio until 2003, when he included it in an exhibition of his work accompanying the launch of his portrait of Micheal Farrell – who died of cancer the previous year – at the Crawford Gallery in Cork. "This fellow I didn't know came up to me saying he was blown away by the show and he had to have one of the paintings. I said there's really nothing for sale, they're all commissioned or borrowed works. Perhaps foolishly I said there are a few I still own. He decided he had to have The History Lesson. He was very persuasive. He even came to Dublin to talk about it. He'd bought a house and they were going to do up a room especially for this picture. I eventually said 'Okay, Okay', and I sold it to him."

Bidding was brisk at the Adam's auction on 28 September. The saleroom, which was established in 1887 for general estate auctions, moved into fine arts in 1923 during the rush to sell off 'big house' valuables after independence. It eventually started embracing Irish contemporary art in the 1970s, and now held four sales of contemporary art annually. Whyte's, originally glass and china merchants, eager to tap into a younger clientele spawned by Ireland's new affluence, followed suit in 2000, while Sotheby's and Christie's had begun holding Irish sales in the mid-1990s.

An increasing number of artists opted to go straight to sale on the open market rather than via a dealer or gallery, where they faced commissions of up to 60 per cent. Ironically, Ballagh had been treated as something of an aesthetic pariah by the art establishment in 1983 when he decided to go it alone rather that sign up with another gallery after the death of his dealer David Hendriks. Now other artists were beginning to follow his lead.

Adam's operates a system where bids are indicated by raising a numbered paddle. The procedure enables it get through up to 100 lots per hour. Early bidding saw a Tony O'Malley painting fetch €63,000, while a Norah McGuinness gouache sold for €27,000, a Peter Collis water-colour for €5,800 and an Arthur Armstrong landscape for €12,000. Just before The History Lesson came up, Jack B Yeats's 1913 oil Lough Gill, Co Kerry realised €29,000.

When James O'Halloran opened the bidding for The History Lesson, several paddles were put up but with the price at €18,000 it became clear that an anonymous telephone bidder would have the final say. "I was resigned to never knowing where this picture had gone," Ballagh says. "You'd get blood from a stone quicker than information from an auction house."

He'd experienced a similar rebuff the previous year when he tried to persuade Ian Whyte to divulge the purchaser of My Studio 1969. "It was my first picture to attract a big price, so naturally I was curious. "Oh, I can't tell you", said Ian Whyte. But I eventually worked out the buyer by default. It was suggested to me that it might end up hanging in a hotel. That's a kind of clue that it was Lochlan Quinn, who owned the Merrion Hotel."

Quinn, along with fellow businessmen Michael Smurfit and Tony O'Reilly, one of Ireland's leading collectors, paid an Agnew's record €2.75 million in London for Louis le Brocquy's *The Family* in 2001, later bequeathing the painting to the National Gallery of Ireland. He is a brother of former Labour Minister for Finance Ruairi Quinn who as a Labour councillor unsuccessfully supported Ballagh in 1976 when Dublin Corporation invoked an old bye-law to prevent him exhibiting a barbed wire pyramid – a protest against internment in the North – at the first Oasis show of outdoor sculpture in Merrion Square.

Ballagh thought no more about *The History Lesson* until the autumn of 2007 when he received a note from David McConnell, professor of genetics at Trinity College Dublin and a pioneer of molecular genetics and genetic engineering in Ireland. It turned out Nobel Prize winner James D Watson, whose discovery with Francis Crick of the double helix opened the way in 1953 for the unravelling of the DNA code governing all human life, was coming to Dublin to be made an honorary fellow of the Royal Irish Academy. "He's interested in talking to you about a portrait," wrote McConnell. "And by the way, you and he have something in common. He owns a painting of yours, *The History Lesson*."

On the morning of the Royal Irish Academy meeting Watson and his wife Elizabeth visited Ballagh's studio at No 5 Arbour Hill, near where Pearse and Connolly and the other executed leaders of the Easter Rising are buried. Watson explained how he learned on the internet about *The History Lesson* coming up for auction. He didn't know anything about Pearse or Connolly at the time. He just liked the image and decided to buy it.

"You know, you'll have to come over to Cold Spring Harbour Laboratory on Long Island and see us there," Watson suggested. "Yeah, that would be great," said Ballagh.

That evening he attended the honorary fellowship ceremony at the Royal Irish Academy meeting room at 19 Dawson Street, which was designed in 1854 by Fredrick Villiers Clarendon and for a while housed the Ardagh Chalice and the Tara Broach before the National Museum of Ireland was established in 1890. The Academy, granted a royal charter in 1786, is Ireland's leading academic body and over the years has included among its members James Gandon, architect of the Custom House, the mathematician William Rowan Hamilton and Oscar Wilde's father, the polymath William Wilde.

McConnell introduced Watson as "truly a giant of our times who was without doubt the greatest scientist of the 20th century, just as Charles Darwin was the greatest scientist of the 19th century." Ballagh didn't know a huge deal about Watson, but was intrigued. "I never thought anything would come of our meeting, but later he contacted me and said, 'When are you coming?' So Betty and myself went over in what in America was late fall."

They stayed nearly a week with the Watsons at Cold Spring Harbour Laboratory, a research institute established more than a century ago in an old whaling town that opens out onto Long Island Sound, about an hour from Manhattan. Watson made it his home after receiving the Nobel Prize in 1962. It has carried out groundbreaking research in cancer, neurobiology, plant genetics,

*James D Watson in Robert Ballagh's*
*studio in Arbour Hill.*
Photo: Robert Ballagh

genomics and bioinformatics, all stemming from Watson's deciphering the double helical structure of DNA.

A 24-year-old researcher, he sat one night in 1953 at a table in a laboratory in Cambridge with a sheet of white cardboard, a hobby knife and paste. He was making molecule models of the four biochemical nucleobases, guanine, cytosine, adenine and thymine. He kept sliding the flat cut-outs around to examine how they might interact and fit together, and soon realised that the adenine could be paired with the guanine and the thymine with the cytosine.

By deduction he and his colleague Francis Crick after years of trial and error had arrived at the double-helix structure of the molecule deoxyribonucleic acid (DNA) of which all living matter is made. The two chains of the "gently twisted" double-helix ladder unlink "like a zipper" and reproduce their missing halves, making possible human existence.

This simple fact – that the essence of human life is carried in a molecule – is one of the major discoveries of the 20th century. It has already revolutionised the study of biology and genetics, not to mention forensic science where it has become popular knowledge through its use in the courts and TV crime programmes. It has led to technological breakthroughs in agriculture and animal breeding and to the Genome Project which in fifteen years created a directory of the genetic code of the human species, opening the way to curing crippling and fatal genetic diseases.

Watson is the first person in the world to have his entire genome mapped, a process that involved three billion different sequences and cost the equivalent of one million euro but which before long is likely to be only a fraction of that. He told the Royal Irish Academy that he is in favour of genetic engineering "as far as it helps humans. The majority of people would benefit from being enhanced genetically. As long as the benefits would eventually be available to all people, I don't think I would have any moral problems with it."

*The History Lesson* hangs in the entrance lobby of the Grace Auditorium at Cold Spring Harbour Laboratory, near a Barry Castle painting of tennis players. Although almost 80, Watson is an enthusiastic tennis player. He has also been able to build up an art collection not from his earnings as a scientist – "you'd be dumb to go into science for that" – but as author of several best-selling books such as *The DNA Story* and, most recently, *Avoid Boring People: Lessons from a Life in Science*.

Going to Cold Spring Harbour and spending time with Watson and his wife was a mind-opening experience for Ballagh who had never spent that amount of time with a scientist before. "You discover that even though Jim has a passion for art and has this very fine collection, he is a scientist. Scientists see the world differently than the rest of us. I liked that. He has a very rational logical way of thinking. I wouldn't think he has any time for superstition or cant. If something is provable it's fact, and that's it. I met several other scientists there, including Sidney Brenner, another Nobel Prize winner and a humorous man, but also with that kind of intense logic which was to me very fresh because in Ireland we tend to be a bit woolly."

This conversation is taking place in Ballagh's studio in Arbour Hill, early in February 2008. He moved here in the early

*Artist Patrick Collins, a previous occupier, in the studio in Parliament Street.*

1990s some years after his attic studio across the Liffey in Parliament Street – where he painted until the mid-1980s – was turned into offices as part of the Temple Bar redevelopment project. It now houses the Disney film company's Irish office.

For a while he tried working at home in 3 Temple Cottages, creating a studio space by expanding into a neighbouring house that came on the market. It's where he painted *Upstairs No 4, The Studio* in 1989. "Running a studio at home just simply didn't work. The space was too small. Also I really do believe that you go out to work and you come home to relax. I found I'd have my breakfast, do a day's work and come down in the evening for dinner and then I'd say to Betty, I think I'll slip up just to finish off something. And the next thing it's half-past-ten. I was working far too much, completely denying any kind of family life."

He was rescued by his daughter Rachel, who was by then studying at the National College of Art and Design in Thomas Street. She noticed a derelict terraced house with a 'For Sale' sign on Arbour Hill, a short walk from their home in Broadstone. Nobody had lived in it for eight or nine years. It had a big yard at the back. Although the going price was £27,000, there were no title deeds. It was a ward of court sale. The person who lived there was so old they'd been put in the care of the state, giving the state the right to sell the property. It took Ballagh's solicitor John Gore-Grimes several months to sort out the legal papers.

Ballagh's intention was to build a studio out the back, where there had once been a pig farm. "There was a lot of agricultural activity in the area. I remember on a Sunday you'd hear the clip-clop of horses. But until I could get the money together I made do with a studio space upstairs, created by knocking down part of a wall between two bedrooms. One big disadvantage was that the front of the building faced south, so when the sun came out I had to put shades on the windows because the sun was too bright. It was like a spotlight."

This is where he painted his 1997 self-portrait *The Bogman* showing him in green rubber boots digging for turf, a reference to Seamus Heaney's early poem about digging. The image is framed by a stone surround and a chiselled Irish inscription which liberally translated suggests that 'you can take the man from the bog but you can't take the bog from the man'. A raven hovers over Ballagh, a reference to the raven that landed on Cúchulain when he was dead. "But I'm not quite dead yet," he says.

When he began clearing the downstairs area to create a space to store his paintings, he opened a cupboard and nearly fainted at the sight of rampant dry rot. Every bit of timber up to the first floor level had to be stripped out and replaced at a cost of around £15,000. "Which meant building a new studio went on the back burner. It was years before I got the money together to build the studio or could find the time to get my head around it."

The airy rectangular studio he now works in was built by George Cooke, a quarry owner he got to know working on some art projects. "We sort of designed it between the two of us. It's just a timber studio, but instead of standard timber sheeting

*Studio with a Modigliani Print* (1976)
*Oil and Acrylic on canvas. 60 x 60cm.*
*Private Collection.*
*This scene is based on the Parliament Street studio.*

we cladded it in shingle, which I think is a more attractive finish." The studio faces onto a gravelled patio with plants and a high brick wall. "I asked for low-maintenance plants. After a few months they were dying. I didn't realise they had to be watered." French windows open out in summer, so he can take a break under a sun umbrella. It's in the middle of the city, but it's like an oasis.

There is also space for his new BMW. Office and apartment block developments have transformed the Arbour Hill area, making street parking impossible. For much of his career he drove a utilitarian Lada, a cheap 'peoples' car that was synonymous with the USSR during the Cold War. The BMW was paid for by royalties from his design work on *Riverdance*, the Irish dance show that evolved from an interval piece in RTÉ's 1994 broadcast of the Eurovision Song Contest to become Ireland's biggest-earning cultural export.

Ballagh is having teething problems with the BMW. He's uncomfortable with anything he can't fix with his hands. "But this is all electronics. Suddenly last week the windows wouldn't open. I was helpless. It's not as if you could get a screwdriver out. If something goes wrong, there's nothing you can do. They had to bring in two modules from Germany. They call it diagnostics."

Pinned up on the wall of his studio wall is a life-size grainy black and white enlargement of a photograph of Watson, a tall man with a weather-beaten face, standing with his arms reaching out, looking directly at the camera as if offering a gift. "I photographed him in all sorts of settings. I had a idea for this stance. He said nobody ever asked him to stand like that before. I said, trust me."

He fixed on the photograph from many he took of Watson in Cold Spring Harbour and also photographs of the tranquil wooded inlet that is his world. For days he's being shuffling the different shots around on his work table – much as Watson did with the pieces of cardboard back in his Cambridge laboratory – looking for an image or compositional shape that might in some way define the man and his work.

"I didn't start thinking about what I was going to do until I got back from America. The portrait started off in my mind very much as a conventional portrait, probably with a vertical format. But I felt it wasn't dynamic enough for what I was after. So I basically converted it to a diamond shape, and suddenly all sorts of possibilities cropped up. The landscape dictated the shape, as it had with the cruciform Noël Browne portrait I painted in 1985."

He fixes a piece of string over the photograph on the wall, pinning it at four points to suggest the outline of a diamond shape so that the full figure of Watson in the foreground forms one diagonal and a backdrop view of Cold Spring Harbour seen from across the water forms the other. Art and pure science, far from being opposites as many might assume, operate on a similar creative level, through flashes of inspiration like this. "I wanted an elegant solution. It's a phrase the scientists in Cold Spring Harbour use in talking about scientific experiment."

Irregular shapes are a recurring feature of Ballagh's work, an aesthetic way – so to speak – of squaring a circle. They provided a solution for his 1971 portrait of Gordon Lambert, the first he ever did, in which Lambert holds a three-dimensional Albers abstract

*Top: James D Watson in Cold Spring Harbour Laboratory.*
*Photo: Robert Ballagh*

*Above: Studio wall in Arbour Hill with a study for the Watson portrait.*

painting. *The History Lesson* employs a triangle shape to add dynamism to what is essentially a simple composition of three men sitting at a table.

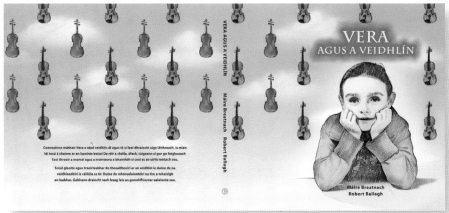

A self-portrait, *The Illustrator*, which Ballagh has put to one side in his studio in order to concentrate on the Watson portrait, is lozenge-shaped. In it he's wearing a 'Fuck The Begrudgers' T-shirt – the phrase is borrowed from Brendan Behan – that he wore in a 2003 painting *Still Crazy After All These Years*. Ballagh decided to paint it as a response to some of the reviews of his 2006 retrospective at the Royal Hibernian Academy.

Declan McGonagle, a curator who had mixed success as director of the Irish Museum of Modern Art and is now director of the National College of Art and Design, maintained while appearing on John Kelly's television arts programme *The View* that Ballagh wasn't a real artist, but a mere illustrator. "I thought it would be a bit of fun to do a painting called *The Illustrator* and express my sentiments in it. I'm someone who's quite proud of being an illustrator."

When the actress Fionnuala Flanagan heard about the McGonagle put-down, she gave Ballagh a book on David Hockney. The dedication said, 'To the merest illustrator of them all – FF'. *The Illustrator* is already framed with the same black wood he plans to use for the Watson portrait. "I made the frame before I made the picture because a frame is so hard to make when the corners are not 90 degrees. With *The Illustrator* each corner has a different angle." Ballagh is pragmatic in his approach to painting, ever ready to improvise a solution. Out of problems, comes invention.

Another unfinished painting is propped beside *The Illustrator*. It's a portrait of the designer Paul Rattigan, a frequent collaborator in work involving digital technology. It's complete except for the face. Ballagh has left the face and hands until last, as always, perhaps instinctively putting himself under pressure so that the work doesn't become routine.

He is working with Rattigan on a children's book by the musician Máire Breathnach about a little girl who likes violins. The cover will show violins falling from the sky like raindrops. "It's a little quote from Magritte's painting of men with bowler hats raining from the sky. In the old days I'd have to paint all the violins. Now I only have to paint a few and Paul multiplies them digitally, giving me different options in terms of composition and colour. Then it's all put on a disc and given to the publishers."

He has never taken to computers. "I suppose I'm antediluvian. I don't have an email address or a mobile phone. I leave all that to Betty. She also handles all our finances. I just pass everything on to her, except for a small bank account I have for things in the studio."

He has an old land-line telephone in the studio and doesn't seem to mind being interrupted when it rings. While we are talking he takes a call from Patricia McKenna, the former Green MEP, about the referendum on the Lisbon Treaty. They're both on the committee of the People's Movement, one of the groups campaigning for a 'No' vote.

RTÉ ring to ask if he'll to take part in *The View*. Somebody else wants him to open an exhibition. The theatre director Ray Yeates has a query about a set he's designing for a play about Captain James Kelly, a key figure in the Arms scandal that caused the sacking from cabinet of Charles Haughey in 1972.

Ballagh's political activism – particularly his opposition to Section 31, and his enthusiastic involvement with Sinn Féin cultural initiatives in the North before the peace process became mainstream – hasn't enamoured him to the art establishment. *The Sunday Times* referred dismissively to "his explicit agit prop style" and argued that his readiness to accept commissions has had the "effect of ensuring that his reputation stayed tangled up with commercial design rather than the world of fine art". Artists, it would seem, should stick to art and leave politics to politicians and pundits.

Ballagh rejects this proposition. He makes no apology for employing his status as an artist to speak out against injustice and the abuse of power. "I have done agit prop, and it was for a political purpose," he says. "I didn't ever consider it art." While he has created posters and slogans in support of political causes and introduced revolutionary images into some of his paintings – notably his reworking of classic works, such as Goya's *The Third of May* and Delacroix's *Liberty at the Barricades*, in a contemporary Northern Ireland context – the main body of his painting work has been personal and self-questioning, while his portraits are iconic inventories of the human landscape of the society in which he lives. As the Irish-born New York art critic and artist Brian O'Doherty wrote in the catalogue for Ballagh's 2003 Crawford Gallery exhibition, "Robert Ballagh isn't a political artist but his art is made by an intensely political person."

No one would suggest Harold Pinter's plays are diminished by his political writings and involvement in protest groups. Similarly, Seamus Heaney has just been speaking out on RTÉ – Ballagh invariably has the radio on while he is painting – against the Irish government's determination to bulldoze a motorway through the ancient archaeological sites of Tara, saying that "a sacred landscape is being desecrated for commerce".

Heaney's utterances as a citizen could hardly be said to sully his poetry. There has always been a dilemma for writers and artists in confronting the horrors of their time. "They are not like speakers on a podium or preachers in a pulpit," Heaney wrote in an essay marking the 60th anniversary of the Universal Declaration of Human Rights. "Because of the artistic imperative they obey, they must do more than utter a commendable sentiment...some kind of turn or twist or swerve, some shift in the mind or the medium has to occur." This inclination to proceed indirectly in his poetry in relation to the politics of his native North has disappointed some Republicans, who see it as a failure to speak out. One Republican jeered that "as long as it's only fucking Tara and some road he'll make a stand".

*Top: Artwork for a banner commissioned to commemorate the 40th anniversary of the founding of the Northern Ireland Civil Rights Association in 2008.*
*Collection: Museum of Free Derry.*

*Above: Artwork for book jacket and poster.*

Ballagh is angered by this criticism. "I know Seamus reasonably well and I think he is right. I am a political animal. I can't help it, that's the way I am. I don't think I make political art as people understand it. Seamus couldn't be a political poet because he's not that sort of human being. But he's an honest poet. And that's all we can expect of artists."

There may be times when an artist has no option in conscience than to become a truth-teller. Pablo Neruda in his poem 'Let Me Explain A Few Things', written in response to the plight of more than a half-a-million Spanish Republicans who fled across the Pyrenees to France to escape Franco's murderous vengeance in the aftermath of the Civil War, declared that he intended to make the exposure of the world's injustices the purpose of his poetry:

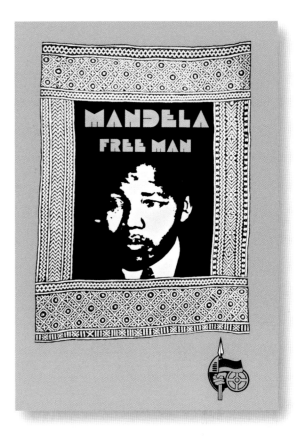

'You will ask: And where are the lilacs
And the metaphysics petalled with poppies
And the rain repeatedly spattering
Its words, filling them with holes and birds?...
You will ask why this poetry
Does not speak of dreams and leaves,
And of the great volcanoes of his birthplace?

Come and see the blood in the streets.
Come and see
The blood in the streets,
Come and see the blood
in the streets!'

Never was this more true that in the late 1980s. An IRA bomb killed eleven people attending a Remembrance Sunday service at the cenotaph in Enniskillen. The loyalist Michael Stone gunned down three people attending a funeral of unarmed members of the IRA shot by the British Army in Gibraltar. Two British soldiers who drove into a funeral cortage were dragged from their car and killed by a Republican mob.

Again the blood was in the streets. Ballagh wasn't going to look the other way.

*Print commissioned by the Irish Anti-apartheid Movement to mark Nelson Mandela becoming a Freeman of Dublin City as well as his release from prison in South Africa.*

On a morning early in August 1988 Robert Ballagh got behind the wheel of his Lada, the Communist answer to the Volkswagen, and drove from Broadstone through the city and out past Dublin Airport, heading North. He crossed the river Boyne, where the Protestant King William of Orange routed the forces of the Catholic King James, the root of sectarian bitterness that divided Ireland for centuries. He negotiated the Border checkpoint manned by British troops. Military helicopters hovered overhead as he approached Belfast. Housing areas along the way were festooned with Union Jacks. He turned off the M1 towards Andersonstown, where Tricolours were flying, and passed Milltown Cemetery before reaching the Falls Road.

He was responding to a letter from Gerry Adams, whose policy role during the 1981 Hunger Strikes and subsequent election as MP for West Belfast led to him becoming president of Sinn Féin, the political wing of the Provisional IRA. Ballagh had never met Adams, who was branded as a terrorist in the Republic – an Osama bin Laden ahead of his time – and banned from television and radio under the draconian Section 31 censorship provisions.

The previous November the Provos had exploded a bomb at the war cenotaph in the Co Fermanagh town of Enniskillen during a Remembrance Sunday ceremony. Eleven people died, all of them Protestants. Many more suffered horrendous injuries. The carnage was captured on video by an onlooker and shown on television throughout the world.

"Where's the glory in bombing a Remembrance Day parade for old age pensioners, their medals taken out and polished up for the day?" demanded Bono, the U2 rock star, catching the public mood before a performance of 'Sunday Bloody Sunday', his protest song about the Northern Ireland Troubles. "Where's the glory in that? To leave them dying or crippled for life, or dead, under the rubble of the revolution that the majority of the people in my country don't want? No more! Sing no more!"

Electoral support for Sinn Féin, which had soared to 43 per cent of the nationalist vote after the 1981 hunger strikes, drained away. Adams was convinced more than ever that political rather than military action had to be the way forward. He entered into secret talks with SDLP leader John Hume, the first tentative steps in what would later become known as the peace process.

There would be years of more blood in the streets before the Provisional leadership – which denied sanctioning the Enniskillen bomb – would be persuaded to give up its armed campaign in return for devolved government in Northern Ireland. The following March the Provisional IRA sent a unit to Gibraltar to plant a bomb during a British military band parade at the weekly changing of the guard in front of the Governor's residence. The British were tipped off. As the three Provo volunteers Mairead Farrell, 31, Sean Savage, 23, and Danny McCann, 30, walked past a Shell filling station on Winston Churchill Avenue in the direction of the Spanish border, they were intercepted by SAS troops and shot dead. Witnesses reported that they had their hands up and were attempting to surrender. They were unarmed and no explosive devices were found on their bodies, which were riddled with bullets.

The bodies were flown back to Dublin and driven North by night for burial at Milltown cemetery on March 16. During the funeral a Loyalist paramilitary Michael Stone, infiltrating the cemetery from marshlands adjoining the M1 motorway, opened fire with guns and grenades, killing three mourners before being overpowered and arrested by members of the Royal Ulster Constabulary.

Two days later at the funeral of one of the victims two British Army corporals drove into the funeral cortege. When they attempted to back out, their way was blocked by black taxis. They were dragged from their car and taken away, stripped of their clothes and shot. As with the Milltown massacre, the incident was caught on television cameras.

"The whole thing was hideous," says Ballagh. "One immediate consequence was that the people of West Belfast were portrayed all over the world as brutal killers and savages. They decided they needed to counteract this bad image and that an arts festival – or *féile* – was the best way to do it. It was in the context of being MP for the area that Adams wrote to me and explained to me what they were trying to do."

A recurring problem in West Belfast was that the first week of August was the anniversary of internment. Every year there were riots. Young people threw stones at British soldiers. The soldiers responded. Many local people got hurt or were put in jail. The community felt a need to provide some sort of alternative to involve young people. "Adams asked me would I support the initiative, and if there was any way I could help out. So I contacted him and said of course I approved of their initiative, and I wanted to get involved in whatever way I could."

Adams first become aware of Ballagh in the late 1970s through a cover he created for *Lost Fields* by Michael McLaverty, principal of a West Belfast school and published in Dublin by Poolbeg Press. "It was just the image of a field, but it was like looking out a window," remembers Adams. "So I became conscious of this guy who was doing this sort of artwork."

Adams was born in West Belfast, one of a Catholic family of ten. His grandfather fought in the Irish War of Independence that led to Partition. His father was shot in an ambush of a Royal Ulster Constabulary patrol in 1942, and sentenced to eight years imprisonment. As a teenager Adams was active in the Civil Rights protests that led to British troops being called on to the streets of Northern Ireland in 1969. He was interned without trial on HMS Maidstone in 1972, but released to take part in secret but unsuccessful talks in London with British Home Secretary William Whitelaw.

"My whole life has been here," Adams says of the Falls Road. "Like any society or community, it has its faults, but it has always had a creative self-help ethos. Out of this came the idea of the *Féile* that would be a genuine people's festival. It was to stage on one level art exhibitions and plays, but on another level also a street party. The idea was to provide a platform for the people who live here, but also that we would invite in others who were in the wider arts world, almost as an act of solidarity. And one of the first people we asked was Bobby."

The Festival's office was in The White House or An Teach Bán, a building beside a roundabout near Kennedy Way. Ballagh cautiously parked his car on the Falls Road and made himself known. "I was fascinated to meet someone who was so reviled in the media in the Republic. But I got on fine with him and discussed all kinds of things, like movies which I discovered he liked. I learned

*Cover artwork for*
*'Lost Fields' by Michael McLaverty,*
*published by Poolbeg Press.*

21

*Judging murals in West Belfast during the first festival or féile in 1988.*

the reason so many of the Sinn Féin leadership enjoyed coming to Dublin was that they could go to the movies. They didn't go to the centre of Belfast because they could be assassinated."

Ballagh gave a talk on art in the Roddy McCorleys, a Republican club on the Glen Road. His job was to adjudicate a competition for the best mural, a mushrooming public art form used mainly as a crude expression of patriotism. "Initially walls in Nationalist areas were covered with graffiti urging support for the hunger strikers. Then slowly images related to the struggle began to be introduced. I find it fascinating that people with little previous aesthetic experience turned to a specific visual art form to tell their own story and to reinforce their determination to continue their struggle against injustice. It rarely happens that art becomes a common point of reference for a social group in that it helps form their political and cultural ideas and indeed articulates their ideals."

Adams took him in a bullet-proof black taxi to visit various mural sites throughout West Belfast. "We went to Andersonstown to see a mural quite near to where the two British corporals were killed. Two young fellows were standing proudly beside a picture of IRA volunteers. I remember Adams talking to them and congratulating them on their effort. He was interested in the way they depicted the volunteers. 'Why did you paint them with balaclavas? You can't see their faces, so you can't see their humanity.' The two looked at him rather sheepishly, and said, 'We can't paint faces.'"

Ballagh promised to return – and he did, conducting a series of mural workshops in which he asked young people what they would like to paint and then helped them bring it about. "It always stuck in my mind because they decided they would do a Happy Birthday to Nelson Mandela on his 70th birthday," says Adams. "And they did this big portrait under Bobby's tutelage, a gable-sized painting which later, when Mandela was released from prison, we photographed and presented a copy to him. He was very pleased. It's really important for people to get a sense of their own dignity in terms of someone like Bobby coming along and judging what they're doing and sharing his expertise with them.

"The murals which had been done initially were fairly basic quasi-religious quasi-military representations, and quite crude. The kids were prosecuted for doing them. But then as they started to pick up the techniques, they realised if they got the permission of whoever owned the gable, it was perfectly legal and the police could do nothing about it. So it developed from where they were operating covertly at night, with buckets and brushes, to gangs of people in overalls with scaffolding and Bobby overseeing it all. It was a whole big lift for young people who may have had some notions that they wanted to be artists, or maybe they didn't even want to be artists, but they were given an opportunity to discover that they had some talent."

Adams quotes from a poem by Bobby Sands, leader of the 1981 hunger strike and one of ten prisoners who starved to death in pursuit of the political status refused to them by the British authorities. The point of the line – 'the men of art have lost their heart' – was that there was no artistic spotlight on what was happening in the North.

"I think there were exceptions to that. I think with Bobby and those others who felt moved to come and contribute to the life of the community here — it was irrelevant whether or not they shared the politics of the community, they recognised that what worked was inclusivity as opposed to exclusivity and alienating people."

He relates this to the whole notion of the bard. "Bobby Ballagh is clearly an activist in the broadest sense of the word, without being at all party political. I think that's what informs his sense of citizenship and public service and engagement with people. It's something I admire. Because if you have a special talent you can just go off to a garret and paint, and if your personality is like that, that's fair enough, and out of that creativity may perhaps result a beautiful work of art. But Bobby has an instinct to get involved. At the time that was in it, it was a brave thing he did. I've not doubt that there was a kick-back, and that he paid for it."

◆

A researcher for a Brian Dobson interview on RTÉ in 2008 was surprised to learn that it wasn't until Ballagh designed the Riverdance set in 1994 that he achieved any financial security as an artist.

"But you represented Ireland at the Paris Biennale in 1969?" "Yes, but I was poor. I was on the dole." "But you were well-known." "You didn't get any money for that. All sorts of prestigious things that look great on a CV didn't put food on the table."

The researcher found this hard to understand. Fame has now come to mean money. But even in the 1980s – perhaps particularly in the 1980s, which saw Ireland spiral into recession – prestige was slow to translate into cash return. Ballagh received international recognition with his set design for the Samuel Beckett one-man show *I'll Go On* at the Gate Theatre in 1985, his debut as a stage designer. He'd been elected to the executive committee of the UNESCO-backed International Artists Association, and was commuting every month to its HQ in Paris. My biography *Robert Ballagh*, published in 1986, was widely read. Yet his paintings, including his portrait of Nöel Browne, were lying unsold in an improvised studio at his home in 3 Temple Cottages. "I was delighted and honoured to be asked to do stamp designs back then, but each one took about a month to paint and paid me £100. And I was delighted to be asked to do *I'll Go On* because earning a living from art was so precarious. But the fee was just £750."

After the death of David Hendriks in 1983 and the closure of the gallery in St Stephens Green, he had decided not to go to another gallery. "Several galleries approached me and I just politely said no. My feeling was I didn't need galleries to sell my work in Ireland. None of them had any real outreach programme. So why would I give 50% to people to do something I can do myself?"

His relationship with Hendriks, who came from Jamaica and opened his gallery in 1956 with an exhibition of Picasso etchings from the Vollard suite, none of which sold, had been particularly close. "I didn't begrudge him the 33% he charged because he was so supportive in the lean days when I wasn't selling at all."

During the day Hendriks used to sit in the first-floor room of the gallery at his desk between two great Georgian windows

*Portrait of Brenda Quinn*
*and her daughters (1986/87)*
*Oil on canvas. 92 x 60cm.*
*Private Collection.*

looking out on the Green, its lush trees reminiscent of summer in the Caribbean. "You'd go in and he always had a seat there for you to pull in and have a chat. I don't know how he knew, but he'd take one look at me, reach into the drawer and take out a cheque book and say how much. He could always read when I had that look on my face. In today's money it mightn't sound much but a few hundred quid back then saved your life over a couple of months.

"The way it worked was he would give you a cheque for whatever you'd ask for, within reason, and there would be no mention of it ever again until you managed to sell something. Or maybe you had a bit of an exhibition and at the end of the account the amount would be discounted. No interest charged or anything."

Ballagh suspected that he was unlikely to find at any other gallery the freedom allowed to him by Hendriks. "The way the gallery system normally works is that you have a one-person show maybe every 18 months. You might have one good idea but you have to make 20 pictures. You invest all the energy in that one idea, and all the rest is flannelling, studies and sketches and things like that. That's how you make a living in that world. It's a kind of treadmill situation. I wanted the freedom to do whatever idea I have and move on to the next project without the pressure of one-person shows and all the attendant work."

After his first sell-out show at the Isy Brachot gallery in Bruxelles in 1973, Brachot had wanted him back for another show 18 months later. All the paintings had been of people looking at paintings on two foot square modules. Ballagh didn't want to repeat that, so the new paintings were smaller and you could see the peoples faces. Brachot was horrified. 'But they are not the same,' he protested.

"Then the penny dropped. He wanted me to turn up with everything exactly the same again. I'm afraid that's the way the art business wants art to be. They want product and they want product that's understandable. When they invest in you, they create a brand and they promote it. Roy Lichtenstein is an extraordinarily intelligent artist but he was trapped in this style he'd invented of the Benday dots, the comic book illustrations. He spent the rest of his life incarcerated in a Benday dot prison. Sean Scully has been painting stripes for thirty years. Doesn't he ever get bored? So many artists seem to get trapped in that situation because they're part of a system of galleries, museums and critics that define what they should do."

Ballagh couldn't have chosen a worse time to go it alone. By the mid-1980s the effects of the 1970s' world oil crisis had led to a global recession, pushing Ireland near to bankruptcy. Unemployment rose from 7.8% in 1979 to 18.2 per cent in 1985, putting a quarter of a million people on the dole. Interest rates were as high as 15 per cent, jeopardising the Irish pound against other currencies. Government attempts to stimulate the economy by reducing tax and increasing public spending proved counter-productive, leading to

Irish Independent

SATURDAY, FEBRUARY 15, PRICE 45p

## The day of champions as we turn to sport

DUBLIN is the centre of the world today for sports fans as Featherweight Champion Barry McGuigan defends his title — and Ireland lines out in the first home defence of their Triple Crown Title.

## A most unlikely fighting Irishman

## The first flare-up!

## A winner

emergency cutbacks in services and tax increases to cover a public finance deficit. Emigration yet again became a scourge, rising according to some estimates as high as 70,000 a year by 1989. Five general elections, three between June 1981 and November 1982, heightened the instability.

"At the time David died I seemed to have no difficulty selling my work. I didn't see why I needed an agent. I ploughed ahead on my own and didn't notice a problem at all until it slowly began to dawn on me that the whole art scene operates around the private galleries. Museums by and large don't buy from artists. They buy from private galleries. Since David died I hadn't sold a painting to any public institution in the country. The long and short of it is when you don't participate in the system you get left out of the system. Having been chosen for the Paris Biennale in 1969, I was never again picked to represent Ireland for anything."

He had become virtually a non-person in official art circles, relying on commissions to generate income. He did a portrait of Lochlan Quinn's wife Brenda and their two daughters. The concept is that the portrait is shown from the back. You just see Ballagh's legs in blue jeans behind the easel – set in the centre of a terra-cotta tiled floor, against the backdrop of a bare plaster wall – as he paints the portrait. The subjects are shown looking at it over his shoulder, Brenda Quinn in three-quarter length skirt and white blouse on one side with a baby in her arms, and the little girl, dressed in a white smock, hands in her pockets, gazing up.

Wilson Hartnell ad agency chief Mary Finan approached him for an image that could be auctioned to raise money for the Irish Kidney Association. He came up with an eye-catching painting of a woman with a bottle of the non-alcoholic drink Kaliber, twisted in a knot. The *Irish Independent* wanted a portrait of the Irish boxer Barry McGuigan, celebrating a second successful defence of his world title. Ballagh obliged even though he wouldn't know a boxing glove from a boot.

Postage stamps provided him with a miniature gallery where his images of everything from a couple of lighthouses and the first Aer Lingus plane to portraits of Arthur Griffith and Cathal Brugha reached the entire population through the letter-box. By the mid-1990s his art would be in everyone's pocket or purse courtesy of his design of the last Irish banknotes before the changeover to the euro.

Michael Colgan's surprise invitation to design a set for the Gate Theatre's innovative Beckett one-person show *I'll Go On* turned out to be the start of a wide-ranging collaboration with lighting designer Rupert Murray. It opened up an alternative art space where he would push Irish stage design in revolutionary new directions, culminating with the global success of *Riverdance* a decade later. But at the time he was just glad to get the money.

*Portrait of Barry McGuigan for a special edition of the Irish Independent.*

*I'll Go On* was directed by Colm O'Briain, former director of the Arts Council, who had just retired as general secretary of the Labour Party. This was to be his comeback. He gave everyone involved in the production copies of Samuel Beckett's three novels *Molloy, Malone Dies* and *The Unnamable*. "We were all supposed to contribute to putting the text together. I remember thinking that if all theatrical shows involved so much work and collaboration I didn't think I'd be able for any more."

O'Briain was keen to sustain a certain narrative logic so that the piece would have a oneness about it. The idea was to follow the inherent structure of the trilogy rather than take excerpts. "The more I absorbed myself in Beckett the more I realised that less is more. Ideally all that was needed was just an actor saying those wonderful words and anything else would be an unnecessary extra. But of course you have to have something else."

Not knowing what was or was not feasible – he had never worked in theatre before – Ballagh came up with the minimalist idea of something that almost is not there, a cube space delineated by a rim of neon light. "Drawing with light is total abstraction. Establishing a space for Barry in this way rather than obeying naturalistic conventions would be much more in keeping with Beckett's work. The least amount of clutter seemed essential. You don't want to presume to add anything to Beckett."

When he was told he couldn't use neons, he asked why not. Nobody could say. O'Briain had an entirely different concept of what the set should be. Ballagh argued with him, but didn't seem to be getting anywhere. One day Colgan looked in.

"How are you getting on?" "I'm having a problem. Colm doesn't seem to like what I'm doing and has suggested something else." "What do you think about what he suggested?" "I don't like it." "Well what are you going to do?" "Ach, I'm weary with it. I'll probably do what he wants." "That's fine, but if you do that, I'm going to demand that you stand at the top of the stairs every night with a sign around you saying, 'I designed this set, but it wasn't the one I wanted to design.'"

So Ballagh dug in his heels. There were some compromises, but essentially he got the set he wanted. "I thought it was quite possible I'd never get to do another set," he says.

*I'll Go On* was invited to Paris for Beckett's 80th birthday the following April. Ballagh was unable to be there. A few days before, Betty fell down the stairs at Caesar's Restaurant in Dame Street. Her skull was fractured. She was in a coma. In those days certain hospitals were on call for accidents, others were not. So she was taken to the Meath Hospital. Ballagh knew nothing about hospitals. He'd never been sick in his life.

"They told me after a day or two that she was coming out of the coma, it's all fine. She was moved out of intensive care into a ward. She was conscious and then slipping back into unconsciousness. I wasn't comfortable with this at all. After a week I said we're not really making much progress here. But every time I spoke to doctors, they said, no, no, everything is fine, it's going well."

One morning when he went to the hospital he met playwright Peter Sheridan. He and Betty were on the board of the City Arts Centre. He was visiting her with his wife, Sheila.

"What do you think?" Sheridan asked. "I'm not happy." "Jesus, I'm not happy either. I wouldn't think she's doing well."

Ballagh realised he had to do something, but didn't know what. He remembered that Eoin O'Brien, who had commissioned him to do illustrations for his book *The Beckett Country*, practiced in the heart and lung department of Jervis Street Hospital. He called him. O'Brien promised to visit Betty on his lunch break. Later in the afternoon he phoned back.

"Betty's on her way to the Richmond Hospital." "Is that necessary?" "It's very definitely necessary. You'll get a call in a short while from Sandy Pate."

Then Pate, a brain surgeon, phoned. "Everything is under control, Mr Ballagh, but I'd like your permission to make an intervention." "What's that?" "Well most people call it an operation." It involved drilling into Betty's head. A couple of hours later Pate phoned back. "Everything is fine. Your wife had a clot."

While Betty was going through this trauma, *I'll Go On* was on stage in Paris. Beckett didn't go to the show, but invited everyone to meet him next morning. According to Colgan, they all arrived and sat down. Beckett was sitting there, waiting and waiting. Then he turned to Colgan and said, "Are we waiting for Ballagh?"

He couldn't have known, but because of *The Beckett Country* – which prompted Ballagh to consult O'Brien – he was indirectly responsible for saving Betty's life.

Betty quickly recovered physically, probably too quickly for her own good. She had lost confidence. There were all sorts of side effects. "I would think that it took her years to fully get over it," says Ballagh. "You can't overemphasise how debilitating an injury like that is. People don't understand because you look all right physically. They think that's it, what are you complaining about."

Months later they travelled together to Iraq for the General Assembly of the International Artists Association, a UNESCO-funded organisation with 82 member countries. Betty, who had been administrator of the Association of Artists in Ireland and attended the previous Assembly in Helsinki, was invited when the Iraqis heard about what they called her 'catastrophe'.

Between official meetings, at which Ballagh was elected to the executive committee and nominated as treasurer – which meant he would be responsible for a budget of several million dollars – there were visits to Samara, the cradle of Western civilisation, and Kerbala, sacred city of the Shia Muslims. At Babylon, Betty found it impossible to walk down the steps. Steps still terrified her.

They couldn't be sure whether or not they ever met Saddam Hussein because there were always three or four men who looked like the dictator to shake hands at official events. It was 1986 and Saddam was at that time an ally of the West, which backed his war against Iran and the Ayatollah Kohmeni. The Industrial Development Authority was out in Iraq, promoting Irish goods. Aer Lingus ran the hospitals. The hotels were full of Irish doctors and nurses. Larry Goodman was selling Irish beef.

Ballagh had never been in a country where the cult of personality was so inescapable. "You arrived in Saddam Hussein International Airport, drove across the Saddam Hussein Bridge and attended meetings at the Saddam Hussein Conference Centre. I wrote about the trip in *the Irish Press* when we got back to Ireland, saying I was uncomfortable with the regime, and I was denounced by members of Fianna Fáil. In 1991 when Saddam invaded Kuwait and the US launched *Operation Desert Storm* and I supported the anti-war movement, the same people attacked me for being a stooge of Saddam. When we were in Iraq we'd visited a leading Iraqi female artist Laila Alattar. Later in the Gulf War a Cruise missile hit her studio and her house. She was vaporised. I signed a petition about her. Sadly, nobody cared."

Through his activities on the executive committee Ballagh formed contacts that led to an invitation to exhibit his paintings in Moscow, Warsaw and Sofia. He became close friends with the first secretary of the Soviet Artists Union, Tair Salahov, who was also a member of the Supreme Soviet and a personal friend of Mikhail Gorbachev. He was invited to attend a Peace Forum in Moscow in February 1987, along with 1,000 leading international scientists, artists and writers.

The day he arrived in the Cosmos Hotel, where all the guests were put up, he came down to breakfast to find himself having bacon and eggs with Gregory Peck, who during the Forum read from William Faulkner's Nobel Prize acceptance speech warning of the nuclear threat to the world. At lunch he sat with Yoko Ono. Because he was an English speaker – but from a neutral country – he was asked to chair an afternoon session of the Writers Union at which the main speakers were Graham Greene, Norman Mailer and Gore Vidal.

On becoming general secretary of the Communist Party of the Soviet Union in 1985, Gorbachev had launched twin policies of perestroika, a reform and restructuring of the political and economic system, and glasnost or openness, a policy of democratising socialism. This was backed by a move towards disarmament and détente with the West, and would trigger a transition to democracy throughout Eastern Europe culminating in 1989 with the fall of the Berlin Wall, but also the break-up of the Soviet Union, which Gorbachev had hoped to avert.

"In my opinion glasnost is real and of enormous significance," Ballagh said on RTÉ's Questions & Answers programme after he returned to Ireland. "It is not window dressing as some cynical critics in the West have suggested. However the final irony is that its ultimate success may depend on those in the West who in the past have been consistent critics of the Soviet Union." He was amazed to discover afterwards that many people felt challenged by this assertion.

The Russian poet Andrei Voznesensky, who had been involved in getting many banned writers published, including Boris Pasternak's *Dr Zhivago*, argued during the Forum that the changes taking place were not a cultural revolution but rather a revolution by culture. He insisted that the changes were not imposed from above but came from the grass roots.

On the final day Gorbachev hosted a meeting in the Kremlin. "Essentially revolutionary changes are under way here," he said. "They are of immense significance for our society, for socialism as a whole, and for the entire world. We want a broad democratisation of all society. Further democratisation is also the main guarantee of the irreversible nature of the ongoing process. We must have a new outlook and overcome the mentality, stereotypes and dogmas inherited from a past gone never to return."

Sadly Gorbachev would be succeeded by Boris Yeltsin, a man – to quote the nuclear physicist Andrei Sakharov, Russia's great human rights activist – 'of a completely lesser calibre', a populist clown who stood on a tank to defy plotters who had put Gorbachev under house arrest in 1991, but in 1993 used the same tanks to storm the Russian Parliament. "What followed was one of the greatest robberies in human history," says Ballagh, "a farce overseen by Yeltsin where all the state industries which belonged to the Russian people were bought for a song by people like Roman Abramovitch who became billionaires overnight, leaving Russia broke and impoverished. Thousands died of hunger and poverty as a consequence, but the whole thing was hailed in the West as a wonderful success. That's why Putin, who is anything but a democrat, is so popular. The economy was in chaos under Yeltsin. Putin stepped in, steadied the boat and gave Russians back some sense of dignity and national pride."

◆

Michael Colgan was back on the phone. Patrick Mason planned to re-set Oscar Wilde's *The Importance of Being Earnest* in Margaret Thatcher's Britain. He wanted Ballagh to give it visual expression.

"The trouble with Wilde is that his plays were adopted as part of the very institutions he satirised," Mason explained. "All the visual clichés that traditionally go with Wilde, the stylish elegance, have merely reinforced this cosiness. It's a play about the English ruling classes, and how they maintain power by lying and cheating while pretending to be very high-principled. The whole 'importance of being earnest' is that you must be anything but earnest to get what you want. It's the classical hypocrisy of the ruling classes. Form is everything. Provided form is observed, you can be as ruthless as you like to get what you want.

"With Thatcher espousing a return to Victorian values, the similarity between the 1890s and the 1980s becomes uncanny. So what's to stop us finding a contemporary style for it? If we're to look at the people in *The Importance of Being Earnest* differently, we have to look at the space they occupy differently. We have to 're-vision' the play. Fundamentally I want to remind people that the play is a satirical portrait of people who are still alive and with us."

To create this effect, Ballagh designed a starkly minimal set of bare marble walls with a slightly raked black and white

The Gate Theatre production of
'The Importance of being Earnest'.
Photo: Tom Lawlor

tiled floor. This was framed by a lavish gilt proscenium arch, and dominated by Winterholder's portrait of Queen Victoria which in reality hangs in the lobby of Buckingham Palace. Permission had to be got from the Lord Chamberlain to use a big copy of the painting, which was created by Oliver Whelan from the National College of Art and Design.

The atmosphere, heightened by the hard-edge silhouettes of Nigel Boyd's Bruce Oldfield-style costumes – the women dressed like Princess Di, the men in double-breasted City suits – is that of a cold rigid society dominated by icons of the monarchy and Victorian morality. "I wouldn't have been interested in recreating a 19th-century drawing room," says Ballagh. "A non-naturalistic set offers far more opportunities in theatre than the traditional style of set. It puts the concentration back on the writer's word. It simply becomes a backdrop for the actors and hopefully creates a mood within which the play comes alive."

It required much research and discussion with Mason before Ballagh come up with a number of models, all the time honing down. "Patrick is very specific. When he takes on a project he really gets involved. He'd call into our house every day to discuss what we were doing, where we were going. When you're doing something cool and minimal, there's no room for mistakes or excesses. Even the chairs have to be meticulously designed to fit in with the total concept. If a character was required to light a cigarette, I had to design a cigarette box and a cigarette lighter and an ash tray."

Aesthetically the play had to be a pleasure. Whether as comedy or satire, Wilde wanted it to be art. So it was a matter of finding another style to heighten the hard edge of the play rather than the traditional camp interpretation that saw the characters as lovable English eccentrics. Initially Ballagh tried designing furniture similar in style to the set, but then decided that if the characters were truly representative of Thatcher's Britain, they wouldn't have high-tech objects in their homes. "I came up instead with a redesign of Hepplewhite chairs painted in gold with off-white upholstery. Even though the set is cool and minimal, we felt it should have an expensive look, the look of privilege."

*The Importance of Being Earnest* opened at the Gate Theatre in July 1987 to approving reviews, and confirmed Ballagh's emergence as an innovative creative force in stage design. It drew on his architectural training and appealed to his penchant for making things. His models for sets were miniature art objects in their own right, inspired by the balsa wood model planes of his childhood. He revelled in the collaborative nature of theatre. "I thought after *The Importance of Being Earnest* that all directors would be like Patrick Mason."

Much of his time in 1987 was taken up by work on the executive committee of the International Association of Art, which

brought him regularly to Paris for meetings, but also to the Soviet Union, Japan, Cuba and Bulgaria. Having persuaded Irish artists to organise professionally by forming the Artists Association of Ireland, he realised that their strength as a small group depended on engaging in international art politics. "Irish artists are inclined to turn to London, New York and maybe France and Germany if they're looking for examples or looking for influence, but I was seeing how art functioned in entirely different countries."

Taking part in a painting symposium in Bulgaria he found that nobody agreed with the Irish tax-free scheme for artists. They didn't see why artists should be more privileged than anyone else. The Artists Union, which regulated the conditions under which most visual artists worked, received no state funding. Its £3 million budget came from its own creative fund made up of sales from craft workshops, publishing revenues and a 2 per cent commission on all art works sold by members. "They didn't need tax breaks or government financing because art was widely used. You couldn't walk into a building that wasn't thick with paintings. Public spaces were festooned with sculpture and murals. Even the smallest towns had first-class galleries. Sales were virtually guaranteed at the ten to fifteen open submission exhibitions held at different venues throughout each year. The jury in each case decided all the prices."

Because Socialist countries were hugely supportive of UNESCO, the US and the UK under Reagan and Thatcher walked out, but stopped short of pulling out of the UN because they felt they might still need it. One of the final straws was when UNESCO declared 'old' Havana part of the 'Patrimony of the World' and gave grants for the restoration of some of the buildings. Reagan was furious. "We're not giving money to an organisation that gives money to Communists," he declared. It didn't occur to him that maybe Havana was part of the patrimony not just of Cuba – which was anathema to the US – but of the world.

All this took up so much of Ballagh's time that by the end of 1987 he found he hadn't painted a single picture. "I'd never had a year with no paintings in my entire career. It took me by surprise. I didn't want it to happen again."

The New Year began with another call from Michael Colgan. Steven Berkoff was coming to the Gate Theatre to direct a production of Oscar Wilde's *Salomé*. There was only one problem. He loathed set designers. All he wanted was a black box. When Colgan asked if he could get someone to design the box, Berkoff refused. "If you ask a designer to do something simply," he said, "he'll inevitably add to it until it becomes his own statement."

Berkoff had allowed only a single chaise lounge on an empty stage when he directed a production of his social satire *Decadence* at the Gate in 1985. Growing up in two rooms in London's East End where the family had to go to the local baths to get hot water had left him with a loathing of indulgence. "It has conditioned my approach to theatre like a genetic code," he said.

Colgan had a hunch that Ballagh's minimalist designs for *I'll Go On* and *The Importance of Being Earnest* – in which nothing was allowed to distract from the acting and the text – might win him over.

*Model of set for the Gate Theatre's*
*production of 'Salomé'.*
*Photo: Robert Ballagh*

31

*Donal O'Kelly and Paul O'Hanrahan in 'The Wake'.*
*Photo: Derek Spiers*

Some weeks later Berkoff agreed to meet Ballagh. Ballagh brought along a model with thick white pillars inspired by Butt Bridge. It didn't at all resemble a black box. Although Berkoff rejected it, he afterwards complained that Ballagh had not brought more ideas. Colgan felt encouraged to ask Ballagh back.

"Beautiful sets are what the Gate excels at," says Ballagh. "The idea of the Gate without a set was unthinkable." What he came up with was a sunken raked tiled area with two tiers of marbled steps at the top of which was a rectangular black table set against a massive backcloth. "We talked it over with Berkoff but I don't think he was really listening or understood what was going on. He seemed to agree."

The set with its different levels was difficult to build. Three days before the first preview it was finally in place on the Gate stage. Ballagh was sitting in the stalls. Berkoff came in. He took one look and bellowed, "I fucking hate it." The carpenters stopped what they were doing as if in mid-sentence. "I should have stuck with what I said," ranted Berkoff. "This is fucking terrible." He began beating his head on the steps. Then he stormed out.

"What are we going to do?" asked a carpenter. "We'll finish it. That's our job", said Ballagh. So they did. By the time Colgan arrived – he had been alerted by production manager Trevor Dawson – Berkoff had calmed down and was back walking the stage and trying out different positions. "I think he likes it," Colgan said. Ballagh replied, "I know he does."

Their next encounter was at the dress rehearsal. By then Berkoff was having problems with the actors. "I think Stephen feeds off difficulties. Afterwards he came over and embraced me and said, 'It's the finest set I've ever worked on.'" *Salomé* went to Edinburgh Festival. The next year Berkoff brought Ballagh over to the National Theatre in London for a production which then transferred to the West End. "Obviously he did like it."

If Ballagh could work with Berkoff, he could work with anyone. Donal O'Kelly was a friend from meetings in support of the Sandinistas in Nicaragua, but he – like Berkoff – had an aversion to sets. "I don't need a set, I just need a table and chair," O'Kelly insisted when he met Ballagh in a pub to discuss the design for Rough Magic's production of his one-man show *Bat the Father, Rabbit the Son* at Dublin Theatre Festival.

The play explored tensions between past and present-day Ireland through a voyage of memory in which a self-made haulage magnate comes to terms with his father, a former Easter Rising rebel and pawn shop assistant. The table and chair could be used to suggest a boat or whatever the performance required. Ballagh produced a model of a metal table and chair which like water would reflect light. He had the idea that the acting area should be a blue platform furling upward like a sail. O'Kelly wasn't happy. He wanted a flat floor rectangle. The eventual set was a clearly defined flat triangle, a compromise of sorts.

The collaboration was successful and O'Kelly and Ballagh teamed up again the following year for a Dublin Theatre Festival production of O'Kelly's and O'Hanrahan's adaptation of *The Wake* from James Joyce's *Finnegans Wake*. This time the brief was even briefer. Since the script was to evolve in the course of rehearsal, Ballagh had little or nothing to go on, either thematically or structurally. He surprised everyone by turning up to an early production meeting with a briefcase from which he emptied a pile of children's building blocks of different shapes and sizes. "Something like this," he told O'Kelly and director David Grant, "only bigger, and perhaps with a marbled finish." The idea was that O'Kelly and co-actor Paul O'Hanrahan could spontaneously arrange and rearrange the shapes to suggest whatever the text prompted, whether streets, interiors, a corpse or even the initials of Finnegan's protagonist. "Robert's design was an essential element of the production," said Grant. "Without it, or had it taken a different form, I am sure the end-product would have been substantively different."

◆

In 1987 the Independent Dublin councillor Carmencita Hederman succeeded Bertie Ahern, the Fianna Fáil TD and future Minister for Finance and Taoiseach, as Lord Mayor of Dublin. She was only the second woman mayor in the city's history, the first being Kathleen Clarke, widow of executed Easter Rising leader Thomas Clarke. During her one-year term she presided over the celebrations of Dublin's millennium and became a widely recognised and popular figure, which perhaps helped clear the way for Mary Robinson to be elected Ireland's first woman President three years later.

Hederman came from the affluent property-owning Cruess Callaghan family and rose to political prominence through her involvement in the Upper Leeson Street Area Residents Association, formed in 1968 in response to the Dublin Development Plan.

Hederman and other concerned residents, including the McDowell family, the architect Martin Reynolds and a barrister Thomas Doyle, feared one of Dublin's most architecturally cohesive and historical suburbs – Ballagh had grown up in neighbouring Elgin Road – would suffer considerable damage if the provisions in the Plan were allowed to stand. Their campaign was so successful that the area was rezoned for residential use only and became a no-go area for the unauthorised property development that blighted Dublin in the 1960s and 1970s.

Ballagh, who had taken part in protests against the demolition of Georgian buildings in Hume Street in the late 1960s, was commissioned to paint her portrait. Apart from his portrait of the contralto Bernadette Greevy – commissioned by Gordon Lambert in 1979 – he had never had a woman as a single subject before. In fact out of 91 portraits, not counting self-portraits and paintings of his family, only nine of his subjects have been women. If a woman featured in any of his commissioned work, it was invariably only as the wife of a successful man, or the mother of his children.

"The fact that I have done so few portraits of women is a huge indication of the nature of Irish society. It reflects a betrayal of the dreams of 1916. Although women always took the radical side in the struggle for independence and were among the most

*Top: The Custom House Murals.*

*Above: Robert Ballagh with the team of young people from Dublin's inner city who worked with him on the murals.*

vociferous anti-Treaty people during the Civil War, the new Irish Free State soon back-tracked on the idea of carving out a role for women in the new Irish society."

The portrait of Hederman differs from conventional civic poses in that the subject is shown from one side rather than head-on, dressed in the blue and green gold-trimmed gown of her office, hands on her lap, while the imposing City Hall dominates the background, drawn in meticulous architectural detail from a dramatic angled perspective.

Restoration work was starting at that time on the Custom House, another Dublin landmark building further down the Liffey. It had been designed in the 18th century by James Gandon, the architect who gave Dublin its distinctive Georgian look. David Slattery, who was in charge of the work, realised that the front of the building would be covered in a hoarding for over a year. He wondered if Ballagh could turn it into some kind of art work. Although Ballagh didn't feel physically capable of undertaking such a large work – it involved two spaces 150 feet wide and 60 feet high – he mentioned it to Independent TD Tony Gregory and to Mick Rafferty, who ran a FÁS training project in the north inner city. They suggested that a team of unemployed inner-city young people might be able to work with him on the giant mural. Ballagh was appointed on a temporary basis as their tutor.

He set up the project in a derelict warehouse known as Stack A which was made available by Mark Kavanagh, one of the developers involved in transforming Dublin's docklands into a Financial Services Centre somewhat in the manner of London's Canary Wharf – a favourite project of recently re-elected Taoiseach Charles Haughey. It was originally used as a banqueting hall for returning soldiers from the Crimean War. Some people still referred to it as the Crimean Banqueting Hall.

Part of the Docklands promotional package had been to restore Stack A as a new Museum of Modern Art, for which it was ideally suited both in its open architecture and central location. One of Haughey's closest advisers Pádraig O Huígin visited the Reina Sofia Museum in Madrid and suggested instead that the recently restored and somewhat similar Royal Hospital at Kilmainham, on the outskirts of Dublin, could more easily be turned around into a modern art space with minimal extra work. "I still believe this was a monumental error," says Ballagh. "I suspect the reason the decision was made was that 1990 was going to be the year of Ireland's presidency of the EU. Haughey wanted to be able to mark his spell as President of Europe with some seemingly grand Mitterand-like architectural gesture."

The value of community art for Ballagh is that it's about process, not product. This is not the view of most of the art community, who judge it exclusively in terms of product. They're critical of the fact that a lot of the work that comes out of community art projects isn't of a quality comparable to work done by professional artists, not realising that that's the whole point of it. "I've worked on a lot of community art projects that may not have produced the greatest art in the history of the world, but the people involved were empowered by the experience, and that's what's important. I'd almost consider it a failure if the end product of a community art project I'm involved with looked like my art. It should be their art."

However the Custom House project was so big he was obliged to compromise this principle. "I couldn't afford to mess around for months trying to develop a concept. So I came in literally with the whole thing planned and the young people worked according to my instructions very closely."

The imagery was a gigantic blueprint of the Custom House arranged on a drawing board with a pencil, ruler, triangle, palette and brush attached. "I designed it in a way that it could be painted by people who had no previous experience, using masking tape, emulsion paint and rollers. I think I learned more about life from them than they learned about art from me. Two of the kids afterwards got jobs with contracting firms – the first new jobs in Sheriff Street for over 25 years, someone joked — another two ended up in St Patrick's Juvenile Prison, and two got pregnant, although not while they were working for me. So it was a very rich experience."

RTE did a programme about it. There were so many expletives that it took ages to record anything. One girl was asked what she'd do if somebody vandalised the mural. "Wha?" she said. "Vandalised, like damaged it." "I'd fucking kill them."

Picking up from where he left off at the Customs House – and at the prompting again of Gerry Adams – Ballagh revisited Belfast to apply what he had learned about the socially empowering value of community art to the plethora of political murals that had become an outlet for popular expression for young Republicans on the Falls Road.

Although he had been castigated for his decision to involve himself in the inaugural West Belfast Festival the previous August – seen by Adams as a way to defuse the communal tension traditionally triggered every summer by the anniversary of internment – he saw it as a small part of a process that might eventually enable the North to find a way out of its twenty-year spiral of violence.

Wearing an 'I Love Belfast' sticker in his lapel, he told local reporters that the significance of the murals was in "ordinary people telling their own stories". He awarded the top prize to Gerry Kelly, known to all by his nickname 'Macara', for a Jim Fitzpatrick-inspired larger-than-life depiction of Nuada the Celtic God of War, and his runners-up prizes went to a portrait of the Gibraltar Three and a tribute to Nelson Mandela by Falls Sinn Féin Youth. He pointed out that art could not really be separated from politics. "I think that the growth of murals here is terribly important, especially with the significance they took on during the hunger strikes. When their stories failed to appear in the media, the people chose to paint them on gable walls."

The fact that the festival largely succeeded in averting the usual street violence and confrontations with the RUC and the British Army seemed to pass virtually unnoticed by the Dublin media, with the exception of Mary Holland, who in her column in the *Irish Times* acknowledged the willingness of artists from the Republic – like Ballagh, Tomás MacAnna and Ulick O'Connor – to make the journey North to participate.

"It would be even better," she wrote, "if some politicians, who are ever ready with instant opinions on what should be happening in Northern Ireland, could also attend. They won't for fear of being branded Provo sympathisers, as though the very air of West Belfast might contaminate their reputations."

*Robert Ballagh with two young
muralists from West Belfast.*

She quoted the Rev Des Wilson's tribute to the spirit of a community which had somehow managed to survive "20 years of unbelievable assault from the military, police, pulpit, newspaper and broadcasting companies, all conspiring to see who could heap the greatest insult on the greatest injury, all vying with each other to be the first to condemn and the last to understand".

Ballagh returned to Dublin determined to campaign in whatever small way he could against the insidious spread of political censorship under the provisions of Section 31 and the culture of denial that treated all Republicans as social pariahs, blindly excluding them from political debate without which there could be no peaceful way forward. "I became more and more concerned with what was going on in terms of Irish identity. I didn't approve of political violence so I'd no objection to people condemning political violence and attempting to counter it. But the kind of hysterical response to it became mixed up with some sort of guilt or shame so that anything Irish was rejected."

A consequence of the blanket censorship operated under RTÉ's rigid application of Section 31was that all the important documentaries about miscarriages of justice to do with the Birmingham Six and the Guildford Four or the killings in Gibraltar were made by Yorkshire TV, Granada, Thames and BBC, not by RTÉ. "I thought this was sad. You had the whole revisionist thing in history which started to try to argue that we disgraced ourselves in 1916, that the Famine was purely an act of nature and that those responsible, namely the British, had nothing to do with it's consequences."

The final straw was when an actor friend auditioned for a part in RTÉ but was turned down because, he was told, Northern accents were too threatening to put on radio. Ballagh's response was *The History Lesson*, an attempt to put back on the table for discussion challenging sociological and ideological issues underlying the 1916 Proclamation that had been swept under the carpet. After a brief award-winning appearance at the annual Oireachtas Exhibition it disappeared from sight, following an Office of Public Works arts committee's intervention to prevent its purchase for display by the Pearse Museum.

Ballagh had gone through similar rejection with his Noël Browne portrait in 1986. The Fine Gael backbencher TD Liam Skelly wanted to buy it and then loan it or donate it to Leinster House, the home of both houses of the Oireachtas. Skelly argued that Dr Browne, who had retired from active politics in 1981, was "one of the outstanding political figures since the foundation of the State and was remembered for the eradication of TB".

Dáil Eireann's powerful Committee on Procedures and Privileges turned down the offer, claiming that it felt bound by a long standing practice according to which only portraits of the 1921 Cabinet and busts of the 1916 leaders and portraits of former Taoisigh could be displayed. One member commented, "If we were to agree to hang Noël Browne, we could be inundated with requests to put up pictures of distinguished former members of the Oireachtas."

Ulick O'Connor, who was on the Hugh Lane Municipal Gallery advisory committee, took up the issue of the public not being able to see the Noël Browne portrait. He proposed its purchase. The response by an influential member of the committee echoed that of the OPW committee to *The History Lesson*: "Over my dead body that artist gets bought."

Several years were to pass before the Noël Browne portrait was eventually purchased by the National Gallery. "Here I had a painting that obviously people wanted to see and yet all the public spaces were closing their doors to me." Browne was widely admired throughout the country. His 1986 autobiography *Against The Tide* had been a publishing sensation, selling 80,000 copies after an initial print run of 1,500 which at the time publisher Michael Gill feared might be too ambitious. At one point Browne, fiercely determined to protect the integrity of his story, took the manuscript back from Gill – or rather the three manuscripts, he couldn't make up his mind which one he preferred. The tear-stained pages were evidence of the emotional stress he experienced in reliving his impoverished childhood. He insisted on having someone he could trust edit the narrative into shape – the "jigsaw" as he called it – and suggested to Gill that I might be acceptable. Three large boxes of typescript were delivered to my house and I spent some months forming a single narrative from the harrowing testimony they contained. Browne seemed to have lost interest in events after his resignation as Minister for Health in 1951, so it was necessary to tape his memories of the later years of his political career to form the final chapters of the book. He came to my house several times and patiently submitted to my questioning, and seemed happy in the "order" that emerged in the final manuscript.

Browne had indicated that he didn't like the idea of his portrait going to any of the private buyers who had approached Ballagh. He preferred the notion of it being in a public space. Eventually in the late 1990s the director of the National Gallery Raymond Keavaney and his assistant Brian Kennedy saw the painting in an exhibition at Kennys Gallery in Galway. They decided to purchase it. Several members of the board of the Gallery were opposed. Rather than have the portrait turned down, Keavaney kept it in storage at the Gallery for over a year waiting for the right moment to propose it. After some changes on the board, he eventually got the purchase approved three years later. "The sad thing is that Noël was sick when it was finally hung in the Gallery. He wasn't well enough to come up from Connemara to see it, and he died before he could make the journey."

Undeterred by the rejection of the Noël Browne portrait and *The History Lesson*, Ballagh decided to embark on a portrait of Michael O'Riordan, founder of the Communist Party of Ireland and a veteran of the International Brigades that fought Franco during the Spanish Civil War. As with the Browne painting, it was a personal undertaking. No one commissioned it. If Ballagh was to rely on commissions he would find himself confined to painting the rich and famous.

"I was always keen to paint Michael," he says. "I thought he had a great face. Both he and Noël Browne stuck to their principles when they were neither popular nor profitable. It seems we don't want to cover the left side of politics in Ireland. In the case of Noël Browne this ran absolutely in the face of reality. Whatever about the politics of Noël, there's hardly a person in Ireland who didn't respect him. It's not as if politicians and decision makers were following public opinion. They actually weren't."

By the time he died in 2006 aged 79 this would also be true of O'Riordan. Tributes were paid by the President of Ireland

*Preparitory drawing of pattern for Michael O'Riordan's tie.*

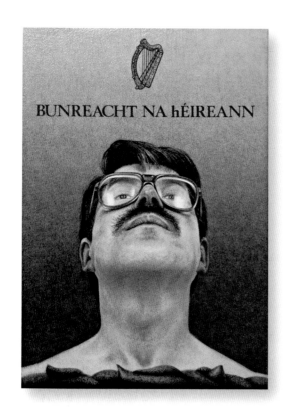

*The Citizen* (1988)
*Oil on canvas. 30 x 20cm.*
*Collection: District Art Museum, Smolian, Bulgaria.*

Mary McAleese, the Taoiseach Bertie Ahern, Sinn Feín leader Gerry Adams and the Labour Party's Ruairi Quinn and Michael D Higgins. But in 1989 it was different. The portrait was unlikely to find a buyer, and it didn't.

O'Riordan was a little reluctant about being painted. Perhaps he thought it was too bourgeois. But eventually he gave in. The concept of the portrait was paradoxical. Here was a defiantly secular politician who fought Catholic Blueshirt fascism on the streets of Cork in the early 1930s, was severely injured on the Ebro front in Spain, was interned in the Curragh during the Second World War, and agitated for social housing to replace Dublin's slums in the 1960s, yet Ballagh chose to depict him in the form of a Russian religious icon, the dominant colours of which are red and green to reflect socialism and nationalism.

Ballagh always asks his subjects if there is anything in particular they'd like to have included in their portrait. "Mick said, 'Well I've been awarded over 40 medals by the Soviet Union.' I thought, oh my God, he's going to want them all in. But he only wanted one, and that was for veterans of the Spanish Civil War." For good measure, Ballagh gave him a flamboyant tie sporting a hammer and sickle, a design inspired by early Soviet textile art.

With unsold paintings accumulating in his studio, Ballagh relied on a variety of art and design jobs to pay the bills. Stamps were a steady earner. His pencil drawing of Arthur Griffith in 1986 launched a series of portraits of Irish statesmen for An Post, which he continued with Cathal Brugha in 1987, William T Cosgrave in 1988 and Sean T O'Kelly in 1989, before completing it with Michael Collins in 1990. He accepted a commission to paint the family of the Austrian ambassador. Dublin City University commissioned a portrait of Minister for Education Mary O'Rourke, who was their chancellor. A Bulgarian museum bought a satirical self-portrait showing him drowning in shit beneath a copy of the Irish Constitution. He painted it out of "total frustration" after the defeat of the Divorce Referendum in 1986.

*In the Heart Of Hibernian Metropolis*, inspired by a Lawrence photograph of O'Connell Street taken in 1904, was commissioned as part of a Dutch project in which twelve European artists were invited to make an image of their native city. It depicts James Joyce in a neat suit and hat strolling past the GPO in conversation with a shirt-sleeved Ballagh. Nelson's Pillar bisects the vanishing point of the picture.

Although without a shilling to his name, Ballagh was paradoxically a man of property. He'd grown up in a rented flat on Elgin

Road. After his marriage to Betty in 1967 they lived in a bed-sit in Rathgar, paying rent of £5 a week. "It was a tiny little shoe-box. You had to put a half-crown in the meter for the lights to go on. If you wanted a bath you had to put another half crown in the geezer." Betty's siblings had moved with her mother to Manchester after her father died, but she refused to go. Although only 16, she preferred to stay on alone at 3 Temple Cottages, the small terraced cottage in Broadstone where she had been born. She moved out after her marriage, but her mother had kept up the tenancy. "It's stupid to have it sitting there empty while you're living like this," she told them on a visit back to Dublin. By then they'd had enough of romantic penury. They moved back in.

Temple Cottages was built in the 19th century by the Artisans Dwelling Company, a private company set up to provide accommodation for tradesmen working in the nearby Broadstone railway station. "Technically Betty's mother was still the tenant, but we took over the rent of 30 shillings a week, which even then was very small. It had been fixed back at the turn of the century. It included maintenance, so if your window got broken, Dublin Artisans fixed it. Obviously this was crazy economics. In the mid-1970s they decided to liquidate their assets. Every tenant got a letter offering a chance to buy out their house for £650. We ignored it. Shortly afterwards we got another letter. The offer was now £750. If we didn't buy it would be sold anyway."

Ballagh didn't have the money. Nor could he get it from a bank. Banks didn't lend money to artists. He borrowed from his parents and from anyone who could help out. It was the best investment they ever made – a single story cottage up the road would sell for €450,000 in 2007. Betty knew all the neighbours from childhood. Although Ballagh was regarded as a something of a blow-in, he too eventually was made to feel he belonged.

Several years later the family next door in No 4 decided to move to Donnycarney. They offered first option on their house for £17,500. Ballagh could just about afford it with savings from his sell-out Isy Brachot show in Bruxelles, of people looking at paintings. "We  physically joined the two houses together by knocking holes in the walls and putting doorways through, and sort of made one house out of the two." This became the subject of two more paintings in his No 3 series, *Inside No 3 After Modernisation* and *Upstairs No 4, The Studio*.

Around the same time Ballagh received a phone call from the potter Stephen Pearce. Before their marriage they'd stayed a few times with Stephen's parents in Shanagarry in East Cork.

He'd told Pearce to give him a call if ever a place came on the market that might be suitable for a summer home. One morning, when Betty was

*The Reiner Family (1988)*
*Oil on canvas. 92 x 30cm.*
*Private Collection.*
*Portrait of the Austrian Ambassador and his family.*

pregnant with their second child Bruce, Pearce called. He'd put in a bid for a cottage in Ballybraher, near Ballycotton. If they were interested, they'd have to make their minds up before that evening. "So we got in the car and drove down. Nobody had lived in the cottage for the best part of a decade. The garden had run wild. There were brambles growing out of the roof. But the price, which included a third of an acre, was just £1,750. We couldn't go wrong, so we bought it."

When Ballagh went back to do a survey, he discovered that what he thought was a tiny cottage was actually quite large. It had eight rooms with a huge living room area. Since they couldn't afford continental holidays, they spent much of their summers there over the next few years, camping in the garden and using contract labour to strip the roof and redo it. "The cottage was around 200 years old. I didn't want to do it up and turn it into something like a semi-detached house on a Dublin housing estate. I wanted it to remain a traditional Irish cottage."

The slated roof was 56 feet long. By the time it was striped half the slates were no longer usable. He was told the only place he could get 3,000-4,000 slates would be from travellers. Eventually he found a traveller who had acquired all the slates from McKenzies, a big store on the quay in Cork which had recently been demolished. The asking price was 75 pence a slate. "I'd never done any bargaining before, but I said no and drove away. After coming back a few times I got him down to 10 pence a slate. I had to hire a driver and truck to collect them. They were all dumped in a field out on the Dublin road near Glanmire. Nobody was there. I could have taken 8,000 slates and no one would have noticed."

Over the years Ballagh would take a few weeks off every so often to carry out restoration work on the house and the garden. He created a studio, the subject of his painting *Highfield* in the summer of 1983. By the late 1980s Rachel, a student at the National College of Art and Design, and Bruce, by now in his teens, were bored spending holidays there. As a surprise, Ballagh decided to bring the family to Cuba, which he had first visited with Betty in 1984. His fee from designing a stamp to celebrate the Bicentenary of the French Revolution paid for the tickets.

"I'd made a lot of contacts there, in particular an artist called Luis Miguel Valdes. We split the holiday between Havana and Santa Maria Del Mar, about 12 kilometres away. When I got bored with the beach I could take the bus into Havana. We hooked up with Lyn Geldoff, a sister of Bob, who was working there as a journalist. There were few tourists then. People would stop you because they never saw anyone from abroad. This was when Cuba was flush with Soviet roubles."

He asked an old farmer aged about 80, who seemed to be -living much the way he had always lived, and probably his family before him, if the Revolution really meant much to him. "Well I have the electricity now," he said, gesturing to a small television set in the corner of his shack. "But your life hasn't changed?" "No, I live the way I've always lived. I don't want to change." "So the Revolution hasn't really meant that much to you?" The old man smiled. "My two grandchildren are engineers," he said.

The myth of the heroic guerrilla – of a handful of men in the mountains with guns, and with a just cause – led to the Che

Guevara delusion that what was achieved in Cuba could be repeated in other countries. But Cuba had been a one-off. Its revolution wasn't imposed, but came from the grassroots. Despite punitive US sanctions and attempted invasions, Castro set about creating a democracy of schools, universities, factories and professions that were open equally to all. "I do not subscribe to the violent version of revolution," says Ballagh. "I'm much happier with the notion of people deciding that they want political change and a better life, and achieving it with the minimum of violence."

◆

Someone from An Post was on the phone. "It has been decided not to proceed with the issuing of a stamp to commemorate the Bicentenary of the French Revolution," Ballagh was told. "I hope you will not be too disappointed."

Apparently thousands of copies of Ballagh's stamp had been shredded and the colour plates destroyed on instructions from the Irish Government. The declaration of an Irish Republic in 1916 had been inspired by the French Revolution and its stirring principles of liberty, equality and fraternity, as had the United Irishmen and the 1798 Uprising. But now it seemed it wasn't worth a stamp.

"I had been given a brief by the Stamps Design Committee which had consulted with the French Government to produce a stamp with a non-violent image. I came up with the idea of a hand holding a torch like the Statue of Liberty from which unfurled red, white and blue ribbons across two stamps. An Post were so pleased they showed it to the French postal services who thought it was probably the best stamp they'd seen from anywhere. They were interested in discussing a joint issue in France and Ireland on 14 July."

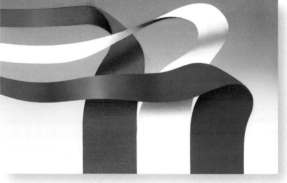

*Artwork for stamps to commemorate the French Revolution.*

41

Ballagh received no official confirmation or explanation for the decision to reject the stamp. Fergal Quinn, the chairman of An Post, promised to "try to find out more" but didn't. There were suggestions that maybe admirers of the painter Louis le Brocquy, who lived in the South of France, may have prompted Charlie Haughey to intervene. Ballagh wrote urging him "to look into the matter to ensure that honest and fair practices prevail". Haughey wrote back saying that he found it "difficult to understand the idea that the Government should not have the right to disapprove of a design. There would be little point in submitting designs to the Government for approval if they were not to be permitted any discretion". He added he would be glad to talk to Ballagh personally about the matter, but attempts to take him up on this offer were ignored. Feeling out in the cold, Ballagh finally reached Haughey's closest confident PJ Mara and warned that if any stamp other than his was issued he would go public. He got a phone call the next day saying Haughey would see him.

"What's this bruised ego, Ballagh?" said Haughey, calling him by his surname as always. "It's not bruised ego. I spent a lot of effort doing this stamp. Everyone seemed to think it was fine. At the last minute it was cancelled and shredded." "All I can say, Ballagh, is that the government didn't approve the stamp."

There wasn't any more Ballagh could do other than mention that An Post had approached him to do several stamps celebrating Irish theatre. "At this stage I'm not prepared to put all the work in and have it cancelled at the last minute." "You'll be alright, Ballagh," Haughey told him, giving him a nod and a wink.

The end of it all was that Ireland was alone in Europe with Britain in not bringing out a stamp to commemorate the 1789 Revolution. Some time later Ballagh met Brian Lenihan, the Tanaiste and Minister for Foreign Affairs. "He pulled me aside and said, 'Whatever happened to that lovely stamp you did?' Although the Government was supposed to have turned down the stamp, he obviously didn't know anything about it. It had been a solo run by Haughey."

A few weeks later Ballagh was in Moscow where the Soviet Union – itself the product of the Russian Revolution – was on its last legs. But there was still time for art. The Irish Ambassador Charles Whelan was at the Central House of the Artist Gallery, close to Gorky Park, to cut the tape to a major Ballagh retrospective, describing it as "a cultural milestone". The critic Mikhail Sokolov was particularly taken by the literary allusions in the paintings, especially references to James Joyce. He remarked on the serendipity of the first exhibition by a Dubliner in Moscow taking place in the same year as publication of the first Russian translation of Ulysses. "I pointed out that in fact I was only the second Dubliner to exhibit there, since Francis Bacon had had an exhibition in 1987. What I didn't add was that I would probably be the last."

Ballagh's realistic technique caused comment since it was perceived as being quite different to the work of most Soviet realist painters. "The general impression seemed to suggest an appreciation of the humour and irony in my work and an overall interest in the autobiographical paintings which frequently examine the relationship between the artist and society."

There were some reservations about the nude self portrait in *Upstairs No 3*, but the female nude of Betty drew most criticism. "This reaction seemed to parallel my own experience in Ireland, so it would appear that, at least in the area of sexuality, official attitudes were similar both in Ireland and in the USSR."

The stimulus of seeing so many of his paintings again together, as if in dialogue with each other, prompted him to embark on a new autobiographical painting. *Upstairs No 4, The Studio* was painted in the stop-gap studio built in the converted upstairs room formed by merging No 3 with the newly acquired neighbouring house. An updating of the series initiated in 1977 with the *No 3* painting and *Winter in Ronda,* it's a double self-portrait split into two irregularly shaped halves. One shows Ballagh clad in a red kimono standing with brushes in his hand and another between his teeth, looking out from a smallish room with an attic window that opens onto a blue sky. Makeshift wooden shelves are attached to the wall.

The other half looks back into *Upstairs No 3*, where he is about to descend the spiral staircase he previously ascended naked from the waist down. He's now wearing blue jeans. A copy of the 1916 Proclamation has replaced the Caillebotte painting and James Connolly portrait that hung on the wall in the previous painting. On the floor is a front page of the tabloid *Irish Press* proclaiming JOBLESS TOTAL REACHES 250,000. "I suppose I was influenced by Brian Friel's *Philadelphia Here I Come* where you've got Gar Public and Gar Private. You've got Robert Ballagh, the artist, and Robert Ballagh, the citizen. It's about the social responsibility of the artist as citizen."

His name is signed in Japanese in the top left corner. "A colleague of mine who has since died but was a wonderful wood block artist in Japan wrote my name in Japanese for me. I was very taken with the tension between traditional Japanese culture and modern Japan when I visited there for a conference, as a guest of the Japanese Artists Association."

As with *The History Lesson*, and the Noël Browne and Michael O'Riordan portraits, *Upstairs No 4, The Studio* didn't find a buyer. It seemed Ballagh had become persona non grata in public galleries. Given the low level of Irish art prices at that time, this was not necessarily a disadvantage.

Joan Miro once said that if a painting stayed in his studio for years it didn't bother him. "I think of my studio as a vegetable garden. Here, there are artichokes. Over there, potatoes. The leaves have to be cut so the vegetables can grow. At a certain moment, you must prune. I work like a gardener. Every thing takes time. My vocabulary of forms, for example, did not come to me all at once. It formulated itself almost in spite of me."

Ballagh works in much the same way. He doesn't dash things off. He's content to let a painting wait until its time has come. He learned to paint on the job. He is his own mentor. The past is his future.

*Visitors to Robert Ballagh's*
*exhibition in Moscow.*
*Photo: Robert Ballagh*

*Robert Ballagh's studio in Arbour Hill.*

Getting to the Ballagh studio at Arbour Hill by car is a complicated drive, particularly if approaching from the south side of the Liffey. The trick is to cross the river by the elegant new Calatrava-designed bridge. Otherwise you get caught in a maze of one-way streets and no-left-turns created to facilitate the Luas tramway. Dublin has grown too fast to accommodate bumper-to-bumper traffic along the quays.

Backing through an archway into the gravelled yard where Ballagh's plants are beginning to bloom is like reaching a haven of quiet. There is an early March freshness in the air. Ballagh is at his easel.

Although he didn't start drawing the figure of Watson until late January, much of the portrait has already taken shape on the canvas. Watson stands in the centre his hands reaching out. He is wearing a green cable-knit jersey. Several of his books rest on a polished wooden surface before him, the titles on their spine, one of which has Ballagh's signature. Across the calm water of the Long Island Sound behind him the buildings and trees of Cold Spring Harbour emerge from a cold grey mist.

Ballagh has been working on Watson's right hand. He once tried to hide hands in his portraits because he found them too difficult. Now he can't wait to paint them. "I kind of rough it in first. The left hand isn't ready yet. This one has a transparent glaze coat over it which I actually apply with my own fingers, dabbing it on like this."

He works the flesh-coloured impasto pigment with his left index finger. "You get a skin texture over it all and when that dries you do a little bit of work building up some of the shadows you missed out on the first draft. This bit is only halfway to being completed. It's a slow way of making a picture." He laughs. "I suppose it has my DNA all over it, which is appropriate."

Everything he does is within the framework of a meticulously worked-out plan. "I still to this day — because I don't know how to do it any other way — organise a painting like an architect would design a building. I plan it out. Then tracing paper goes down on the drawing board and I draw it up like a blueprint."

With the drawing complete, he finally put the canvas up on his easel, resting it on a point of the diamond, and started painting, first the wood area and the books, then the background and then the figure. There's a beautiful shine to the curved surface of the wood that makes you want to run your hand over it. "That sort of thing I can do so easily now. But it comes with 20 or 30 years of effort trying to do it. You're inclined to forget how difficult it was, but once you develop the skills it's not hard to do any more. Of course all it does is slow down the job, but maybe that's worthwhile."

Originally he was just going to give Watson an ordinary plain sweater. "I remembered how long it had taken to paint Noël Browne's intricate Aran sweater. There was a huge temptation to avoid going through that again. But then I realised that the cable pattern is sort of a helix, so there was an echo thing going on there. I knuckled down and started painting. When I started doing the jumper I painted in the shape with a flat colour. Then I applied a glaze coat and a stipple coat over it to bring up the textures of the material. If you saw it before that went on, it would have seemed very bland. The sweater had a really pale green shade to start with.

I put a stipple on top of that, and then the cable pattern, and then finally the shadow glaze. It probably took a month or a month-and-a-half just doing that. I'm kind of happy with the way it turned out."

There had been no particular reason to ask Watson to stand with his arms reaching forward. But back in the studio when Ballagh started to make drawings from the photographs he had taken at Cold Spring Harbour the stance suggested an answer to the problem of working an image of the double helix into the portrait. "I wanted to come up with an elegant solution that would appeal to the scientific mind. I knew I could paint a double helix, but that would be too literal. So I thought of creating a double helix hovering in front of him so that he might seem to be reaching for it. This could be done by etching it on the surface of the glass of the picture frame. It would be there but it wouldn't be there. It would just float in front of him."

He shows me some sample strips of glass offering different etched versions of the double helix. They have been prepared for him by an art glass company based in Ashbourne. "They said the pattern would show better against a dark background. So my plan was to paint a dark background. But when I tested it, it came up much better against a light background." He holds a piece of glass for a moment before the painting. The etched image stands out beautifully.

The wide landscape in the background, which is allowed full scope by the irregular shape of the canvas, has been painted in grisaille, a style of painting in greyish tints in imitation of bas-relief – the word is derived from *gris*, the French word for grey. "I painted this in enormous detail. There are hundreds of little trees in there. But I wanted to haze it with a stipple glaze and, of course, this makes the trees almost - but not quite - disappear."

The delicacy of the painting has the soothing effect of drawing in the eye so that you become immersed in the visual possibilities and the beauty of the trees glowing through the haze. "That's the whole thing about glazing. What's underneath no matter how obscured still glows through. Of course the difficulty of it is you can't make any mistakes because any mistake will glow through too."

The glass required to achieve the double helix effects will be weighty, so he has a joiner working for him on a hardwood frame that will be strong enough to hold it. All kinds of elements are involved in the portrait: carpentry, glasswork, paint, glazes, drawings, photographs. Ballagh's delight in making things defies the current curatorial penchant for conceptual art in which the object – if there even is one - has come to matter less that the idea it represents. "This philosophical inversion has created a situation where art is no longer perceived as a skills-based sensuous engagement with materials but rather the result of conceptual decision-making by the artist."

He refers to a quip in Tom Stoppard's *Artist Descending a Staircase* that "imagination without skill gives us contemporary art". Stoppard gives himself the last word, saying the term artist isn't intelligible to him if it doesn't involve making.

Not everything Ballagh makes is art, of course, nor is it intended to be. A completed model of a stage set Ray Yeates has

*Three major survey exhibitions of*
*Robert Ballagh's work.*
*Top: Konsthall, Lund, Sweden 1983*
*Centre: Galerie Dap, Warsaw, Poland 1987.*
*Above: Central House of the Artist, Moscow, USSR 1989.*

*Photos: Robert Ballagh*

45

*Captain James Kelly* (2009)
*Oil on canvas. 60 x 60cm.*
*Private Collection.*

commissioned for the *Our National Games* play is on his work table. It's a split-level structure designed to allow the action to open upstage on a warmly lit dance in the officers' mess before switching to a coldly lit cell below where Captain James Kelly is being interrogated after his arrest in 1970 on charges of conspiracy to import arms into Ireland. His arrest followed the sacking of two ministers and the resignation of another in Jack Lynch's Fianna Fáil government, two of whom – Charles Haughey and Neil Blaney – were arrested but subsequently acquitted on the same charges.

The implication of the play is that Kelly has been set up as a scapegoat. It's written by Gerard Humphries, a barrister and former Army officer and friend of Ballagh's, whose previous writing has been in Irish. "It's gone through a fierce number of rewrites. I think it's actually now beginning to turn into a real play rather than a play which is just an exposition of events and very strong opinions. It has found a personal dynamic to engage audiences. Certain people come out of it badly, including 'Honest' Jack. The one thing we can be sure of is that an awful lot of people didn't tell the truth at the time. Maybe the play will encourage some kind of debate."

Some photographs of finely drawn hedgerows are on Ballagh's work table. They are from an exhibition by his daughter Rachel at the Stephen Pearce Emporium in Shanagarry. After graduating from the National College of Art Rachel exhibited lens-based work in Temple Bar. "Her images were not done digitally but all very carefully staged in a studio. I remember picking up a load of stuffed magpies for her from a taxidermist in Laois. She used back projections, sometimes with her own image in silhouette and the magpies flying around."

For the past six years Rachel has lived in the cottage in Ballycotton where her work has taken a radical shift. "She returned to something I always thought she was very good at, which is drawing and sketching. She has sold several pieces and has been asked by the Sirius Gallery to take part in a group exhibition. Her subject is basically the flora and fauna of the Irish hedgerow, but done in a personal way. Even though they are quite detailed drawings, they're not botanical but kind of imaginative and charged with personality."

Ballagh had put her onto a quotation from Charles Darwin's *The Origin of the Species*: "It is interesting to contemplate an entangled bank, clothed with many plants of many kinds, with birds singing in the bushes, with various insects flitting about, and worms crawling through damp earth, and to reflect that these elaborately constructed forms, so different from each other and dependent on each other in so complex a matter, have all been produced by laws, acting around us."

The challenge to decode these "laws, acting around us" inspired the discovery by James D Watson and Francis Crick of the double-helical structure of DNA, the chemical that carries the genetic information of chromosomes and has led to the $3 billion human genome project aimed at completing the human DNA sequence. This raises the possibility of everyone being able to know their DNA make-up and what genetic strengths or weakness they might have, although whether they would want to be saddled with

this information or not is debatable. In the wrong hands it could lead to many people being classed as uninsurable – much like the stigma of the untouchables – although one suspects Lawrence Sterne's character Tristam Shandy, the subject of a Ballagh mural in 1975, would prefer it to the worry of trying to work out whether he was born at the right hour and under the right star.

Not that DNA has eliminated chance from life. Chance even played a part in its discovery. Watson maintains that if he'd chanced to fall in love while he was doing research in Copenhagen in 1950 he might never have gone to Cambridge and teamed up with Crick. Rather than wait for model makers at the Cavendish laboratory in Cambridge to make tin models of the four nucleobases – again by chance – he tried to make his own with cardboard and eventually stumbled on the solution through trial and error. "When you look at the photographs of this model made all those years ago, it's a real Meccano job," says Ballagh. "It brings home the kind of adventure in that scientific discovery. Watson and Crick were a bit like the early explorers. Right across the scientific world, a lot of people were zeroing in on DNA."

Pure science in this sense has a strong affinity with art. Although rooted in the empirical it arrives at truth through flashes of inspiration. "The support systems of pure science and art are not dissimilar either. Pure research, the same as making art, is an expensive business and requires either private patronage or state funding, which can often be very difficult to get. Obviously great scientific discoveries have commercial spin-offs later but take place entirely outside the market and the so-called real world."

The Ballagh portrait of Watson will celebrate the fiftieth anniversary of Trinity College's genetics faculty, set up in 1958 with the help of a £15,000 donation from the Irish Sugar Company which was then run by Lt Gen Michael Joseph Costello. It grew over the years to embrace the Smurfit Institute of Genetics through the help of major benefactors like Michael Smurfit, Chuck Feeney, the Irish-American billionaire who made his fortune as a pioneer of duty free shops and then gave most of it away, and Dr Martin Naughton.

But for now the Watson portrait has no face. Not until Ballagh has applied all the layers of glazes and shadows to the rest of the picture will he take the plunge and try for a likeness that captures the essence of the man who through his research has helped solve the secrets of life. He has every mark and blemish of the face charted much like the contours of the sea bed. But how this will translate into paint depends on the flick of his brush and what he puts in or leaves out. "It's always been this way for me," he says. "I put myself in a spot from which the only way out is to get it right."

Above: Betty and Rachel Ballagh
in a photograph taken by Fergus Bourke
as part of his 'Kindred' project.

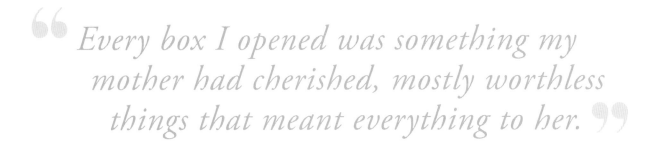

Ballagh had a habit of dropping in on his parents Nancy and Bobbie at their flat in Ballsbridge once or twice a week. His father didn't have the energy to play golf any more. He seemed run-down and tired. Nancy had begun to forget things.

Early in February 1990 he found them sitting in the front room with their coats on. "What's going on?" "It's very cold." "Why didn't you light the fire?" "I was too tired to get the coal."

He brought up some coal and lit a fire. He'd never worried about his father before. "He'd always been fit as a fiddle. I'd ask him if he needed help. No, no, he'd say, everything is fine. That's the kind of guy he was. He never complained. But at that moment I felt a sudden dread."

Nancy had become obsessed with money. "She sewed a little purse on a string around her neck and would always have a £20 note in it. I didn't know what she was thinking of. In fact she was in the early stages of some kind of dementia. Nowadays we'd call it Alzheimers. But we didn't realise it. We just didn't spot what was going on, and my father not being able to cope with it. When you're old and you're looking after someone it drains you."

His mother had stopped working when she got married. That was the tradition in Ireland in the 1930s. The woman's place was in the home, according to the Constitution. His father worked all his life as manager of the shirt department of Ferrier Pollock in what is now Powerscourt Centre, on South William Street. When the company went bust, he lost his pension. "Every time I go in there I still see him standing behind his old counter. His ghost is still there."

Because their flat was on a ridiculously low fixed rent of around £5 a week they'd never thought of buying a house of their own. All this ended when the publican Paddy Madigan took a test case as a landlord to the Supreme Court which ruled that a landlord was entitled to the market price. "Rent control went out the window. My parents found they now had to pay £100 a week and had to look for rent allowance benefit to cover it. They went from a fairly comfortable middle-class life to an old age in penury."

A week or so after finding his parents alone in the cold, Ballagh and Betty attended an opening in the Taylor Galleries on Kildare Street, where Micheal Farrell, Louis le Brocquy and Tony O'Malley regularly exhibited. Afterwards they went with friends to Tobin's pub in Duke Street. He got a message to phone his mother, which he did. He couldn't make much sense of what she was trying to say. "There's something about your father," she mumbled.

When he got to the flat, a few people were already there. He walked into the room. "I saw my father sitting there, and immediately I knew. He'd had a stroke. He wasn't moving and there was a look of absolute terror in his eyes."

They got an ambulance for him. He was brought to St Vincent's Hospital in Merrion. He was there a couple of weeks. He seemed to be improving. The doctors were hopeful that he would get through it. Nancy couldn't be left on her own. "I'd stay with her two or three days and Betty would look after the home situation. And then she would come in and look after Nancy for a couple of days and I'd go and bring the kids to school and all that."

One night he was in Ballsbridge with Nancy. The phone rang. "There was a nurse in floods of tears saying Bobbie had had a massive heart attack and was dead. I lay awake all night wondering how I would tell my mother her husband had died."

He got up early in the morning and prepared breakfast for her. "I've got bad news," he told her. "Bobbie died during the night." "Oh," she said. She didn't seem upset. She didn't do anything. She just carried on. She seemed to be in another world.

It rained during the funeral at Star of the Sea Church. Much of the art world was there and many old friends of his parents, offering their condolences and talking under umbrellas before accompanying the hearse to the graveyard, a sad but necessary ritual.

Nancy was in hospital. They had to find somewhere for her when she came out. She couldn't live on her own, but they couldn't look after her at the cottage in Broadstone, which was already doubling as a studio as well as a home for Rachel and Bruce. "I went around Dublin trying to find a place where she could have proper care. They were all either ghastly or didn't have any vacancies. It's only when you have to deal with the problem yourself that you realise that the care of old people is so under-resourced and neglected."

Then he found a rest home in Dundrum. "I knew my mother would like it because she always liked things neat and tidy. I talked with the matron. 'Oh, we'd love to have your mother.' 'Have you a vacancy?' 'Oh yes, no problem.' 'Put her down. As soon as she comes out of hospital I'll contact you.'"

He drove home in a hurry to tell Betty their problems were over, that he'd found a wonderful place. "The first thing she said was, did you ask the price? I'd forgotten. Betty phoned up and said thank you, putting down the receiver. She turned to me and said that the price of the home was twice what I earned in a year."

His mother never got out of hospital. The Gate Theatre was bringing *Salomé* to Charleston in South Carolina. Ballagh had to fly over for a production meeting. It was just for three days. The doctor told him it was okay to go. On the second day there was a call from Betty. Nancy had died with Betty at her side. An only child, in less than three months he'd lost both his parents.

"Because of all the things you have to do to get through two funerals, I thought I was coping as well as could be expected. It wasn't until about six months later that it really sank in. I suddenly had this realisation that I'd never see them again. Their landlady had been very kind. But after some time she phoned up and said I'm afraid you're going to have to get all their stuff out. I need to rent the place."

He called the furniture removal company Beverley Smiths to bring it all to the cottage in Cork. He loaded everything into boxes, their whole life, and followed the van down. "We unloaded it all. They drove away. I was on my own. I started unwrapping things. Every box I opened up was something my mother had cherished, mostly worthless little things that meant everything to her."

Ballagh was back at his easel upstairs in No 4 within a couple of days, painting a poster – and also the programme cover – for a new Frank McGuinness version of Chekhov's *Three Sisters,* which Adrian Noble was directing at the Gate Theatre. In discussions with designer Bob Crowley he came up with the idea of a variation of a Magritte repeating image in which one sister looks into a

*The Three Sisters* (1990)
*Oil on canvas. 60 x 60cm.*
*Collection: The Gate Theatre.*

49

mirror in which there is the reflection of another sister looking into a mirror in which the third sister is reflected. On the mantelpiece against which the sister leans is a green-covered copy of a book with the title of the play in Russian. The sisters are portrayed in the play by real life sisters Sorcha, Niamh and Sinéad Cusack, whose father Cyril Cusack plays the army doctor Chebutykin.

The production was both a critical and a social triumph, bringing together on stage for the first time the Cusacks, one of the great Irish theatrical families. The painting still hangs in the box-office at the Gate.

It was joined on the wall in the hallway not long after by a portrait of Oscar Wilde commissioned by Michael Colgan to celebrate the success of *Salomé,* by now one of the Gate's most popular touring productions. Instead of the usual image of an older slightly blousy Wilde, Ballagh used for reference a less familiar photograph taken while he was still a student in Oxford. He posed him against a wall of gorgeously-patterned, deep aquamarine William Morris wallpaper of a type popular at the time. Wilde had written an essay 'The Soul of Man under Socialism'. Like other English socialists, Morris deplored the dark satanic mills of the Industrial Revolution and sought to reawaken respect for workers and their traditional crafts by bringing back into fashion handmade furniture and hand-painted wallpaper. "The irony of their movement, as Wilde might have appreciated, was that the only people who could afford this sort of thing were the fabulously wealthy people whose fortunes were created by the mills and factories that scarred the English landscape."

An entrepreneur Brian Loughney approached Ballagh to paint a portrait of Charles Stewart Parnell to evoke the historical associations that inspired the popular Kitty O'Shea pub franchise. During the campaign for Home Rule in the late 19th century Parnell's authority in the British House of Commons had been undermined by revelations of his adulterous affair with Katherine O'Shea. The only stipulation Loughney made was that the portrait should make some reference to her. Ballagh came up with the ingenious idea of inserting a tiny portrait of her dangling from a fob-watch chain on Parnell's waistcoat. Outside the paned window against which Parnell stands are clusters of ivy leaves, a homage to James Joyce's short story in *Dubliners*, 'Ivy Day in the Committee Room'.

◆

A notice appeared in newspapers saying that "a group of concerned citizens" was going to meet in Liberty Hall to discuss ways of commemorating the 75th anniversary of the Easter Rising in 1991. It had become apparent that the Government was anxious to avoid any official ceremonies that might be regarded as politically inappropriate, if not provocative. Ballagh decided to go along to the meeting and found himself elected chairman of an organising committee.

He'd taken part in a highly effective 'Parade of the Innocence' in Dublin the previous year in the immediate aftermath

**The New Revised History of Ireland**

*In 1847, two peasants debate the benefits of a low starch diet.*

of the release of the Guildford Four, which highlighted the plight of the Birmingham Six who were still languishing in British jails through a similar miscarriage of justice. He got involved in this and other initiatives for what he believed were cultural reasons rather than political reasons, using the term cultural in the broadest sense.

*The History Lesson* had been a statement of intent. "I was trying in my own small way to challenge some of these attitudes in an artistic fashion." He followed up with a series of graphics satirising the dreadful anti-Irish illustrations published in *Punch* magazine during the Famine. He called it *A New Revised History of Ireland*. One of the pictures showed two dilapidated peasants in conversation. Underneath a caption read, "In 1847 two Irish peasants discuss the benefits of a low-starch diet." For his contribution to *In A State*, an exhibition in Kilmainham Jail where artists were invited to examine Irish identity, Ballagh created an installation called *Pages From Irish History* in which the graphics fluttered down into space like pages in the wind.

The 'Parade of the Innocence', choreographed by the film director Pat Murphy, was the first political parade in Dublin to take place in the carnival atmosphere of street theatre. Up to then it had been difficult to galvanise people around a political issue because they were afraid of being labelled Provo supporters. The fact that it was in protest against miscarriages of justice that had already been highlighted by British lawyers and in the British media seemed to legitimise participation and attracted a substantial turnout of writers, artists, actors and celebrities. Ballagh organised a huge INNOCENT banner which he and Donal O'Kelly attempted to raise on O'Connell Bridge, but a gust of wind caught it full on and in trying to prevent it blowing away he lost his glasses in the Liffey.

The success of the parade provided a model for the 'Reclaim the Spirit of Easter' project. "One of the things we said right from the start was that we weren't interested in the military aspects of 1916. What interested us were the ideas of the people of 1916 encapsulated in the Proclamation, which promised to cherish all the children of the nation equally. This goal seemed to stand in stark contrast with the Ireland we were living in at the time."

Ballagh designed a logo featuring a dove rising from the GPO, a symbol of the ideals of the people who had fought and died there. A tribunal was held which charged "that the nation had failed to cherish all its children equally". Submissions were made by the unemployed, travellers, youth groups, environmentalists and others. The Mansion House hosted a debate in which Senator John A Murphy and Jim Kemmy TD spoke for the motion "that the concept of a United Ireland is an impediment to peace" while Senator Eamon O'Cuiv, a grandson of Eamon De Valera, and Bernadette McAliskey opposed.

They realised that if the 1991 Easter parade was to grab the popular imagination it would need to reach beyond political activists and become a family event with banners and floats and lots of street theatre and ancillary events, culminating with a pageant outside the GPO. A new more wide-reaching national committee was formed under Ballagh. Its members travelled out around the country establishing committees to organise events. Local councils were encouraged to pass motions of support. An Post agreed

to issue a commemorative stamp, but the St Patrick's Day Parade stalled on the idea of a commemorative float on the grounds that it would be "inappropriate".

Dr Eoin McKiernan, the founder of the Irish American Cultural Institute, in the official programme for New York's St Patrick's day parade, bemoaned the silence of the Irish Government on Easter Week and asked, "Has Charlie Haughey himself acquiesced in the new revisionist philosophy that seems apologetic about Irish nationhood?"

As Easter Sunday approached Dessie O'Malley suggested that "Mr Ballagh's committee serves the interests of the provisional IRA." Senator Shane Ross claimed that "the 'Reclaim the Spirit of Easter' is menacing". Ballagh was constantly harassed by the Special Branch. One day as he was walking home from a committee meeting along Parnell Square an unmarked police car mounted the footbath. Two detectives jumped out and pushed him against the railings, and frisked him. They demanded to see identification. "I showed them a driving licence. They drove off. The whole purpose was intimidation."

Another time he called into the Sinn Féin HQ to pick up a speech that a friend had typed up for him. As he drove home he didn't notice he was being followed by a Special Branch car. As he entered into the cul-de-sac in Broadstone where he lived, they turned on their siren and flashing lights and pulled him out of the car outside his house. "What are you doing?" they demanded. "I'm going home for my dinner," he confessed.

This was at a time when the secret Hume/Adams peace talks were taking place and Ballagh with others was talking to people like Gerry Adams, Martin McGuinness and Pat Doherty, arguing the case for a movement away from the physical force tradition to non-violent politics. "It was of course terribly private. Yet I was being labelled by the media as a supporter of violence. I found it at the time very frustrating and very hurtful."

The day got off to a damp start with an open-air concert at the top of Parnell Square featuring leading musicians Jimmy McCarthy, Donal Lunny, Mary Stokes, Paddy Glackin, Declan Masterson, Noel Hill and Tony McMahon. As the parade led by a pipe band progressed along its route, actors proclaimed extracts from appropriate speeches. Jer O'Leary climbed up beside the statue of Big Jim Larkin to exhort the working classes to rise up. On O'Connell Bridge Brendan Caldwell assumed the persona of James Connolly, while at the bottom of Grafton Street Olwen Fouere and Ailish Connolly became Countess Markievicz and Maud Gonne. Outside the Dáil, Paul Bennett as Patrick Pearse read out the 1916 proclamation.

All this was a rousing prelude to the gathering at the GPO, where Ballagh addressed a crowd of over 20,000. "There were those who said it could not be done," he roared. "There were others who said it should not be done. Let's give them your answer loud and clear. Let them hear it in Leinster House – are you proud to be Irish?" "YES", roared everyone. "Let them hear it in Westminster." "YES." "Let them hear it in Bruxelles." "YES."

*Top: 1991 Parade to commemorate the 75th anniversary of the Easter Rising.*

*Above: Robert Ballagh addressing the crowd in front of the GPO.*

This was followed by a pageant written by Tomás MacAnna. A mock funeral procession, led by a piper, marched slowly on stage, carrying a coffin with Éire RIP inscribed on the lid. Actors symbolising the political, legal and academic elements that wanted to bury Irish history made their point, before a judge played by Kevin Reynolds declared the Rising "completely illegal." At which point the coffin burst open and a woman representing Ireland emerged.

That evening the six o'clock RTÉ news gave the event 32 seconds as its last item – as if an event that took over the centre of Dublin was of minimal news value - while the camera focussed on one face in the crowd, the Sinn Féin President, Gerry Adams.

◆

A warder poked his head round the door of the Provo recreation room in the high security wing of Portlaoise Prison. He was looking for Robert Ballagh. "You're ten minutes late. Tommy is going mad upstairs waiting for you." Someone quipped, "He's got forty years. What's the hurry?"

Since Ballagh had already wrapped up the art class he was giving, he gathered his things and headed up to the next landing. Tommy McMahon was waiting in an empty cell he was allowed use as a studio. He always complained Ballagh spent too much time talking politics with the Provos. He was eager to talk art.

Ballagh was in jail every Thursday to give three classes under a visiting artists programme sponsored by the Arts Council, an idea pioneered by Campbell Bruce of the National College of Art and Design several years earlier. His routine was to start each day with the murderers, rapists and drug pushers, a category known sardonically as ODCs or ordinary decent criminals. "One of my students was the drugs baron Larry Dunne. He was a bit lazy, but did interesting work."

Then he'd move up to the Provo section, where about 20 of the 100 or more inmates showed an interest. "Their set-up was highly organised, being an army. They had an education officer who met me and explained that some of the boys were doing the Leaving Cert and A-levels, and needed help."

His final class was attended by "unattached political prisoners" who were in either small organisations like the INLA, or were unconnected with any group. They included Dominic McGlinchey, who was later murdered, and also Peter Pringle, charged with the murder of a garda during a robbery but eventually released after 14 years when it was established that the evidence against him had been fabricated.

Tommy McMahon was serving a 40-year sentence for his part in the assassination of Lord Mountbatten, a cousin of Queen Elizabeth. Mountbatten, who had presided over the partition of India, was blown to bits by a remote-controlled bomb while sailing his boat off the seaside village of Mullughmore in Sligo in 1979. Later the same day 18 British soldiers were killed in an ambush in Warrenpoint.

McMahon had broken with the Provos while in prison. He immersed himself in his painting. "He wanted to get every

little bit of help or information that I could give. He was released in 1998 under the terms of the Good Friday Agreement. I met him a while ago. He's still painting. He lives in Monaghan."

Ballagh had been told he'd need full security clearance to give the classes. To his surprise he got it. While the Special Branch were busy harassing him in Dublin, he not only had the run of Ireland's most tightly guarded prison but was told when he finished teaching that he could go back in any time he liked.

"I remember I counted one day the number of locked gates I had to go through before I got to the high security wing, an area no member of the general public was allowed enter. It was 35. Many are air-locked. You open one and go into a space where you wait until it closes and the next one opens. Sometimes I would have a lunch in the staff canteen. I'd be talking with the warders. They asked me with some interest what did I think of such and such a prisoner's work."

He was allowed bring in his own equipment for classes, everything except black paint. "But you can't paint without black paint." "No, it's forbidden."

The reason it was banned was that a prison escape had used artist's black paint to dye uniforms made by the prisoners. The same applied to the wooden-handled badger brushes Ballagh used to create a smooth finish. "People think I use an airbrush or some kind of mechanical technique but it's all actually done with these brushes. I was allowed to bring them in to show to the lads. They would be carefully noted when I brought them in and when I brought them out. Several of the lads were so taken with them I decided when I was finished I would give them a few. They're quite expensive and sometimes hard to get. I got a few. I drove down to Portlaoise and I went to leave them in. By then I'd got to know everyone.

"There's a problem." "Why?" "We can't give any wooden objects to prisoners." "But they've only small wooden handles." It turned out that in the past brush handles had been hollowed out and used to smuggle in Semtex.

During the Civil War the prison – which dates from the Victorian era – was first used to house Republican prisoners, one of whom was my father. He set fire to his cell hoping to burn down the building, but because it was solid bricks and mortar the only damage was to beds and blankets. As punishment the prisoners were forced to sleep out in the yard in the middle of winter. He then joined a hunger strike, fortunately with a similar lack of success.

Things were more humane by the 1990s, particularly during John Lonergan's term. "The atmosphere wasn't bad. I never talked as much politics in my life. I didn't mind being there. You don't mind when you get out every night."

◆

"Is there anything in particular you'd like?" "The only thing I've ever been interested in all my life is sailing." "Forget about that, Liam. I can't do a portrait of you as a sailor." Ulster Museum fine arts curator Ted Hickey had asked Ballagh for a portrait of the Derry architect

*John Medlycott* (1991)
*Oil on canvas, 46 x 76cm.*
*Collection: Mount Temple Comprehensive School.*

Liam McCormack. He was gradually building up a representative collection of portraits of people who made a significant contribution to the arts in Ireland, the centrepiece of which was Edward Maguire's iconic study of Seamus Heaney.

McCormack invited Ballagh up North to stay for a few days. He lived by the sea in Greencastle, next door to playwright Brian Friel. He had a telescope hanging on the wall in his room. This offered Ballagh a way of satisfying McCormack while fulfilling the requirement to show him as an architect. On the wall behind McCormack he painted a picture within the picture, a portrait of his grandfather who had been a ship's captain. It shows a tall man in a formal suit standing by a window that looks out on to the Foyle, holding the telescope in his hand. It's a subtle variation of the window motif that is a recurring feature in Ballagh's imagery.

McCormack is sitting at a table with a sheet of paper, a scale rule, a pencil and a rubber. "Obviously the tools of his trade he'd use and I would use, although not any more. Architecture is all computers now." He has a model before him of one of his commissions, the Meteorological Office at Glasnevin in Dublin. Ballagh had wanted it to be the church at Burt in Donegal, generally regarded as one of the best buildings in Ireland. But McCormack chose the Met Office, partly because it was his only major commission in Dublin but also because he had been overruled in terms of the finish for the building by accountants and engineers and quantity surveyors who said what he wanted was too expensive. They applied a thin stone material instead and assured him it would be perfect. After a short time it warped and fell off. For years it was covered in tarpaulin. "I don't know if they got it finished for Liam to see before he died. But he had this strong feeling about it. The model shows it as it was intended to look."

Soon after Ballagh undertook a more modest commission, a portrait of John Medlycott who was headmaster of Mount Temple Comprehensive School in North Dublin where Bruce went to school. Mount Temple started out as a Protestant private school but opted to go public when comprehensive schools were introduced, much like Avoca in Blackrock which became Newpark. "It still had that ethos. You'd get very posh Protestants going to school with kids from the flats in Ballymun. Bono went there and U2 was formed there."

The school had a policy of putting up portraits of its headmasters. "The budget was very small, so the picture was very small. Again, I asked what he'd like me to put into it. He was very proud of trees he'd planted in the grounds. So that gave me the picture."

Although Ballagh's style and technique is suited to large canvasses and theatre sets, he shares with the Dutch painters a delight in small meticulously rendered detail. Medlycott is portrayed in close-up, a bearded bespectacled man in a tweed jacket and tie with the firm but understanding bearing of a teacher, standing amidst the trees, the texture of which is beautifully observed. It's a simple but effective image, an example of how the challenge of a commission seldom fails to bring out the inventiveness in Ballagh.

By contrast Samuel Beckett's *Endgame* for the Beckett Festival at the Gate Theatre draws on his pop art origins and the power of an iconic three-dimensional image. Not that he had much freedom in this case. The director Antonio Libero had been

a close collaborator of Beckett's. "Like everyone who has anything to do with Beckett, he had very fixed notions of how the play should be done. He wanted a roof on the set, which means you can't have any overhead lighting. Rupert Murray, the lighting designer, hated this obvious restriction but nevertheless, with great ingenuity, managed to light the set beautifully."

Ballagh's solution was to have walling that tapered in and a roof that tapered down to create a claustrophobic space within which Barry McGovern's Clov and Alan Stanford's Ham could play out their existential relationship. The Gate brought the production to the Barbican Centre in London and later to the Melbourne Arts Festival, along with *I'll Go On* and *Waiting For Godot*, directed by Walter Asmus with a set by Louis le Brocquy. "I don't know whether I would have done it differently if I hadn't been working with someone who had worked with the master and was very sure of the way it should be done. But it's my favourite Beckett play so it was a joy to do it."

To lighten up after Beckett, the Gate turned to Shakespeare and the innocent joy and passion of *Romeo & Juliet*, updated to the Italy of the 1930s and directed by Alan Stanford. The lovers were played by the young actors Darragh Kelly and Hilary Reynolds. The set was a slightly stylised village square. Rupert Murray lit it beautifully. The girls all had lightly coloured cotton dresses. The ambience was warm and Italian. "Alan was going for realism. He wanted the smell of freshly baked bread wafting off the stage. We'd soundtracks of birds twittering. It was more the geometry I found interesting. There was a rake on the stage, and a building with a little portico. I got the artist Jack Kirwan to paint a sort of classical mural and make it appear aged and dusty."

The tragedy of youthful life snuffed out would also find an echo in a painting of *Icarus* that Ballagh did for the cover of a catalogue for the Dedalus Press, a small poetry imprint run by John F Deane. It shows a slightly singed feather floating down after Icarus has flown too close to the sun.

*Robert Ballagh on the 'Romeo and Juliet' set.*

◆

"You're very good to come up," said an old farmer sitting beside Ballagh. They were in a hired bus with volunteers just arrived from Dublin to help local people rebuild Border crossings blown up by the British Army for "security reasons". "And what's your name?" "Ballagh." "That's a Protestant name. But we won't hold that against you."

*The set of 'Romeo and Juliet' 1991,*
*a Gate Theatre production.*

Many towns like Clones were dying because the cratering policy cut them off from their hinterlands and markets. Farmers trying to bring cattle from one field to another often had to travel 40 miles through check-points. Children going to school down the road were forced to make lengthy detours.

Ballagh was involved through his chairmanship of the Irish National Congress, a non-party political organisation formed to advance "peace, unity and justice". Local communities had applied to it for help. He decided to respond "because it was essentially a non-violent protest".

Among others taking part were Neil Blaney, the independent TD for Donegal who split with Fianna Fáil after being sacked from the Government by Jack Lynch during the Arms scandal, and Kevin Boland, who had resigned at the time from the Government in sympathy with him.

Ballagh first become aware of Boland in the 1960s when he responded to the ransacking of Georgian houses in Ely Place by saying that "we shouldn't worry about these houses, sure weren't they the homes of belted earls". So he wouldn't have had a high regard for him then for cultural reasons. But he got to know him later and began to realise he was a man of principle. "He was what you would call a narrow-gauge nationalist." Jack Lynch, who he met through Gordon Lambert, was different. "I always found Jack Lynch a bit of a phoney. I felt he was a very ineffectual and weak leader at a time when the country needed strong leadership."

Ballagh had been up to the Border several weekends with his shovel. "We'd fill in a road and the British Army would come back and crater it again the next day." The Ballaghs came from the particular area of Monaghan towards which the bus was now heading. "The British not only blew up the road but also dynamited a little stream so that it flowed along the damaged road. The locals cleverly pushed an old car into the hole and filled over it so that the water could flow under."

They'd almost finished the job when Ballagh heard a loud whirring noise. He saw two helicopters land in a field on the Northern side. A platoon of paratroopers with red berets advanced down the hill, their faces blackened. "I heard an order being given. They dropped down on their knees. I was busy with the shovel. An officer walked straight up and stood a foot away from me. He said: 'I'd stop doing that, sir.' I started quoting European law about freedom of movement. Then I heard the click of safety catches being taken off. 'I would advise you to step back, sir,' he said. He mentioned something about this being a zone of security. I stepped back. Boland was standing right beside me. 'God, this is great Bobby.' 'What?' 'We could get arrested and it'll be in all the papers.' 'Speak for yourself,' I told him. I don't intend getting arrested.'"

Ballagh noticed that while the day-trippers from Dublin were being very Bolshie, the locals had gone very quiet. "All that was needed was for some eejit to do something stupid and the whole thing could have blown up. Thankfully it passed off peacefully."

Not so a confrontation at Lackey Bridge later in February 1991, outside Clones and just down the road from playwright Eugene McCabe's farm. This time the locals had JCBs. A RUC snatch squad arrived almost immediately and weighed in with batons, dragging away people. One youth was taken into custody streaming blood. The mood was turning ugly. Ballagh was standing on the riverbank. "Stop it, lads," he said. What the others couldn't see was a load of British soldiers in the cornfields as back-up.

The entire incident was extensively reported in the *Fermanagh Herald*. It had been filmed by Tommy Collins, who later turned it into a documentary *Dragon's Teeth* (the title was a reference to the obstructions the British Army built across roads). There was talk of police brutality. "I don't think we should complain," said Michael McPhillips, one of the local organisers. He'd checked the video. "The lad was hit on the head by a rock thrown by one of our people. He was looked after by a RUC doctor and allowed home the following day."

Ballagh was back a few weeks later to speak with Neil Blaney at a public rally beside a bridge that was blown up near Belturbet. They arrived on the southern side and the rally was on the northern side. It would have taken nearly an hour to find a way around. Somebody sequestered a small punt. The two men rowed across together. "It's like Washington crossing the Delaware," Ballagh joked to Blaney.

Robert Ballagh had been painting for a quarter of a century. He was arguably one of the best-known living Irish artists. Yet none of his work was on public display anywhere in Ireland, apart from the Ulster Museum in Belfast. *The History Lesson* and Michael O'Riordan's portrait still lay unsold in his studio, from where *Upstairs No 4, The Studio* had a brief outing for the European Dimension exhibition celebrating the Irish presidency of the EU in 1990. His widely reproduced Noël Browne portrait had finally been purchased by the National Gallery, but there were still no plans to put it on view. None of his paintings hung in the Hugh Lane Municipal Gallery.

It was left to the department store Arnotts to put this right. For several years Arnotts through Bill Kelly had sponsored the National Portraits Award show, which was run by the painter Jackie Stanley and Betty Ballagh. To Kelly it seemed odd that that while Ballagh was frequently invited to exhibit abroad, notably in Sweden, Poland, Russia and Bulgaria, no Irish gallery seemed interested in showing his work.

Kelly came up with the idea of 'Robert Ballagh: The Complete Works', an exhibition featuring not only Ballagh's paintings and graphic works but also his work as a stamp designer, photographer and theatre designer. It ran throughout February 1992 and occupied Arnotts' fourth-floor exhibition space. To reach it, the public had to take an escalator up through the perfume and fashion areas, as if emphasising Ballagh's disassociation from the art world of which he was once central.

Frances Ruane suggested, in her review in the *Irish Times*, that the venue was "consistent with the painter's proletarian outlook. Exhibiting in the heart of northside Dublin is certainly a way of reaching a new viewing public." She maintained that Ballagh didn't get into his stride until the late 1970s "when he was able to shake off the influence of American Pop Art" but since then "his technical skill, particularly in the use of three-dimensional space, light, and the subtle handling of paint, had improved rapidly".

She particularly admired *Upstairs No 3* and the Michael O'Riordan portrait "probing the personality of his subject, portraying his strength and restlessness. Pictures like this one establish that Ballagh can paint great pictures, not just clever ones."

The catalogue included assessments of Ballagh's contribution to photography, as well as theatre and stamp design and architectural prints. Film director Kieran Hickey argued that the photographs in his 1981 book, *Dublin*, "belong not to a tourist guide-book but to something more private, secret almost, and unintelligible to outsiders – a record of a genuine world, evidence of the stubborn survival of a timeless local character. Dublin has never been seen like this: one has to go back to the pictures taken by Robert French in the thirty years before the First World War, and to the work of Neville Johnson soon after the Second, to see such a record of the face and fabric of the city."

Gerry Dukes, who had collaborated on *I'll Go On* as an academic adviser, argued that Ballagh's work as a designer "offers us a redefinition of the function of theatre design, predicated as it is upon close reading of the dramatic text and responsiveness to its nuanced meanings. What his designs ordinarily do is to deliver a set which is both an appropriate space for such an action and a visual expression of the meanings of that action."

Despite its success, the exhibition did little to change the apparent disregard for Ballagh by much of the official Irish art establishment, which was increasingly preoccupied with conceptual, video and installation work. It would be another decade before Ballagh exhibited again in Ireland. When the critic Dorothy Walker's "comprehensive" survey, *Modern Art in Ireland*, was published in 1997 by Lilliput Press, no reference was made to any of Ballagh's work after 1980 and then only in passing in a list of Irish artists participating in the 1980 Rosc exhibition.

Judy Friel, a director and friend, sent Ballagh a copy of *Misogynist*, a complex new play by Michael Harding she was putting on at the Abbey Theatre. He read it with bemusement. "I really don't get it," he said. She'd sent the script to Rupert Murray, too. "I don't get it," he said. But she insisted. "I really want you and Rupert to work on it. Come to the rehearsals. Then you'll get it." So they did, sitting in the back. "What's this all about?" said Ballagh afterwards. Murray just shrugged. Even after the dress rehearsal and the opening Ballagh was still confused. "Harding seemed to be working all sorts of things out in his head about sexuality, maleness and all that. I have to confess I didn't get it."

Harding possibly would take that as a compliment. Born in Cavan, he went straight from school to a seminary in 1971, gave up after several months to qualify as a teacher, worked at Loughan House for some years and then as a youth officer in Sligo. He went back again to Maynooth and after ordination served as a curate in Fermanagh. He later resigned all his clerical responsibilities

*The Red Cow, Clondalkin* (1981)
*Photograph from Robert Ballagh's*
*'Dublin' published by Ward River Press.*

The Abbey Theatre 1992 production
of 'Misogynist'.
Photo: Fergus Bourke

so that he could write full time, and was nominated for the 1987 Irish Book Award for his first fiction *Priest*.

With his thick red beard Harding looked as if he'd be more at home playing a gig with the Dubliners than saying Mass. He relished the anarchy and irrationality of the human condition and sought to find a form to explore this on the stage. He was drawn to the notion of theatre as an event, something that just happened. "That engages people in a way that is untouchable by other means," he told me. "It doesn't have to be a place where you translate some other thing, where you put some treatise or argument."

His debut play *Strawboys* at the Peacock in 1987 – the title derived from an Irish folk ritual, an idea of acting out communal experiences – was refreshing in its defiance of preconditioned expectations of what a play should be. *Misogynist* perhaps took this leap of the imagination beyond where audiences seemed prepared to go, despite the seductively visceral impact of Ballagh's monumental purgatorial set.

Ballagh designed it as a trompe l'oeil Escher space of impossible stairs that seemed to have no end, which could be seen as representing the inside of the actor Tom Hickey's head. Although the play is at its core a one-man show, all sorts of other things were thrown in. Dervla Kirwan played a young woman Hickey is obsessing about. Her costume was a little surplice that was like a baby doll nightie. Over a dozen women who were naked under their monk's costumes had been coached by Colin Mowbrey to sing *Te Deums* in Latin as they filled the air with incense.

"I've noticed in the past when a play is proving difficult there's an assumption it can be solved by throwing more money at the set," says Ballagh. "All sorts of things that were new and radical at the time were attempted. A huge TV set in a packing case was lowered on to the stage and Tom had a camera and was filming himself only to appear on the big TV screen. A statue of the Infant Jesus of Prague was placed on each step of the main stairway. I remember going to the Catholic Repository. 'Do you have a Child of Prague statue?' 'Oh yes.' 'Could I have a dozen, please.'"

Gay Byrne reviewed *Misogynist* on his radio programme the next day. "I've never heard a worse review. Not only did bookings collapse, people were ringing up cancelling bookings. The play came off after three days."

Up river on the other side of the Liffey, in the heart of the old city known as the Liberties, the Tivoli Theatre on Francis Street put on shows of a much less esoteric nature. It was run by Tony Byrne, who grew up there and went on to play soccer for Ireland. "Johnny Giles, the footballer, was one of his best friends. He'd go on and on about never getting any grants like the Gate or the Abbey. I said to him, 'But Tony, they don't put on shows like *How's Your Wobbly Bits??*' But he just didn't see it. The whole class thing was going on in his head – that he's been discriminated against because he was working class."

Byrne commissioned Ballagh to do a set and poster for a Niall Toibin one-man show. Toibin was one of Ireland's most loved actors, renowned for his impersonations and charm as a raconteur. The poster was a straight-forward head portrait showing him against a red-brick wall on which the title of his show *Takin' Liberties* is chalked, like graffiti.

"Tony was going to put it up all over the town. It never appeared anywhere. And then he refused to give me back the art work. 'I paid for it, it's mine,' he said. 'No,' I said, 'you paid for the image, you didn't pay for the oil painting.'

Another sore point was the use made of Ballagh's set. "The week before Tony had *The Dickie Rock Show* and he put it on my set. And after the Toibin show he had Brendan O'Carroll and my whole set was painted in luminous colours. So he got three shows out of one set and kept my art work. Some while later we bumped into each other. 'Oh, you'll be very pleased,' he said. 'You know that painting you did of Niall Toibin? His daughter got married and I gave it to her as a wedding present.'

Ballagh was on safer ground when Groundwork Productions commissioned a portrait of John B Keane to coincide with their production of his play, *The Field*. The idea was that after its unveiling by Brenda Fricker, who starred in Jim Sheridan's film version of Keane's *The Field*, it would hang in the Gaiety Theatre. Keane, rooted in the rich story-telling tradition of his native Kerry, captured the grief and laughter of Irish rural life in plays and prose that spoke the language of the people and articulated their concerns, gaining his insights while running a small pub with his wife in Listowel. He didn't flinch from tackling issues of rural poverty, emigration and sexual frustration, arguing that "the writer's greatest asset is his indignation".

The life-size portrait, based on countless photographs of Keane taken by Ballagh, who visited him in Listowel, is a picture within a picture, creating the illusion of a framed painting on a wall. In the background is Ballybunion strand, where Keane often walked when he wanted to be alone. But Keane has one foot out of the frame and on the parquet flooring of the illusory room where the painting hangs. The lush Victorian wallpaper implies that it's a theatre. "The idea is to suggest a playwright who has the ability to bridge art and life."

Much the same could have been said of Ballagh. Life can hardly get more real than the money everyone has in their pocket. As if being given high security clearance to work with IRA prisoners in Portlaoise Prison while under surveillance by the Special Branch was not irony enough, Ballagh now found himself entrusted by the Central Bank with the task of designing a new series of Irish banknotes incorporating features that would rule out any possibility of counterfeiting.

The replacement of the existing banknotes, which had been in circulation since the changeover to decimalisation in the 1970s, was forced on the Central Bank by radical developments in printing and colour reproduction technology which made forgery far easier. Ballagh was one of a dozen leading artists invited to submit designs. His proposals were selected by a jury who judged each of the entries anonymously. In creating the designs he worked closely with the long-established German banknote company Geisicke & Devrient, who manufacture printing plates. Although the Central Bank printed the notes at Sandyford, it didn't have the highly specialised facilities for preparing its own plates.

"The design problem was to find a way to put in all the new security features and still come up with something attractive. We're talking about a note little more than half the size of the existing note but with over twice as many security elements and a lot of lettering too. "

The image had to incorporate areas of micro-lettering, too small to be detected by the naked eye, together with intricate patterns. There had to be a see-through motif, elements of which would be on either side of the note with the full image only becoming apparent when held up to the light. Ballagh also had to allow for a circular feature incorporating a hidden image – the letters IR – which similarly can only be seen when the note is tilted to catch the light. A silver security thread had to run through the note: in any illegal attempt to reproduce the note, the silver would come out black.

Three different types of printing would be involved: an intaglio or raised method (that can be felt by the fingertips) for the portrait, the litho-simultan process for the backgrounds, and then a letterpress technique because it's the only printing press that can change the numbers every time the note goes through. Each of the notes also had to have a strong predominant colour as well as a distinctive raised symbol to facilitate easy identification by the blind.

Ballagh decided that the key to a successful banknote design was a good portrait. Each note would be dominated by a striking, full-face image of the subject, aligned to the right to allow space in the background for associated biographical imagery. Taken in conjunction with the reverse side image, the banknote offers – as in most of Ballagh's portraiture – an inventory of the subject's life

For the £20 note, the first in the series to go into circulation, he worked from a contemporary mezzotint by John Gubbins of Daniel O'Connell as a young man, which he found in the National Gallery. The background is a landscape of Derrynane, Co Kerry. His work as a lawyer who successfully campaigned for Catholic Emancipation early in the 19th century is suggested on the reverse side by an elevation of the Four Courts, the background to which is the pledge to repeal the Act of Union signed by O'Connell and others in 1845. The dominant colour is violet, with browns and shades of blue.

Finding a suitable image of James Joyce for the £10 note proved more challenging. The Central Bank insisted on a smiling portrait of Joyce, yet no such photo existed. Ballagh had to invent a happy Joyce. It was set against a panoramic view of Dublin city and parts of counties Dublin and Wicklow drawn in the 19th century by TR Harvey. The reverse side carried a reproduction of one of the fourteen heads sculpted by Edward Smith for the Custom House. This head of Anna Livia, said to represent the Liffey, along with the opening lines of *Finnegans Wake* are overlaid on part of a 19th-century map of Dublin.

With the £5 note, the problem in portraying Catherine McAuley, the foundress of the Sisters of Mercy, was to avoid being too severe while finding a way on such a small canvas to suggest the extraordinary range of her commitment to the poor. "She was a Mother Teresa of her day and I wanted to do justice to that." He adapted a posthumous portrait which he set against a view of the

Mater Misericordiae Hospital in Dublin. The back of the note features a classroom with three children. The first verse of the poem 'Mise Raifteri an File' – quoted from a version in Songs Ascribed To Raftery by the Protestant scholar Douglas Hyde – is written on the blackboard. A map of Europe without national boundaries hangs on a wall.

A new portrait of Hyde, the first President of Ireland, features on the £50 note, with a drawing of Áras an Uachtaráin in the background underlined by a design from the interior of the base of the Ardagh Chalice. A traditional piper features on the reverse side overlaid on a 16th-century manuscript from the collection of the Royal Irish Academy and imprinted with the crest of Conradh na Gaeilge, an organisation for the propagation of the Irish language founded by Hyde.

For each banknote Ballagh had to provide a tiny painted portrait and a very precise drawing to enable engravers in Germany to get the anatomical details absolutely right. He worked closely with the chief engraver Antonio Lopez, one of only a handful of people who could do the work. "The engraving is done same size. If you make a mistake, you throw it in the bin and start again. There's no way to make corrections. You have to be on top of your game all the time. If you come in the morning and are not feeling good, you go home again."

Lopez was due to retire and move home to Avila in Spain, but stayed on to do the last note. "He did such beautiful work. It's not just because it was my work he was engraving. If you look at the quality of his portraits on our notes as against portraits on many other notes, they're streets ahead. Punters probably didn't notice but if you have an eye for those things, you see the quality. The thing about wonderful craftwork like his is that it's not original. It's always a copy of something."

After he retired Lopez did a beautiful engraving of a Dürer self-portrait and gave it to Ballagh. "He knew I loved Dürer. It had been a wonderful learning process for me. The challenge increased with each note. When I started I had a relatively clear playing field. But the design decisions I made for the first note established a style and a format which I had to continue in the others. I was limited by my own rules."

The £20 note, which became legal tender on 13 November 1992, was launched by Bertie Ahern, then Minister for Finance, at a reception in the Central Bank's Fort Knox-like premises in Sandyford. His surprising likeness to O'Connell was joked about in newspapers the next day, one of which demanded: "Why did Ballagh put Bertie on the £20 note?"

Ballagh's banknotes remained in circulation until Ireland adopted the euro in 2002. "When I started I knew nothing about banknote design. When I finished I was an expert, but an expert in an art form I'll probably never use again."

*Artwork for the poster for 'Féile an Phobail'*
*(The West Belfast Festival).*

"Would you like to go for a walk?" said Gerry Adams. "Yeah, great," said Ballagh. It was lunchtime on a beautiful summer's day early in August 1993. Ballagh had been hanging an exhibition of his portraits at the Belfast Institute of Further Education. It housed St Thomas' Secondary School in the 1960s. Author Michael McLaverty was one of its headmasters and Seamus Heaney taught English there.

Each August the BIFE was taken over as a venue for plays and exhibitions by the West Belfast Festival, which was rapidly growing into one of the largest community events of its kind on the island. Ballagh had designed a poster which became its emblem – a flower bursting out of a concrete block to become a dove of peace.

On visits North he'd often meet Adams for a chat in the Rock Bar on the Falls Road. "I got to know him a bit. We got on fine. We talked about a lot of things, mostly art and movies." There's a reference to the Rock Bar in Neil Jordan's *The Crying Game*. Stephen Rea, as an IRA gunman who holds hostage a black British soldier, played by Forrest Whitaker, mentions that it's his favourite bar. "A lot of Republicans didn't like *The Crying Game* because it ends with an IRA volunteer falling in love with a fellow, but Gerry thought it was terrific. He'd grown up on movies."

A black taxi was waiting outside. "Come on, get in," said Adams. "Where are we going?" "Have you ever been up the Black Mountain?" The mountain is the western end of a ring of hills around Belfast that eventually turns into Cavehill to the north.

Ballagh noticed the road getting steeper and steeper. Suddenly the black taxi wouldn't go any further. "The driver kind of scratched his head and said to Gerry, 'This is as far as we can go.'" It transpired the door panels had been filled with concrete as armour plating, so the taxi weighed a ton.

They got out and walked the rest of the way, just the pair of them. Sinn Féin had lost substantial ground to John Hume's moderate nationalist Social Democratic and Labour Party in the 1992 Westminster elections, ending up with no seats to the SDLP's four. It was a backlash to the Enniskillen bombing. Many Protestants voted for SDLP West Belfast candidate Joe Hendron rather than a unionist in a successful attempt to oust Adams. He was deeply engaged in secret talks with Hume and was moving the republican movement away from the physical force tradition. He asked Ballagh if he thought this would benefit Sinn Féin. Ballagh said he didn't know if it would benefit Sinn Féin, but that it would certainly benefit Ireland. "I think he was a bit disappointed that I didn't say Sinn Féin would benefit hugely from it. But I think in fact they have."

There were a few small houses near the top. "Gerry knew the people, because he brings his dogs up there a lot. I'd never been there before. All of Belfast was spread out below us. It suddenly came to me. This is the picture. I'd been thinking at some stage I would do a portrait of Adams. That day crystallised an image of him up there looking out over Belfast. He didn't know, of course, what I was thinking."

When Ballagh got back to Dublin he was contacted by Labour TD Michael D Higgins, a long-time campaigner for human

rights in many parts of the world and first recipient of the Sean McBride Peace Prize of the International Peace Bureau in Helsinki in 1992. After the 1993 elections the so-called 'Rainbow Coalition' appointed Higgins minister of a newly created Department of Arts, Culture and the Gaeltacht. Earlier that year the Supreme Court had upheld a High Court ruling that RTÉ had wrongly refused to broadcast the views of Larry O'Toole when he represented fellow trade union members in the Gateaux bakery dispute on the grounds that he was a member of Sinn Feín.

"Higgins believed that Section 31 was an impediment to moving the peace process forward. He told me he was really fighting hard to get it lifted, but not having much success in cabinet. "Is there anything you can do at Aosdána to help?"

Aosdána had been formed by Charles Haughey in 1981 as a sort of Irish Academy for people who have achieved distinction in the arts and, according to commentator Fintan O'Toole, as a way of deflecting criticism of his political actions. Ballagh, one of its 200 members, reminded Higgins that it had criticised Section 31 and called for an end to its 22 years of direct political censorship at a previous annual general meeting. "I can put down a motion calling for this to be reaffirmed." "Oh, that'll be a great help," said Higgins.

Motions have to be submitted to the governing body – the Toscaireacht – a month before the meeting. Ballagh did so and was seconded by Ulick O'Conner. What he hadn't realised was that since the previous meeting, several new members had been elected to Aosdána who were strongly anti-Sinn Feín and anti-Republican. When Ballagh rose to propose his motion, there was an immediate protest by the painter Gene Lambert who said he would not tolerate listening to the motion without Ballagh immediately condemning the murder of women and children.

It was like being harangued at one of Senator McCarthy's hearings in the 1950s. "I'd thought we'd struggle through but then Brian Lynch pops up and wants to put down an alternate motion that my motion only be taken after a full discussion on my politics. I couldn't understand how all this could be happening, since any such motion ought to have been submitted a month before. It went on and on. Finally I decided, against my principled feelings, that I would make a declaration. I had no problem in saying that I'm opposed to political violence, but I felt it was grossly unfair. It had never before been demanded of any member to make statements of where they stood on political issues."

Afterwards Ballagh wrote to Adrian Munnelly – who as head of the Arts Council was registrar of Aosdána – saying his experience at the meeting caused him to question any future active involvement on his part in the affairs of Aosdána. Lambert and Lynch were told by the Toscaireacht to apologise. Lynch didn't but the following March Lambert eventually did. "While I would not attempt to deny the views I expressed at our last meeting, I am very sorry for the tone and manner in which I addressed you. I wish to apologise unreservedly." By then it was too late to dissuade Ballagh. "My belief in Aosdána as a forum for civilised debate was damaged and unfortunately nothing has happened since last September to restore my faith in the

*Gerry Adams (1997)*
*Oil on canvas. 76 x 152cm.*
*Collection: Belfast Media Group.*

organisation," he informed Munnelly. "Consequently, I feel that my decision not to play an active part in the future work of Aosdána must stand."

The incident effectively drove him out of Aosdána. "I made a decision not to resign. I said I'd become effectively a non-playing member. I didn't attend meetings. I didn't nominate people for membership." By putting Section 31 back in the headlines, the controversy provided Higgins with the ammunition he needed. He announced on 11 January 1994 a cabinet decision to scrap the offending orders imposing the Section 31 censorship restrictions, although the legislation itself was not repealed. From midnight on 19 January, radio and TV reporters were legally permitted to interview Sinn Féin representatives. Higgins subsequently succeeded in his stated ambition to double the Arts Council's funding during his four years as minister. He kick-started an Irish film industry by re-establishing the Irish Film Board, and set up the Irish language television station Telifís na Gaeilge, or TG4 as it was later renamed. He appointed Patricia Quinn as the Arts Council's first woman director. He is still a member of Parliament and a published poet.

◆

The studio in Arbour Hill was finally up and running, if not in the way Ballagh had hoped. The terraced house at No 5 which Rachel had spotted for sale was a bargain at £30,000, but the expense of eradicating dry rot downstairs meant that he couldn't afford to go ahead yet with his plan for a studio extension in the back yard. He had to knock down the wall between two rooms on the upper floor to create a painting space.

The windows faced south which meant that he had to put up blinds to keep out the sun. But at least he was back in the situation he preferred of being able to leave home in the morning and go to work somewhere else. The only problem was that between his political commitments, theatre work, stamp designs and other commissions there was little time left for his own painting.

Ireland had come out of the economic doldrums. Trade benefited spectacularly from the 'single market' created by the Maastricht Treaty in 1992, lessening dependence on the British market. After a run on sterling forced Britain out of the European Exchange Rate Mechanism on 'Black Wednesday' in September 1992, Bertie Ahern smartly bit the bullet and went to Bruxelles to agree a 10 per cent devaluation of the Irish punt, promptly easing the pressure on exporters. From being the 'sick man' of Europe — with the International Monetary Fund in the late 1980s close to taking over the economy — Ireland was on its way to becoming one of the wealthiest by the late 1990s. A potent combination of a low-cost labour market, low corporate taxation and the provision of subsidies and investment capital encouraged high-profile technology companies to locate in Ireland. GNP growth took off, ranging

from six to eleven per cent between 1994 and 2000, while unemployment fell from 15 per cent in 1992 to 3.5 per cent. The Morgan Stanley 'Celtic Tiger' was born.

Extravagance became the new virtue. Nothing expressed it more stylishly than a display of tableaux vivants at the RHA Gallagher Gallery to launch a new range of Cutex cosmetics. Ballagh and Rupert Murray were drafted in by Mary Finan of Wilson Hartnell PR to replicate a form of entertainment that was popular among glittering New York society in the 1870s. The idea was to create living versions of famous paintings.

Ballagh opted for Vermeer's *The Girl with a Pearl Earring*, later to be celebrated in a novel and a film, and Renoir's *La Loge*, in which a man with opera glasses and a smartly dressed woman preen themselves in a box in a theatre. Ballagh built screen walls with two frames, and the spaces inside the frames were cut out. Actors who looked like the original subjects were hired to dress up in similar costumes and adopt the same poses, which Murray then lit just like the paintings. On arrival at the gallery the glitterati were treated to champagne or fizzy pink glasses of Kir Royale. Liveried footmen ushered the guest upstairs where a string quartet played baroque music in semi-darkness. The gallery director Ciarán McGonagle, dressed in a velvet smoking jacket, showed a slide of *La Loge*. Red velvet drapes were swished back. There was the painting, a living illusion. The same trick was repeated with *The Girl with a Pearl Earring*. "Apparently, with these magic new lipsticks, powders and creams, you too can look like a woman from a Renoir or a Vermeer painting," commented Miriam Lord in the *Irish Independent*. "Is this the new face of public relations? Or is it just PR gone mad?"

The bottom line was that it got lavish media coverage.

Ballagh kept a foot in reality by designing a production of Donal O'Kelly's play *Trickledown Town*, which the Calypso Company staged at the City Arts Centre. It was a flamboyant thriller set in a debt-strangled Jamaica where the World Bank and the International Monetary Fund have imposed punitive cutbacks. "It's a challenge to the neo-liberal theory that free-market conditions generate trickle down wealth to the poor. The play suggests the opposite." Any parallels with poverty in Ireland were purely coincidental.

An Post decided to bring out a series of stamps celebrating Irish Nobel Prize winners. The subjects of the five stamps would be George Bernard Shaw, WB Yeats, Samuel Beckett, Sean MacBride and Ernest Walton. Each was portrayed on a gold medal aligned to one side of the stamp to allow room for an image symbolic of their works. Ballagh gave Beckett an empty pair of boots, and for MacBride doves fly free into a blue sky, while Shaw has a poster of the first production of *Pygmalion*, Yeats a quotation from a poem, and the nuclear physicist Walton a chain reaction with a formula written on it. The Walton stamp was Ballagh's favourite. Sadly it was never issued. An embarrassed An Post official belatedly discovered that he was still alive, and there was a policy of not putting live people on stamps. A year after the four other stamps were issued, Walton died aged 92.

*Robert Ballagh beside a 'tableau vivant'*
*version of Renoir's 'La Loge'.*

Ballagh shared a distinction with Walton. Following the International Forum in Moscow in 1987 a Swedish academician proposed him as a fellow of the World Academy of Arts and Sciences and he was duly elected. When he read the list he noticed that the only other Irish person who was a fellow was Ernest Walton.

Having lost one stamp, Ballagh unexpectedly got back another. To mark the occasion of *L'Imaginaire Irlandaise*, a major festival of Irish culture in Paris, An Post decided to issue a stamp. Ballagh produced another version of the French Revolution stamp shredded in 1989. He had the last laugh.

As summer came and with it the 25th anniversary of British troops moving onto the streets in the North – and the British government effectively assuming responsibility for all security there - Ballagh was caught up in the 'Time For Peace, Time To Go' campaign. "Basically the argument was, let's have some peace and the way to have peace is if you lot go." He designed a *Slán Abhaile* (Safe Home) print showing troops leaving much the way they arrived, with good humour. The image was soon painted on gable walls all over the North. British investigative reporter Peter Taylor used it on the cover of a book about the Troubles. "It became a ubiquitous image. I even saw it on television in Germany. For me, what it was doing was underpinning the importance of non-violent political action. Apart from addressing the British, it was saying to the Republican community that there was another way."

The campaign was largely ignored in Dublin, provoking Ballagh to write to the *Irish Times* pointing out that "at this critical stage in the peace process if those nationalists who are committed to non-violent political action cannot get their point of view across, and are constantly harassed and marginalised, what sort of message does that exclusion send to those engaged in violence about the efficacy of non-violence?"

Along with the musician Cormac Breathnach he decided to organise a concert for peace. They booked the National Concert Hall. The NCH cancelled the booking, claiming they were entitled to do so if a proposed event threatened either the building or the safety of the public. Breathnach and Ballagh decided to contest the decision. The case was heard at the High Court by Declan Costello. A garda superintendent with whom Ballagh had had some dealings when organising marches was prepared to testify that the venue was not at risk. The NCH produced an affidavit by unnamed members of the Special Branch saying lives were at risk. Costello ruled in favour of the NCH.

The Royal Hospital Kilmainham agreed to host the concert and it took place, without any trouble. Undaunted, Ballagh went ahead with a 'Parade for Peace' which, following the strategy of the Easter Rising anniversary, culminated with a pageant in front of the GPO written and directed by Tomás Mac Anna. Ballagh's set took the form of a cardboard British barracks covered with camouflage netting which collapsed when the Red Choir of Cardiff burst through the walls singing 'We Shall Overcome'.

Ballagh was accused in the Dáil of being a fellow traveller and giving comfort to the Provos. Elsewhere Dessie O'Malley, leader of the Progressive Democrats, made a speech claiming Ballagh and his committee represented the heart of the Provo propaganda machine. John Hume came under even more vicious attacks for talking to Gerry Adams.

The peace process prevailed. Adams convinced the Provisional IRA of its effectiveness. Within two weeks they declared an indefinite ceasefire on condition Sinn Féin would be included in political talks for a settlement. Although the ceasefire broke down after 17 months, with the explosion of a bomb at Canary Wharf, it marked the beginning of the end of the IRA campaign.

◆

Ballagh wasn't a big fan of the Eurovision Song Contest. Because an Irish song had won in 1993, RTÉ were obliged to host the 1994 event. It took place in the vast Point Depot on the Liffey docks. Ballagh tuned in to the television coverage just to see the interval. "The host country always used it as a means of selling their country. I was interested to see what sort of image we were going to present of ourselves."

Previously when Ireland hosted the event, the time was filled with tourist views of Ireland. Not this time. The compere, Gerry Ryan, stepped forward and just said, without any rigmarole, 'Ladies and gentlemen, *Riverdance*!'

And it happened. In just seven pulsating minutes Michael Flatley and Jean Butler danced traditional Irish culture into an eye-grabbing global brand, helped by a mesmerising Bill Whelan score. "I think along with 500,000 other people I was completely blown away." The next day he rang his friend Bill Whelan to offer his congratulations. He was not to know that *Riverdance* would change his life.

◆

James Watson looks as if he's been punched in the face. "He has a sort of imperfection on his upper lip," says Ballagh, sifting through photographs he took at Cold Spring Harbour. "I'd be kind of happier with his mouth closed, but his wife Elisabeth would like him smiling." Capturing Watson's smile is a key to the portrait.

Ballagh has been working on the face for some weeks now, filling in the meticulously detailed contour map he drew of Watson's features. Every age spot and skin blemish had to be charted. "I need to know where they are, but I can then play them down a bit without being dishonest. They're there and they're not there. They give me all the information I need to know."

Painting the face, even at this rough stage, has brought alive what up to now has been primarily an exercise in technique, a setting of the stage for the final act of the portrait – the likeness. Imbued with this kiss of life, the beautifully textured wood, the books, the landscape backdrop, the figure with the outstretched hands should fall into place and assume a meaning beyond the sheer

*Top: Slán Abhaile (1994)*
*Limited edition print produced as a fund raiser*
*for the 'Time for Peace, Time to Go' campaign.*

*Above: Slán Abhaile mural on a gable in*
*Ardoyne, North Belfast, painted by local artists.*

virtuosity of their execution. The way Ballagh paints is a bit like sculpture. "You're kind of modelling and adding to it, except with clay modelling you take away as well as add stuff: in painting you are adding on little glazes and building it up slowly, one on top of the other. If you rush it you can overdo it and make a mess of it."

Although time consuming, it has become quicker than it once was. The traditional oil glazes were all based around linseed oil, which was fine except that they took forever to dry. Once he started using glazes he chose a glaze medium developed by Windsor & Newton called Liquin, which is a modern alkyd resin. The beauty of it is that it's very similar to linseed oil or the traditional mediums, but it dries within a day. Sometimes if there's good weather, it will dry out in twelve hours. "I did a little bit of work on Jim's face this morning. Tomorrow morning it'll be dry and ready for a bit more work. The portrait can progress along like this."

To facilitate what is called the scumbling effect – a form of texturing – he uses an impasto made by Windsor & Newton which has the quality that any mark he makes holds. "A lot of contemporary mediums – particularly in the house-painting range – are designed so that when you apply the paint the brush marks will smooth out because nobody wants streaky walls in their houses, whereas for this effect you want the complete opposite. You want every mark you make to hold. I've found it a very useful medium. I can daub it on with my fingers so you get the texture of a fingerprint, which I think enriches the painting."

Each stage of his evolution as a painter has seen him playing to the strength of whatever techniques he has mastered. The flat pop art surface applied quickly in his early paintings was dictated by the use of acrylics, before he found the confidence to turn to oils. Brush strokes were anathema to him then: not anymore. Always a model maker, he now has the confidence to treat each painting as a carefully sculpted tactile hand-made object. All of which, of course, takes time. He's being working on the Watson portrait nearly four months, bit by bit, day by day. "That's the way I work. It's a long distance journey with many stops, waiting for things to dry so you can inch forward again."

Between all the stops he has time for others things. The campaign for a 'No' vote in the referendum on the Lisbon Treaty is gathering momentum. Last night he was at the launch by the American political activist Susan George of *The Peoples of Europe*, a book against the treaty for which he wrote a foreword. He also designed a fund-raising print *Mise Éire* for the People's Movement, one of the leading ad hoc groups fighting against ratification of the treaty.

Susan George is based in France where she is prominent in an organisation called ATTAC – Association for Taxation of Financial Transactions to Aid Citizens – which opposes globalisation and neo-liberal economics, and in particular what she calls the "maldevelopment' policies of the International Monetary Fund and the World Bank. Ballagh shares with her a distaste of the one-way bias of free market economics. "The state is not supposed to intervene, we all must survive in the market, but when the banks get into trouble, the state is expected to dig into the taxpayer's pocket and bail them out. It's anything but a free market."

He rejects Lisbon as "a manual for neo-liberal economics", pointing out that in the Charter of Fundamental Rights the treaty uses "affirmative verbs in matters dealing with competition, saying there WILL be this, there WILL be that, but when it gets to the rights of citizens it lapses into the subjunctive, we hope that, or the people have the right to engage in work, not the right to work". Its obtuse provisions conceal "a kind of ache for empire".

While the French will never have an empire again, nor the Germans or the British, together they might make one; that seems to be the vision he detects lurking in EU Commission President Barosso's claim that "with the Lisbon Treaty we have the dimensions of empire". The defence part of the treaty, if passed, lays down that all European states "must increase their defence budgets," in other words build up their armies. "What do you do when you've got armies? You go to war. The whole thing sniffs of 19th century imperialism."

Ballagh has just become a grand-father for the second time. Two nights ago Andrea, Bruce's wife, gave birth to a baby boy, Ethan. "They saw an Ethan Hawke movie years ago and thought that's a lovely name, if we have a son we'll call him that." Their little daughter is called Ava. "After Ava Gardner?" Ballagh enquired. Bruce just looked at him. "Who's Ava Gardner?"

He keeps being surprised by how unalike Rachel and Bruce are. "It's all to do with the times you grow up. Rachel would be largely interested in much the same things I'd be interested in, art and politics. The 1960s was a significant period for me. There was this feeling that the world was going to change for the better, not just for the few. There was a huge optimism. I often think Rachel's a 1960s person in the wrong time. She grew up before Thatcher and the whole 'me' generation thing and the notion that there's no such thing as society, get on your bike. But Bruce was a teenager in the Thatcher years.

"He never had any great interest in art. He was determined to get on. He loved sport, and played junior tennis for Leinster, although sadly my father, who had played tennis for Ireland, had died by then. As soon as he left school, he got a job selling mobile phones. He was particularly interested in the motor industry, and worked for a company selling commercial vehicles. Earlier this year he and a pal decided that instead of making money for someone else they'd set up their own company. He has a settled middle-class view of life, whereas if Rachel didn't have any money next week, it wouldn't bother her in the least."

No doubt where and when someone is born has much to do with how they live their life, but what they might be capable of is predetermined by DNA. Ballagh bumped into Phelim Drew a few days ago. He's the actor son of the Dubliners singer Ronnie Drew. His wife has just given birth to twins. One of her grand-fathers was a twin. "It has to be there," Ballagh says. "Twins don't pop up out of the blue."

James Watson had his DNA sequenced for scientific purposes. There's nothing in his genetic make-up he doesn't know. It cost hundreds of thousands of dollars to find out. Even if the process of decoding eventually becomes much cheaper – and Harley

*Mise Éire* (2006)
*Limited edition print commissioned by the
Peoples Movement to raise funds for their
campaign against the first Lisbon Treaty referendum.*

71

Street clinics are already offering for £825 a personalised read-out of 42 genes that will allow you, according to the promotional hyperbole, "take control of your life and your health" – it's not something Ballagh would want to know about himself. He prefers to continue being surprised by life and by his children.

"It's all in this," he says, holding a sample strip of glass up to the light. By incorporating both sand blasting and etching he's finally found a way to capture the spiral effect of the double helix so that when it is set into the frame of the portrait it will create the illusion of a shimmering concept that Watson is about to grasp. "It's deep etched and every two rings are sand blasted to create a sense of depth." The glazier is now working on a full sheet of glass. Ballagh has dropped all his other work so that he can finish the portrait and have it photographed by David Davidson, who for years has photographed all his work. He wants to rush a print to Cold Spring Harbour as a birthday present for Watson, who was 80 on 6 April.

"When I finish a picture I know there are bits I've made a balls of that didn't work. It takes me a long while before I can sit in judgment on it as an independent thing in its own right. I just keep seeing the things I struggled with. This particular one was a desperate struggle, which was self-inflicted. If you look closely there's a very strong weave in the canvas. You can see it going through Jim's head and other places."

He's never had that in a canvas before. He just stretched the canvas, primed it and started working. It was only when he was half way through that he noticed the canvas wasn't like the canvas he usually uses. "As a consequence, every part of it was a battle against the canvas. It's a different weave. It all looks the same until you stretch it and prime it. That was a real battle. Nobody would know about it, but I do. I began to think I was losing my touch."

He never finds any part of a painting easy. But this proved a little more difficult than usual. "The little tricky things I've learned to do over the years weren't coming as easy as they did before. For ages I thought, it's all deserting me. But then I realised it was the bloody canvas." It will require extra care when Davidson makes photographs of the picture. "With a certain light the imperfections show up quite a lot."

He steps back from the easel. "Jim looks different in different lights. I'll hang him on a wall and leave him there." Working against the weave may have pushed Ballagh that little bit more, but it doesn't show. Watson seems wonderfully relaxed, standing before the soothing, almost ethereal, stillness of Cold Spring Harbour. "Even though it's an old man's head, there's a bit of a sparkle in it, isn't there?" says Ballagh.

Moya Doherty has a reputation for shaking things up. Born to Donegal parents but reared in Dublin, she ran Ireland's leading independent television production company Tyrone Productions and provided much of the more challenging drama and entertainment programming on RTÉ. She was determined to come up with something radically different for Eurovision 1994, a competition notorious for the dah-dee-duh mediocrity of its songs. The seven-minute interval slot offered an opportunity to grab the attention of 500 million viewers with an electrifying dance number that was Irish in a very modern and exciting way. And she knew that with champion Irish-American step dancers Michael Flatley and Jean Butler she could deliver just that.

Flatley was the best dancer of his generation, and he knew it. He came from Chicago and learned his first Irish dancing steps from his grandmother Hannah Ryan. When he was 17 he became the first non-European to win the All Ireland World Championship. He toured with the Chieftains in the 1980s and first danced with Butler – who grew up in Mineola on Long Island – when she made her debut at 17 with the Chieftains at Carnegie Hall in 1988.

Both were fired up by an awareness of the power of Irish music to speak to a wider audience. Their choreography for Eurovision daringly broke away from the stiffness of rural dance with a succession of virtuoso leaps and jumps. The staid buttoned-up lace collars and chaste costumes with interlacing Celtic motifs and Tara broaches characteristic of traditional Irish dancing gave way to provocative low-cut body-hugging dresses with flimsy skirts for the girls and unbuttoned bare-armed shirts with tight leather pants for the boys.

High-kicking to the whirring rhythms of a Bill Whelan score sung with intensity by the Celtic choral group Annua, Flatley and Butler burst onto the vast stage of the Point Depot in an exhilarating act of liberation – a casting off of centuries of repressed sexuality and puritanical insularity and re-branding Irish culture as a spectacle for mass global entertainment.

Ballagh was friendly with Whelan, who played on keyboards with Planxty and had composed the group's interval piece at the 1981 Eurovision – and also scored Pat O'Connor's 1984 film *Lamb* with Van Morrison. After calling up to congratulate him, Ballagh thought it would be the last he'd ever hear of *Riverdance*. But a couple of months later he received a call from Doherty. She was considering doing a theatrical show based on *Riverdance*. "Would you be interested in becoming involved as a designer?" "Yes, of course." "Well, I'll get back to you."

Months more passed, and he hadn't heard anything. He presumed either she'd forgotten about him or the project wasn't happening. But then she phoned again.

"We're having great difficulty getting finance, but we still want you to be involved. Would you able to hang in there?" "Certainly."

He discovered later Doherty had approached RTÉ for support, but they wrote back, "Dear Moya, Thank you for telling us about your project to put on a theatrical show based on *Riverdance*. We regretfully have to decline because we see no commercial future in such a project." She wasn't prepared to leave it at that. Her persistence eventually convinced RTÉ to change their mind

*Michael Flatley and Jean Butler in the 1994 Eurovision interval piece – 'Riverdance'.*

*One of a series of paintings used as back projections on the 'Riverdance' set.*

and come on board, along with others. By then Doherty and her director husband John McColgan had mortgaged their house to get the project off the ground.

Part of RTÉ's contribution to *Riverdance* was to design a set for the Point. But Doherty still wanted Ballagh involved. "Her idea all along, right from the time I spoke to her first, was to use back projection. She really felt the important thing was the dance. The notion of scenery or anything getting in the way of the dance was a no-no. She wanted to denote scene changes through immense images projected behind the dancers. She asked me to do the artwork."

Putting the whole financial package together had taken so long that once the green light was finally given there was much less time before the actual opening night than Ballagh would have liked. Up to 50 images would be required, which wouldn't be possible using the slow technique he normally used in his paintings. He suggested photographs or computer graphics. Doherty was adamant that all the images must be hand-painted to realise her vision of *Riverdance* as a show that respected the tradition of the music and the dance. Everything about it had to have integrity. Ballagh realised he'd have to devise a different way of painting.

"I came up with a wet-on-wet method, which Renaissance artists called *alla prima*. You literally do a painting in one go, one picture a day. When it works, it's great, when it doesn't you throw it in the bin. The attrition rate is quite high. And that's how I produced most of the images. I did fifty or sixty small 2 foot by 1 foot oil paintings which were then photographed so they could be rear-projected onto a screen behind the dancers. In the beginning we thought we'd get maybe six weeks work out of this project and then we'd all go on to something else."

For inspiration he turned to Casper David Friedrich, the 19th-century German Romantic painter whose fascination with light influenced his 1976 portrait of Joseph Sheridan Le Fanu and the *contre jour* (into the light) approach of his 1984 self-portrait *Highfield*. "When I had to create an image for the scene where Michael Flatley came flying out from the wings – which Michael said had to be like the arrival of the Ice King – I remembered the famous *Sea of Ice* by Friedrich, so I did an adaptation of that as a slide and it became part of the show."

At the same time Ballagh was executing the images, Whelan was busy composing the music and Flatley and Butler were putting together the choreography. They all improvised as they went along, each responding to what the other was doing. "Every week a new tune popped up. I remember going with Moya to Ringsend Road Studios, near the Grand Canal, where Bill played and sang what he had written. On another occasion a courier arrived at the studio with a cassette. I'd be listening to it while I painted, wondering does this sound blue, or does that sound green."

Most of Ballagh's experience of working in theatre was that you got one crack at designing a set and even if you felt you

could have done it differently, it's only up for a few weeks and that's it. "The wonderful thing about the success of *Riverdance* is that right from the start we could develop and improve it." The first full-length *Riverdance* opened at the Point on 9 February 1995 and was a sell-out throughout its five-week run. "It was far from the finished project, but it was as good as we could get it in that time. Not that it really mattered. People were so enthralled and so excited, Flatley and Butler could have been dancing in the street and nobody would have noticed."

Doherty gambled on moving *Riverdance* to London. She sent Ballagh and McColgan to check out two possible venues, the old Wembley arena and The Odeon, Hammersmith. "The problem with Wembley was that audiences had to go through turn-styles to get in. It wasn't a theatrical type of experience. John was very much against it. Prince was playing while we were there. I remember this diminutive little man coming to the venue in a purple suit. It was hard to imagine *Riverdance* there."

The Odeon Hammersmith was very down at heel. It was an art deco cinema now being used for rock concerts. "I was a bit depressed by it, but the Apollo Group who owned it said that if *Riverdance* went in they'd do a complete refit. And they did. They spent several millions getting it right. When *Riverdance* finished there they brought in other quality shows. The whole venue was lifted on the back of the success of *Riverdance*."

In London RTÉ were no longer involved with the set design, which meant that as well as providing the imagery Ballagh was now the designer. He was told to spend whatever he needed to spend, so he brought in the London company Imagination with Chris Slingsby to look after all the projection work. "The show had to be completely redesigned for the space because there wasn't room to use back projection. We had to use front projection. This meant building a new false proscenium and building out into the auditorium to create a bandstand. One projector was up high behind the existing proscenium, projecting down onto a screen behind the dancers, and another was in the theatre's projection box, projecting onto the false proscenium. The whole thing was a changing mosaic of projected images. It created a wonderful intimacy, but was difficult for the dancers to exit because, being a former cinema, there was no wing space."

Again *Riverdance* was a spectacular sell-out. Plans were made for a long run. But it went back to the Point, this time with Ballagh in charge. Whereas Hammersmith was small, the Point was vast. "We looked at it and said let's try and really use this whole space. The one thing I couldn't alter, and it never altered, was the choreography and where the entrances and exits were: it was a given that there would always be steps upstage in the centre. So we put in three huge screens – there had to be two entrances upstage – on which the images kept changing behind the dancers, and I created more images based on spirals from Newgrange which were painted on the flats that separated the screens."

*One of a series of paintings used as back projections on the 'Riverdance' set.*

Never mind that the passage graves at Newgrange were built long before the Celts arrived in Ireland, they just seemed right. The spiral motifs were seldom used or seen up to then. *Riverdance* was to turn them into a widely used symbol of Irishness. "One of the crew, an English guy, came up to me and said he'd seen someone wearing a tie with a spiral. You should sue him, he said. I told him I'm afraid the copyright holder of that design died three thousand years ago!"

When *Riverdance* returned to London it ran into its first crisis. There was a dispute with Flatley. "I found him fine to work with, but apparently he was becoming difficult and making more and more demands. A lot of people were saying to Moya, you have to give in to him because he's the star. At a certain stage she just said no, that's the final offer, if he doesn't accept it he's out. I thought it was very courageous of her."

They were rehearsing for the opening in the Hammersmith Palais, an old dance hall across the road from the Apollo. Ballagh was aware negotiations had failed, but none of the dancers knew. Moya asked everyone to gather and announced that Michael was gone. "There were tears and wailing, but the show went on. It didn't seem to affect things. Colin Dunne came on in Michael's place. No one asked for their money back. In hindsight it was probably a good thing, because it meant the show wasn't dependent on a star."

Flatley set up his own rival show *Lord of the Dance*, followed in 1998 by *Feet of Flames* and in 2005 *Celtic Tiger*, all of which were successful without damaging *Riverdance*. It seemed *Riverdance* had pioneered a global audience for a whole new dance entertainment genre rooted, much like Guinness or Jameson, in a popular conception – some might argue misconception – of Irish culture. This became clear when *Riverdance* travelled to New York City to perform at the legendary Radio City Music Hall in March 1996.

"The big gamble in London was that we knew ex-pats would support us, but couldn't be sure English people would like it. It turned out they liked it even more than the Irish. Moya was now making the same gamble in America. To cover her bet the show opened on St Patrick's Day, so there was a lot of hype around it."

Radio City put on their own Christmas and Easter shows, but apart from that normally rented the theatre out for awards ceremonies or to performing artists like Johnny Mathis for Friday and Saturday shows. "Just do a weekend," they advised Moya. "You'll never fill it for a week. 6,500 a night is a lot of people." But she was absolutely insistent. "Okay," they said. "It's on your own head." *Riverdance* sold out for the entire week.

The turning point was when McColgan, who was the director, had the idea of an invited audience for the dress rehearsal rather than doing it cold. He told Radio City he wanted to open it to all their staff. They agreed but said to do so they'd need to bring on more staff. Between staff and their families there was an audience of 2,500, a wonderful cultural mix of Irish, Italian,

Asian and African Americans that brought the house down. "That was the stage when we realised there really was something special about *Riverdance* that went way beyond appealing just to an Irish audience."

The show was co-produced with the Really Useful Group, an Andrew Lloyd Webber company. "They organised the people who would work on the show. We had to employ a union carpenter. I couldn't talk to the crew because I was non-union. I'd have to say to this fellow, could you get them to move that over there a little bit. He'd go over and talk with them. That's how it started off. What I found was if you played the game, the rules were relaxed. We developed a very good working relationship. It was my first real involvement with the American theatre world."

"What's wrong with being popular?" John B Keane laughed when some critics dismissed his plays as low art. Marie Jones was in some ways his Northern equivalent. She grew up in East Belfast's working-class Protestant community and left school at 15. The fact she never went to university made her a cultural outsider in a Belfast where theatre was traditionally the preserve of the educated middle classes. In her thirties she set up the all-woman Charabanc Theatre Company in the 1980s out of frustration at the tradition of English actresses being brought in to play roles in Belfast theatre. When she approached Martin Lynch to write a play for Charabanc, he urged her to write one herself out of stories she used overhear her mother tell when she was a little girl. So she did.

Ballagh admired her defiance of a cultural snobbery that belittled her because of her appeal to ordinary audiences. He designed a set for Marie Jones' version of the *The Government Inspector* for the West Belfast Festival. Gogol's comedy of errors about officials of a small provincial town in Tsarist Russia desperately trying to cover up their local misdeeds at the rumour of the arrival of an incognito inspector from the capital, had telling parallels to the situation in Ireland.

"The sectarian demarcations in the North meant nothing to me when I'd drive up to there. Apart from maybe not going into East Belfast at night, I'd go anywhere. But it was different for people living there. I remember before the opening of *The Government Inspector* we were rehearsing in rooms on Ravenhill Road, which is a very middle-class and safe area. I was talking to a young costume designer. 'Oh, I'm rattling,' he said. 'Why?' "I've never been in West Belfast.' He was really scared about going there. But artists tend to transcend cultural barriers. Here was a working-class Protestant playwright finding an audience on the Catholic working-class Falls Road."

The staging of 'Riverdance' in the Apollo Theatre, Hammersmith, London.

Ballagh worked with Jones again when DubbelJoint Productions, which she helped set up, premiered her play *A Night in November* at the West Belfast Festival in 1994. A Protestant dole clerk Kenneth McCallister, disgusted by the sectarian hatred of the crowd when the Republic of Ireland qualified against Northern Ireland for the World Cup in a showdown match in Belfast, becomes an Irish fan and decides to fly out to New York with the Republic's supporters for the finals. The minimal set provided three levels to represent the terrace against the backdrop of a football crowd. The rostrum is painted red, white and blue which flips to green, white and orange when the action switches to Dublin Airport. Kenneth's closing lines before flying off into the unknown are, "I am free of it, I am a free man…I am a Protestant man, I'm an Irish man."

The following year DubbelJoint brought Jones's play *Women on the Verge of HRT* to West Belfast. The title is a twist on Pedro Almodovar's 1988 Oscar-winning *Women on the Verge of a Nervous Breakdown*, although its take on the theme of women becoming old and being forgotten is much more personal than political. It toured for several years, eventually transferring to London's West End.

Ballagh went straight from the West Belfast Festival to the Edinburgh Festival, where Kenny Glenane had commissioned a set for a new production of Joe Orton's *Loot* at the Royal Lyceum Theatre. He'd met Glenane through Donal O'Kelly, who had another play *The Business of Blood* – a true story about the arms industry – for which he was also building a set. Calypso Productions were putting it on at the Project Arts Centre as part of the Dublin Theatre Festival in October, which meant Ballagh was involved in three festivals almost at the same time.

*Loot* was a wildly eccentric production. "Kenny wanted to do it like the cartoons of Chuck Jones to the extent that all entrances had little mini-trampolines to allow the actors to boing–boing onto the stage. The sets all had zany proportions, so that everything was distorted and strange. The actors I think found the whole thing mad and were a bit uncooperative. They were terrified they'd literally break a leg."

While Charles Stewart Parnell was going into circulation in 1996 as the new face of the Irish £100 note – the final denomination designed by Ballagh in the currency series launched by the Central Bank in 1992 – his demise was already sealed. With the introduction of the euro on 1 January 2002, the Irish punt would cease to exist. It was to be replaced by euro notes, which would become the common currency in all fifteen countries qualified for membership of the euro zone. Each country was invited to submit entries for the design of the new notes. Ballagh was commissioned by the Central Bank to design Ireland's entry. Although the choice was questioned by some, under the conditions laid down by the European Central Bank only experienced banknote designers could submit designs. Ballagh was the only Irish designer with banknote experience.

He was faced by a dilemma, which he resolved pragmatically. "I still don't think the euro is necessarily a good thing. The

loss of our own currency marks a loss of sovereignty and a further loss of control over our economic destiny. But I have to say the fee that was offered was sufficient to assuage any doubts about the project."

His Irish banknotes were all hand-drawn and hand-designed. Each one took about six months to complete and involved several trips to Germany to supervise the plate making process. There were no computer graphics used or any kind of shorthand techniques. A requirement for the euro submission, however, was to design all 28 fronts and backs in the same length of time. Obviously computer technology would need to be involved. "I worked with a graphic design company called Image Now. I'd bring in drawings, they'd scan them. It was the only way you could get that quantity of work out with sufficient quality in that period of time."

Right from the start he faced a major obstacle. "There could be no national or gender bias in the design. I asked if the notes could feature cultural icons like Shakespeare, Goethe, Beethoven, Dante and Cervantes. No, no, that's national bias. I asked about architecture – I wanted to put something like Newgrange in my designs. No, no, that's Irish, you can't do that. I understood the criteria, of course, but now that we're all a part of Europe, famous buildings or cultural figures surely belonged to all of us. They didn't see it that way."

He finally chose to depict animals on one of the series, echoing the indigenous animals on the much-admired coins Ireland used to have. On another he featured fictional portraits, alternating male and female from note to note up to the €500 note, which had a male and a female. "There was no licence for creativity or imagination, unfortunately. Back when I was designing my first note for the Central Bank, I was given a statement issued by the head of the German Bundesbank who said that a banknote is a security document, not a work of art. The briefing for the euro notes issued to all the invited artists was the size of a telephone directory. All the security features had to go into the design first. They were more important than the image. So you have watermarks, and silver threads and this, that and the other. When you've got all that done, maybe then you can do something nice graphically in terms of an illustration."

All the designers were invited to Frankfurt to hear the result of the competition. The winner, an Austrian Robert Kalina, got around the restriction of not being able to base a design on any existing building by inventing a series of bridges, gateways and windows that correspond to specific periods like the Renaissance, Baroque and Rococo. Mary Finan, who represented Ireland on the judging panel, admired the symbolism of the bridges. "It was a sophisticated and appropriate design. It stood out among the entries."

Ballagh admits to being a bit miffed at not being picked. "But when I got to Frankfurt I was less disappointed because there were several wonderful designs that were not picked either. There's no reflection on Kalina, but the brief ensured that the currency design chosen would avoid rows and offend no one. The danger is that it ends up pleasing no one."

*Designs by Robert Ballagh for the Euro.*

Bertie Ahern became Ireland's youngest Taoiseach when Fianna Fáil returned to power in the June 1997 elections. The Labour Party ousted the Tories in Britain, putting Tony Blair in 10 Downing Street. The IRA reinstated its 1994 ceasefire in July. The secret talks going on in various forms since the late 1980s between Gerry Adams and John Hume and later involving both Dublin and London, took on a new urgency. "The irony was that even at this time Adams was a pariah," says Ballagh. "Being the sort of person I am, I thought if everyone hates him that's reason enough for me to paint him."

Since the day he walked with Adams to the top of Black Mountain he'd imagined portraying him in a wide-angle joined-together triptych rather like a medieval altar piece. His idea was to place Adams not on Black Mountain looking down on West Belfast, but on Cavehill looking at all of Belfast, evoking an association with the founding there by Henry Joy McCracken and Wolfe Tone of the United Irishmen, a revolutionary movement that sought to transcend religious differences in the struggle for freedom from England.

There was only one difficulty. Adams didn't want to be painted. "I told Bobby you don't want to do a portrait of me, but he persisted," says Adams. "He said you don't have to do anything, all you have to do is let me come and take a photograph. Eventually I said okay."

But Ballagh found it hard to set up a photographic session. His way of contacting Adams was through his personal aide, Siobhán O'Hanlon. "She died tragically young of cancer. She would have been at the Downing Street meetings that led to the Good Friday Agreement. Blair's long-time chief of staff Jonathan Powell thought highly of her. She was a powerful woman with great integrity. I said to her I have to get to Gerry to take some photographs. Oh, leave it with me, she said. Months passed. He's very busy, you know, she said. Then one day she phoned. "Can you go to Monaghan today?" "Yeah." "He's talking at a meeting there. He can give you a little time."

Ballagh headed North, a two-hour drive. He brought Adams out into the car park of a hotel where there was large boulder. It was the nearest they could get to being on a mountain top. He asked him to put one foot on the ground and the other on the boulder and spent about ten minutes taking photographs from different angles, a stance that was a quote from Casper David Friedrich's *Wanderer Above the Sea of Fog*.

The portrait places Adams in the centre of a wide landscape with a high sky and the city of Belfast simmering below. "I was a bit embarrassed by it, to tell the truth," says Adams, who saw it several months later when he was in Dublin and visited Ballagh's studio in Arbour Hill. "I always admired his *Noël Browne* and the quirky bit with the stones. This was at a time when we hadn't made as much progress in the peace process as we have now, so it is flattering that he would have me looking from Cavehill in this sort of visionary way. There you go."

The following Easter the Good Friday Agreement was signed. It established "an exclusively peaceful and democratic" framework for power-sharing in Northern Ireland and marked an effective end of the IRA campaign of violence. Both the British and the Irish governments endorsed it, as did the electorates of the North and the Republic in May. "When I started the portrait, Gerry Adams was the devil," says Ballagh. "By the time I had it finished he was sainted, and was voted the most popular politician in the country."

Although Ballagh's images were reaching hundreds and thousands of people not just in Ireland but around the world – whether through *Riverdance* or the Irish currency notes and stamps – he had become in some way the invisible man of Irish art. "If you wanted to see any of my work in Dublin you'd have to go to the theatre. My *John B Keane* portrait was hanging in the Gaiety, *Oscar Wilde* was in the Gate and *Brendan Smith* was in the Olympia. But exhibiting art in those kinds of venues didn't seem to merit a mention."

Official Irish art had become mainly conceptual and preoccupied with video and installation work: paintings, invariably abstract, barely got a token look in. Drawing seemed almost a term of contempt. Ballagh's brilliantly executed, jokey, realistic commentary on Irish life and identity seemed anathema to this exclusionist aesthetic.

"When exposure is not available for you in some arenas, you can't just stop doing art. I went in another direction, which in a way was a very post-modernist initiative. I made art by and large for either myself – as with the Gerry Adams or Michael O'Riordan portraits – or for people who wanted it, people who would phone me and ask me to make it. I was a kind of artist in the medieval tradition, a journeyman artist. It was a much more modest role in some ways. In some ways I found it intellectually more honest than becoming famous for embalming dead sheep."

This is not to de-legitimise any form of art experience. What he was against is the way much of it is curated and written about and presented. A tiny little tributary in art was getting all the attention. "My feeling was that modernism had run its course. It was like watching a terminally ill patient. So many things on show to us – apart from being boring in themselves – had all been done before. We really were at the rag end of modernism. But nobody seemed to have noticed.

"I always thought the visual arts were about visual aesthetics and things that were supposed to look beautiful or challenging. So how could you have visual art when you had to read about it? Or visual artists who worked in sound? Or visual artists who worked in performance?"

All of which added to the irony of Ballagh designing the set for Christopher Hampton's translation of Yasmina Reza's play *Art* at the Gate Theatre. To provide a visual context for the action, a comedy of manners in which three men argue over the purchase of a virtually blank modernist canvas for 200,000 francs, Ballagh created a pastiche of three different modernist styles. "I found the play interesting in that the idea of a blank white canvas being outrageous is a little old-fashioned to anyone who remembers the furore caused by a Dublin councillor Ned Brennan when the Hugh Lane Gallery purchased an Agnes Martin back in the 1970s."

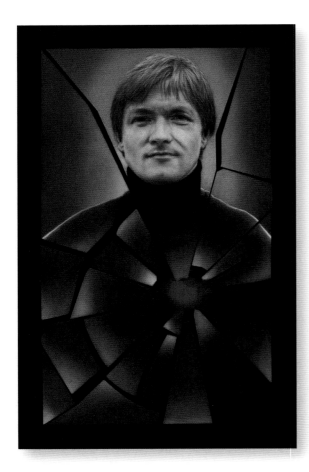

*Is there any evidence anywhere that you may have supported violence?*

*Pat Finucane (2009)*
*Oil on canvas. 92 x 60cm.*
*Private Collection.*

"Is there any evidence anywhere that you may have supported violence?" "I am absolutely positive there isn't." Ballagh was able to back up this assurance to his solicitor James McGuill by producing various speeches he'd made supporting peace. Together with musician Cormac Breathnach he was suing the *Irish Independent* for libel over an article in which Bruce Arnold seemed to suggest that they were propagandists for the IRA. This had been published in the context of their failed attempt to stage a Peace Concert in the National Concert Hall in 1994.

"If it was just me I'd have let it go, but Cormac was determined to go ahead. I remember Adrian Hardiman, the senior counsel, advising that we could not bank on a jury at that time being able to put out of their mind prejudices about the Provos in making their judgement. So we decided to wait."

After the peace process gathered momentum in 1999 and with the ceasefire holding firm, Breathnach decided it was time to go to court. The case was still within the statute of limitations. Under the laws of discovery, the *Independent*'s lawyers had to show McGuill some of the evidence they were considering using in court. "They had stuff I believe they could have only got either from Irish or British Intelligence. One was a statement by Des O'Malley, a former Fianna Fáil minister who had formed the right-wing breakaway Progressive Democrats, in which he said that Mr Ballagh and his committee for 'Reclaim the Spirit of Easter' represented the interests of the IRA. The *Independent* was planning to use this in court. These were just allegations. There was no evidence. There was no smoking gun in my past."

The case was settled out of court, and they were awarded £30,000 damages. He had become accustomed by then to being a target for disapproval. He could even see the absurd side of being harassed and tailed by the Special Branch while entrusted with responsibility for the security-sensitive design of the Irish banknotes. It hadn't surprised him to be attacked for his opposition to Section 31 or for taking part in campaigns such as 'Reclaim the Spirit of Easter' and 'Time For Peace, Time To Go' – that was all part of the cut and thrust of politics – although he could have done without abusive phone calls that led to the Gardai advising him to go ex-directory, and it worried him to read in *Hot Press* that "somebody out there has let it be known that he would like nothing more than to kill Robert Ballagh".

He had never made any secret of his views and was ready to debate them in public, although apart from Michael McDowell and Paddy Harte, few public figures were prepared to engage with him. Instead he found himself being labelled by association, as when Senator Shane Ross claimed the organising committee for 'Reclaim the Spirit of Easter' was "heavily infiltrated by fellow travellers and could be hijacked by the Provisional IRA or one of its front organisations".

It was particularly frustrating to be accused of supporting or condoning violence at a time when behind the scenes he was actually doing everything he could to encourage Sinn Féin to reject the bullet for the ballot. Soon after the *Irish Independent* article, *The Sunday Times* published a humorous "blaggers guide" in which Shane Hegarty noted that he had been "accused of representing the 'arty' wing of the IRA". Ballagh wasn't bothered too much about it, but John Gore-Grimes, a solicitor and a long-time friend, said that it was a serious libel and advised him to sue.

There are areas where you can be critical and harsh in what you say about people, because nobody is going to die as a result, but in relation to the North, loose talk can cost lives. In 1989 a Catholic solicitor Pat Finucane, who had represented republicans and taken the British Government to court several times over human rights abuses, was assassinated by masked loyalist paramilitaries in front of his wife and children two weeks after Tory MP Quintin Hogg alleged in the House of Commons that certain solicitors were sympathetic to the republican cause.

Aware of this Ballagh decided to sue, and he won. *The Sunday Times* settled out of court for £35,000 and published an apology acknowledging the allegation had been highly offensive, and that "while Robert Ballagh holds strong republican views, he has never supported or condoned the use of violence to achieve political objectives and has been a consistent advocate of the peace process in Northern Ireland. We unequivocally accept that Robert Ballagh has never been a member or supporter of the IRA or any other illegal organisation. We apologise to Robert Ballagh for the distress and embarrassment caused, and have agreed to pay him a sum of damages and his legal costs."

Betty disappeared from his paintings after *Upstairs No 3* in 1982. He depicted himself alone in subsequent autobiographical works. Perhaps for that reason he decided to celebrate her birthday in 1999 by painting a small miniature head-and-shoulders portrait. He intended it as a companion to a similar circular vignette he painted as a birthday present in 1979, when she was 30. It is a simple close-up showing Betty bare-shouldered except for a necklace. Her head is turned to one side, looking upwards pensively. The background is attractively grained wood.

"She didn't like it. It's sitting at home, although I notice it's not hidden behind things any more. I think she has learned to live with my portrayal. I must do Betty at 60 and see if we can please her more."

The format of a circle set within a square had been effective when he painted silhouettes of marchers in 1969. He also used it for his prize-winning James Connolly acrylic in 1971. It's simple and direct and is particularly appropriate for small-scale portraits because it rules out the necessity for background detail.

To portray the assassinated Catholic solicitor Rosemary Nelson he chose the same round format he used for Betty, but framed with a painted stone ring on which the Irish words *'Guth an Phobail'* (voice of the people) are carved. Nelson, a 40-year-old mother of three, was killed by a car bomb outside her home in Lugan, Co Armagh in March 1999, put there by a loyalist paramilitary group calling itself the Red Hand Defenders. Allegations were made that elements within the RUC had colluded with her killers. The portrait was commissioned by the Campaign For Justice for Rosemary Nelson.

Some months before her murder, she had testified to a committee of the US Congress investigating human rights in

Northern Ireland that death threats had been made against her and her three children. The British government had been warned of the threats by the UN. A subsequent inquiry revealed in September 2008 that the RUC Special Branch had been recording the "minutiae of her life" for almost three years before her murder, abusing the legally privileged talks she had with Republican clients while acting for their defence. Rory Phillips QC, lead counsel for the inquiry, asked, "Why was the Special Branch recording information of this kind relating to Rosemary Nelson's private life, including details of her family, friends, people who worked in her solicitor's office?" He also noted that despite this, there were no "reports, notes, memoranda or documents produced by E3 (the Special Branch's republican desk) containing analysis of the intelligence on Rosemary Nelson".

Ballagh used another variation of the format – a half circle, or *lunette* – to portray Bernadette Devlin, iconic leader of the 1968 Civil Rights marches. She is shown leaning forward, clutching a bull-horn in her fist. Behind her it's possible to make out details that evoke the Battle of Bogside of 1969: some B-Specials approaching a group of youths, and graffiti on a wall proclaiming 'You Are Now Entering Free Derry'.

A circle enclosed in a black square dramatised – like a spotlight – a small portrait of playwright Brian Friel, whose Tony Award-winning play *Philadelphia, Here I Come* inspired the dual-self portrait used in *Upstairs No 4, The Studio*. It was commissioned by impresario Noel Pearson, who managed Ballagh in his days as a bass guitarist. A shot of Friel tilting his spectacles down to peer at the camera, it featured as the poster for a Friel Festival Pearson was putting together in the Abbey and the Gate and also New York. The lenses of glasses reflect white clouds in a blue sky.

Ballagh switched to an isosceles triangle format for Rory Rapple, son of the financial journalist Colm Rapple. Asked by his parents what he would like for his 21st birthday, Rapple chose to have his portrait painted by Ballagh. He wanted it to include his mandolin, his favourite book and an Irish setting. Ballagh obliged, sitting him on a chair, with stone-walled Connemara fields behind.

During the campaign to repair Border roads dismantled by the British Army, Ballagh got to know Neil Blaney reasonably well. For a while they were both involved in a think-tank to discuss Articles 2 and 3 of the Irish Constitution, which Unionists wanted removed. "We thought they were an important part of the Constitution, not to be discarded lightly. We used meet in Anthony Coughlan's rooms in Trinity."

When Blaney died in 1998 a local committee was set up in his constituency in Donegal, which he had represented in the Dáil throughout his political career – first as a Fianna Fáil Minister and then as an Independent after his dismissal from government. It decided to commission Ballagh to commemorate him with a portrait. After several trips to Letterkenny to discuss it, it became clear they wanted something of Donegal in the background. When Ballagh asked where, Joe Gallagher, who owned a shop in the main street, offered to show him. "Betty was with me, and he drove us along the east side of the Fanad Peninsula to a place called Portsalon. It was absurdly gorgeous. I took loads of photographs. My idea was to paint him with his famous pipe, and the beach and the sea

*Brian Friel (1998)*
*Oil on canvas. Diameter 30cm.*
*Private Collection.*

behind him. One of the details that appealed to me was a road snaking through the landscape known to all the locals as the Blaney Road, because he got the grants from Europe to build it."

The wide-angle painting has some similarities with the Gerry Adams portrait. It hangs in the Letterkenny Institute of Technology, which he was also instrumental in establishing. Politicians of all hues attended the unveiling.

A paper Ballagh wrote on Articles 2 and 3 of the Constitution caught the attention of Hugo Flynn, who decided to have it published. Flynn, whose family was involved in the *Irish Press*, had civil engineering projects in West Africa. One of his ways of spending the considerable money this earned him was to build golf courses in Ireland, notably St Margaret's Golf Course in North Dublin. He wanted Ballagh to be his artistic adviser in a far more ambitious project in Druid's Glen near Newtownmountkennedy in Wicklow. "Great care was taken with the ecology of the area for example. They decided against disturbing the migrating pattern of the birds. It involved a lot of work planting and moving trees."

Woodstock House, where the Duke of Wellington's brother used to live, was to become the clubhouse. One of the tenants before it fell into disrepair was Rod Stewart. "Hugo said we must put our mark on the house. He wanted a bronze version of the 1916 Proclamation in the hall with a garland of Easter lilies around it. I made that for him. On the walls of the beautiful winding staircase I did drawings of the seven signatories of the 1916 proclamation. There were so much space to fill I had to sub-contract some of the work. Hugo created a *Seomra na mBan* for famous Irish women. My Bernadette Devlin portrait is there, along with portraits of Mary Robinson and Countess Markievicz."

During excavations a tunnel was found which had been built from the house to the edge of the property, so that when people working in the house or on the estate were coming to work they didn't disturb the view. "I got a fellow who worked in the wax museum to make a life-size model of a servant girl emerging from the tunnel, and Jim Harkin, who had done a lot of work at Ardmore studios, dressed the space as a pantry."

Flynn also commissioned Ballagh to create a stained glass window of the Famine. "I worked with a studio in Galway. The design is divided in two. One half has all the flowers growing and the tubers are fine, and in the background comely maidens are digging the spuds. The other half shows everything rotting and dying, as well as evictions and people emigrating." With the help of a young sculptor from Leo Higgins's C.A.S.T. foundry, Ballagh created a life-size bronze 1798 Pikeman to stand at the first tee. "The whole thing was a bit of adventure, considering I never had any interest in golf."

Ironically he would become involved in another much bigger golf project in 2006 – designing a structure for the opening ceremony of the Ryder Cup at the K Club in Straffan. His idea was to create a shell-like arena with canvas and cables that would look well not just on the ground but shot from above by television helicopter cameras. All the back-stage dressing rooms were to be accommodated in smaller tents. His model was a strikingly beautiful image giving an impression of weightlessness, a complete departure from the usual black-box bandstand used for rock concerts which tend to be all façade but an unseemly mess behind.

*Top: Rosemary Nelson (1999)*
*Oil on canvas. Diameter 60cm.*
*Collection: Druid's Glen Golf Club.*

*Above: Pikeman (1998)*
*Life size bronze figure.*
*Collection: Druid's Glen Golf Club.*

Regrettably it failed to get approval. It was his last collaboration with Rupert Murray, who died soon afterwards. "His early death was a huge tragedy. We had a really exciting creative partnership. We sat together in the dark in countless theatres all over the world, working on shows. I remember joking once that the only other person who spent more time in the dark with Rupert was his wife Shelagh."

◆

Marie Jones and Pam Brighton believed theatre could be rooted in the lives of its spectators, much as Paul Mercier and Roddy Doyle had demonstrated with the Passion Machine Company operating out of the St Francis Xavier Hall in north Dublin in the late 1980s. DubbelJoint aimed to attract audiences who would not normally go to the theatre by convincing them that their own everyday experiences had far more drama than anything they could see on the television soaps. Following the success of *A Night in November* – and working mostly with women from West Belfast – they created *Bin Lids*, a title inspired by a tradition that caught on when internment was introduced in the early 1970s, when women would go out on the streets banging their bin lids to warn people that the Brits were coming. They also did it when Bobby Sands died.

Ballagh was brought in at the early stages of rehearsal when it was been improvised. "We did it as a promenade production. The audience all came in and stood around. There were five different stages surrounding them and the actors moved about from one to the other. The people who were at the play were the people whose stories were being told."

This led to some highly emotional moments during the staging. There was an incident from the period after the breakdown of the early IRA ceasefire in the 1970s in which a little girl going out to get milk was shot by British soldiers. "The girl's parents were at the play. This was the first time their daughter's story had ever been told. Of course they were in tears."

The whole thing was powerful in terms of community theatre. The second half of the play started with the election that led to Bobby Sands winning a Westminster seat which of course he couldn't take. When the audience came back after the interval the cast circulated among them dressed in clothes of that period. "They were handing out leaflets VOTE BOBBY SANDS and asking, do you need a lift, can you get to the polling stations yourself? One old lady replied, 'No I'm fine, I'll get there myself.' They were all caught up in the immediacy of it."

After its premiere at the West Belfast Festival, *Bin Lids* transferred to New York where it was identified as part of a vogue for testimonial theatre in which the spectator is placed in the position of receiver of the testimony. Cut off from an audience familiar with the experiences being evoked, it did less well. "The reception history of *Bin Lids* demonstrates that any attempt to formulate the spectator as an engaged 'witness' may collapse under the multiplicity of response," said Karine Schaefer, who made it the subject of an academic case history.

*Stones in His Pocket* made up for this disappointment, although not initially. A two-hander written by Jones and directed by her second husband Ian McElhinney – by whom she has two children – it centred on a couple of extras hired to appear in a Hollywood production that has taken over a small town in Kerry. The comedy is in the contrast between the romanticised Irish 'authenticity' they are helping to provide with the actual reality of their lives. The two actors in the play perform all 15 characters, male and female, switching roles at times in mid-sentence. It called for a minimalist open set and a few representative props. It opened at the Lyric Theatre in Belfast in 1996 and also played at a community hall in East Belfast and at An Cultúrlan on the Falls Road, without success. Ballagh designed the first production at the Tivoli Theatre in Dublin, which also failed. After much rewriting and modifications it resurfaced in 1999 with a set by Jack Kirwan, reaching the West End's New Ambassadors Theatre via the Edinburgh Fringe and London's Tricycle Theatre. Audiences took to it so spectacularly that it moved to the large Duke of York's Theatre, where it remained for three years while the original cast of Conleth Hill and Sean Campion took it to Broadway. It was nominated for three Tony Awards in 2001, and has since been produced all over the world. Ballagh sent Jones a congratulatory card, "Now you've got your own *Riverdance*."

The Prince's Trust, a personal project of Prince Charles, came up with the idea of inviting artists and musicians to paint masks for a charity auction. Someone at *Riverdance* volunteered Ballagh, without telling him for what: he was just asked to paint a suite of 19 *Riverdance* masks, which he did. Sting's mask fetched the biggest price at the auction, followed by the *Riverdance* suite which was bought on behalf of Moya Doherty. It now hangs in her boardroom in Merrion Square.

All the contributors, a Who's Who of famous Brits, were invited to a personal opening arranged for Prince Charles. A publicist phoned Ballagh. "Isn't it wonderful, I'll see you there." "No, you won't." "But why?" "I'm in Ireland." "You can fly over." "I can't take time off simply to meet Prince Charles."

His response was in the same spirit of Seamus Heaney, who demurred in verse to his inclusion in *The Penguin Book of Contemporary British Poetry*, "My passport's green/No glass of ours was ever raised/To toast the Queen."

*Riverdance* at Radio City had been so successful that it was followed by an American tour. The scale of the show meant there were only about a dozen venues in the States large enough to stage it. After playing Boston three times, the imperative was to come up with a version of the show that would be just as exciting but could play in 2,000-seat theatres with smaller stages. Ballagh and Rupert Murray went back to the drawing-board.

"To our chagrin we had to jettison the projection. It just took up too much space. In those days back projection was relatively unsophisticated. We needed a huge space behind the screen which pushed the whole set downstage. Another problem was that in order to have space for the dancers, we needed to put the band on a specially built bandstand in the auditorium. This resulted in a massive number of seat losses, or 'seat kills' as they called them."

*The Riverdance Suite of Masks (1996)*
*Gold leaf, acrylic and oil paint on ceramic.*
*Private Collection.*

Ballagh's solution was to build a two-story bandstand centre-stage that accommodated all the musicians on two levels. Instead of back-projection he relied on a lot of traditional theatrical effects, like flying in gauzes and painted drapes. Vancouver was the first to see this new theatre-friendly *Riverdance*. There were worries people might see it as a diminished version of the original, rather than appreciate it for its difference. But right from the start it went down a treat and toured the US in that format for the best part of ten years.

"The interesting thing about all of this for me as a designer was that *Riverdance* never seemed to be a finished project. There was always a new version to fit a new situation. I travelled with it to Australia, Mexico, Japan and China, all the time adjusting the set to suit the circumstances and the any new numbers that were introduced. The music seems to have the capacity to transcend the local and become universal. I've watched the Irish people getting it, the English getting it and then the Americans. When we were in Tokyo we thought, maybe this time they won't get it. But they went mad for it, too."

He did an interview with a Japanese journalist. "Which of the images did you specifically do for Japan?" "Well, none." "But what about this red sun? What about those gold panels?" "They've always been in it." "But they're so Japanese."

He had a similar encounter when he was building sets for a Broadway version. Touring sets always had to be light-weight and easy to dismantle, so a lot of the scenery was covered with printed canvas. Since the Broadway show was intended to last for 18 months, they decided that the flats instead of being printed fabric would be like Neolithic panels, with spirals carved into simulated stone.

"I remember going to the Scenic Workshop in upstate New York to check out what they were doing. The guys were all working away from my drawings and samples. 'It's looking good, lads.' 'Uh-huh. You're the designer?' 'Yeah.' 'Tell me, what's it about? Is it some Native American show?' I thought how universal such iconography can be".

To the craftsmen, the spirals seemed like Native American iconography. It seems that *Riverdance* for whatever reason, whether the music or the dance or the imagery, always touches a common chord. Back in Ireland it came to be seen by many as embodying the confidence and gung-ho entrepreneurship of the Celtic Tiger Irish economy, but to others it represented a 'Disneyfication' or 'McDonaldisation' of Irish culture. In their sociological study *Cosmopolitan Ireland,* Carmen Kuhling and Kieran Keohane acknowledged that it "brings millions of spectators to their feet, waves of rapturous applause, cheering, weeping hysteria", but wondered "when audiences leap to their feet ...what is it that they are straining to see or to hear?" Neo-Marxists might argue that it was "a mass-produced global product cynically created for a homogenised global audience" while cultural nationalists accused it of being "inauthentic", but somehow these perspectives did not "capture the way in which it has become a source of a positive identity for Irish people".

Whatever the verdict, there can be little doubt that there never has been a project like it in the Irish cultural sector and probably never will be again. Its influence can perhaps be measured by a documentary film *A Bronx Tale*, which is about an Irish woman who got a job in a Bronx school, a run-down building where the kids were either Hispanic or African-American. Trying to think of something interesting for them to do, she started teaching Irish dancing. The kids absolutely lapped it up. They formed a company called Celtic Dreams. She even started teaching them Irish.

"So you have all these black kids saying '*Conas atá tú?*' They began to mix Irish dance with hip-hop and salsa, a wonderful expression of youthful exuberance. I do believe that there's something in the music and the dance that appeals to people at a deep human level."

*Riverdance* changed Ballagh's financial situation dramatically. It was the first project he'd ever been involved in as a visual artist that delivered royalties. Up to then, even if he got a fair price for a picture, that was all he got. "Now suddenly I was involved in a situation where any night there was a performance anywhere in the world I could expect a royalty. It was to allow me time and freedom to paint without worrying about having to pay the bills."

The potted plants in the studio are yellow from lack of water. Ballagh doesn't seem to notice. He has already started another painting. It's a pop art version of Theodore Géricault's monumental *Raft of the Medusa* in the stylised manner of his 1970 series *The Rape of the Sabines, Liberty at the Barricades* and *The Third of May*. It's taking him days to fill in the black lines delineating the shipwrecked figures, which he has drawn on a wide canvas stretched out along a wall. "It's dreadfully tedious. You have to paint one side of the black line and then the other side, and fill it in, maintaining a consistency of width throughout. I don't know how many miles of black line you end up painting on something like this."

The Watson portrait is lying against the wall within its large glass frame. It is too heavy to lift onto the easel so that it can be seen upright in it's proper diamond format. "I don't want to take a chance with my bad back. All those early years bending down to paint have taken their toll."

The portrait will be unveiled in Watson's presence at a dinner in his honour at the Department of Genetics in Trinity in September. Watson is delighted with the likeness. Watson's wife Elizabeth loves it too. She got the smile she wanted. There is a wonderful life-like immediacy to it that shows no sign of the elaborate planning that went into its capture.

With every portrait Ballagh draws the face in particularly fine detail. "Every hillock and bump is there, and when I start painting I put in probably more detail than is necessary and then gently glaze over it. At one stage Watson looked far too wrinkly, but I feel it's better to put everything in and then take things out than go at it the other way round."

Any adjustments he might make in the course of the portrait are likely to happen more in the painting stage than in the drawing stage. "I suppose it's similar to the way an architect's blueprint might change a little bit in the course of putting up the building. But it's only a little bit. The actual structure is fixed. When I get to the stage of actually moving to canvas it would be very rare for me to change anything radically, such as moving the position of an arm up or down. But there are millions of little things that might change in the course of painting, like a bit more shading here or a bit less there."

The original drawings for all his paintings are quite small. He later has them blown-up to scale. "The technology that exists now wasn't around when I was starting out. I used have to enlarge my pictures by the traditional squares method. You square up a drawing and then draw bigger squares on your canvas in order to enlarge it. But now I just take them to Hacketts print shop in Lower Baggot Street and get them enlarged by photo-copying. What you see on the wall is a blown-up version of a small drawing of *Raft of the Medusa*."

Getting the scale right is not easy. Usually he needs to have the blow-ups done two or three times before they feel right. "The first blow-up of *Medusa* was only a foot or so bigger than now, but it looked completely overblown. The irony is that Géricault's painting is about three times the size of this, about 24 feet wide whereas mine is less than 8 feet. In terms of contemporary art there are very few spaces that can accommodate large paintings any more."

The dealer Damien Mathews prompted the idea of looking back to earlier work. A few clients were interested in the history paintings Ballagh did in the 1970s. They wanted another *Third of May* or a *Liberty at the Barricades*. "I'd no interest in doing the same thing again, but I began thinking it might be interesting to work on some other painting."

He had chosen *The Third of May, The Rape of the Sabines* and *Liberty at the Barricades* as references because they commented on events in their own time similar to events unfolding in the North. Géricault's *Raft of the Medusa*, which caused outrage when it was displayed at the French Salon in 1819, is the true story of a shipwrecked French frigate *La Méduse* which before it sank was abandoned by its captain and officers. They took the only lifeboats, leaving behind 150 passengers and crew who managed to put together a makeshift raft. Only 15 were still alive by the time they were rescued. The rest had either starved or drowned, the survivors eating the dead to stay alive.

Géricault was a prime mover of 19th century Romanticism in France, as another Ballagh favourite Casper David Friedrich was in Germany. Although Ballagh never had sympathy with the romantic conceit of the artist as a misunderstood outsider starving for his art in a garret – even if this was at times his own lot – his work is clearly influenced by a romantic insistence that what is beautiful comes from composition, paint, colour and lighting. Ballagh's readiness to engage with society echoes the romantic ambition to tear down barriers between art and life and embrace new techniques of reproduction, such as photography, as a means of enabling art to speak to and be accessible to all, not just to connoisseurs.

*Raft of the Medusa*, with its powerful blend of emotion and realism, was intended as an indictment of French political corruption and failure of leadership. "It seems an appropriate metaphor not only for Géricault's own time but also in the context of so many things that are happening in Ireland today, particularly the corruption emerging from the tribunals. There's a really depressing failure of leadership in contemporary Ireland."

With the decisive rejection of the Lisbon Treaty on European reform in the referendum on 6 June – the 'no' vote had a majority of 109,164, despite the electorate being urged by all the main parties and the media to say 'yes' – there's a feeling that this result will be ignored. Brian Cowen, who became Taoiseach in May after a disgraced Bertie Ahern was forced to resign over revelations of dubious financial matters, keeps stressing that Ireland "does not wish to halt progress in Europe". There's much talk of Ireland being in "uncharted waters". With international capitalism showing signs of collapse through the excesses of its own unregulated neo-liberal free-market chutzpah, the unfortunates abandoned on Géricault's raft may soon all too aptly represent the poor and the marginalised left behind by the Celtic Tiger.

Ironically the French European Minister Jean-Pierre Jouyet blames "American neo-cons" for the defeat of the referendum. No doubt he is referring to the participation of the ad-hoc Libertas party, led by businessman Declan Ganley whose company is involved in US military contracts in Iraq, but Ballagh and others on the left campaigned for a 'no' vote because they believed Europe

*Detail from*
*Raft of the Medusa* (2009)

*'The Joyous Wake and Burial of
Patrick Ireland and the Rebirth
of Brian O'Doherty'.
Irish Museum of Modern Art, May 2008.*

was being taken over by neo-liberal laissez-faire economics and advocates of military involvement with NATO.

Everything seems to be going full circle. The arguments that brought Ireland into the Common Market in 1971 are being used to alienate it from the EU. The belief in change that characterised the 1960s – and was personified by Fidel Castro and the Cuban revolution – has turned to scepticism. The North has evolved through bitter struggle from unionist domination to democratic power-sharing government. With *Raft of the Medusa*, Ballagh is now back where he started as a painter.

"I'm revisiting a technique I used long ago but this time around, because of the various skills and techniques I've picked up, the straightforward flat colours with black lines are somewhat modified. I'm introducing a bit of toning and a little bit of textural work. There were no faces in my early paintings in this style but now there are. I don't want them to be overtly naturalistic because the whole approach is quite stylised, but at the same time I want to be truthful to the original painting. Hopefully it will still have that pop-ish minimalist quality to it."

This sense of life going around before ending up back at the beginning, only differently, found wry expression on Bloomsday 16 June when Ballagh took part in public readings from James Joyce – the master of circuitous thinking – at Meeting House Square in Temple Bar. He'd hoped to intone *Introibo ad altari Dei* (I will go unto the altar of God), the famous opening passage of *Ulysses*, but was told that this was the prerogative of the Minister for Arts, Martin Cullen. So he opted instead for an account of Leopold Bloom at home in Eccles Street, preparing his breakfast. "I was more nervous campaigning against the Lisbon Treaty, and that went well," he said, before stepping out onto the open-air stage.

Afterward he joined other participants, among them John Boorman, the Israeli writer David Grossman and Miriam Ahern, ex-wife of Bertie Ahern and mother of the romantic novelist Cecilia Ahern, for Gorgonzola cheese and Burgundy wine at Davy Byrne's public house on Duke Street, as was the practice of Bloom on his perambulations.

On a more political level Ballagh experienced déjà vu a few weeks earlier acting as a pallbearer at the funeral of the artist Patrick Ireland in the gardens of the Irish Museum of Modern Art in Kilmainham, and then as witness to his re-incarnation in the person of Brian O'Doherty. After graveside orations and a keening recital by Alanna O'Kelly, and as the coffin of Ireland was being lowered into the freshly dug ground, O'Doherty stepped forward with outstretched arms. "Thank you for peace," he proclaimed. "We are burying hate in a ceremony of reconciliation celebrating peace in Northern Ireland."

O'Doherty took Patrick Ireland for his name as a painter at the 1972 Exhibition of Irish Living Art at the Project Arts Centre. It was a gesture of protest over the gunning down of 13 civilians by British troops in Derry on Bloody Sunday. Ballagh's contribution to the same show was chalk outlines of dead marchers in pools of blood on the gallery floor. O'Doherty, who was then editor of *Art in America* and a leading New York critic, vowed that he would continue to sign his art works 'Patrick Ireland' until the British military presence was gone from Northern Ireland and human rights were restored. "That time has now come," he said at Kilmainham. "I want my name back." The coffin of Patrick Ireland contained a manikin with a life mask of O'Doherty made back in 1972 which was now Patrick Ireland's death mask. The headstone on the grave reads, Here Lies Patrick Ireland.

Ballagh had been involved with sculptor Brian King in the original 1972 performance. They carried O'Doherty on stage on a stretcher, then painted his prostrate white figure green and orange. "So I was happy to assist in the burial. It's nice to live long enough to turn full circle."

> *"Art is above politics but not above humanity."*

The first performance of Stravinsky's *Le Renard* by the Ballets Russes in Paris in 1920 gave a socialite couple Mr and Mrs Schilf an excuse to host a supper bringing together the four men of genius they most admired – Pablo Picasso, designer of the sets, the dancer Vaslav Nijinsky and the writers Marcel Proust and James Joyce. Sadly the evening was a fiasco, right from the moment they introduced Proust to Joyce. "This is James Joyce, the Irish writer." "I regret I do not know Monsieur Joyce's work." "Well, I don't know yours either."

Later Joyce preferred to forget the incident. "Joyce never mentioned that unlikely party to me," Samuel Beckett informed Micheal Farrell. Undeterred, Farrell went ahead and immortalised it in a spectacular wall-long 5½ foot x 13 foot painting *La Fête* which he exhibited at the Taylor Galleries in Dublin in 1984. "It really doesn't matter whether the party took place or not," Farrell said before his tragic death in 2000. "It's just an excuse for a pictorial image."

Long before post-modernism became fashionable Farrell rejected purely formal art for art's sake to explore a way of painting that referred to a reality beyond itself. Like Robert Ballagh he dared to reconnect with earlier traditions of Western art, employing literary allusions and even puns to establish a dialogue with the viewer. Picasso lurks in *La Fête* near a coat-stand from Farrell's series of *Café Triste* prints. An oddly sinister bottle is at Proust's elbow. Behind him an image of Howth Head, inspiration for Molly Bloom's soliloquy. There's a suggestion of Farrell's 1960s hard-edge abstractions in the patterns of Nijinsky's costumes. "And we know for certain he couldn't have been there. By then he was in the madhouse."

Farrell became a painter almost by accident, having gone to St Martin's College of Art in London at 16 to study commercial art. He won a scholarship to New York where he plugged into the vogue for monumental hard-edge acrylics inspired by the abstract motifs in the medieval illuminated manuscript *The Book of Kells*. He took pride in the significance of having himself been born in Kells, claiming that "no pictures of any value concerned with real problems of picture-making have been made in Ireland since *The Book of Kells*, a masterpiece devoid of all mist, wind and whimsy – perfect in harmony and uncompromisingly direct".

Ballagh might never have become a painter if Farrell hadn't taken him on as an apprentice on murals he was doing for the National Bank building on Dame Street. He didn't just teach techniques he had picked up in New York: he nurtured in Ballagh an attitude that encouraged him to take on the art world and strike out on his own. After the brutal suppression of the civil rights protest in the North, Farrell felt unable to continue with an abstract art form that denied him the scope to identify with the cause of justice and to express his repugnance at what was happening – and Ballagh took a similar stance. "Art is above politics but not above humanity," Farrell said. He doubted if art could make effective general statements about the world. "You can't deal with everybody's business. Political statements have to be in a limited sense. Like Simone di Martini in Sienna, who was political and religious, but only about the town of Sienna. Generalised political art becomes impersonal and loses its power."

We last met at what turned out to be his last major Irish exhibition at the Taylor Galleries in 1994, although he continued to keep in touch with lively letters from his home in Cardet in Provence, which he shared with his second wife Meg Early.

The power and scale of his exhibition was astonishing coming after a five-year period during which he was in and out of hospital in France, undergoing 11 operations for cancer of the throat. "Chemotherapy doesn't work," he said. "The knife is the only way. Of all the guys I've been to the hospital with, I'm the only survivor. I'm a lucky lad."

This defiant exuberance was evident in the paintings and sculptures. On legal advice the gallery felt unable to show a piece depicting a man wearing only a bishop's mitre being pleasured by a naked woman, together with several accompanying lithographs and drawings on the same theme: the reference was to a recent Episcopal scandal. Far from being gratuitous, the outrageously explicit image came out of Farrell's long-held belief that art ought to be a commentary on society rather than just its toy. Ever since his marvellous *Madonna Irlanda* series in the early 1970s, humorously inspired by Boucher's portraits of Louis XIV's Irish mistress Miss O'Murphy, he resorted to art – much as Ballagh did – to conduct a playful visual dialogue in public with himself about the whole nature of his art and its relationship with Ireland and the world he lived in.

Because he had managed to evade death for so long, when it finally caught up with him everyone was taken by surprise. Ballagh's sadness and sense of loss filtered into a personal painting he was working on at the time, a memory picture evoking his father before he knew him. He called it *The Orchard of Nostalgia*. Although his father as a young man is the subject, he is a relatively small figure in white flannels holding a tennis racket, placed off-centre in the background of the lozenge-shaped painting. The picture is dominated by the lower part of Ballagh's body, his legs in blue jeans stretched out in a hammock as he lies back reading a copy of Che Guevara's *Socialismo y el Hombre Nuevo en Cuba*. The optical effect is to put the viewer in his vantage point, looking out over the top of the book on a freshly mown lawn where a handmade balsa wood model airplane from his childhood lies, while through the apple trees there is a glimpse of his cottage.

*The Orchard of Nostalgia* somewhat belatedly picks up on *Highfield*, which Ballagh painted in 1984, the second in what has become a series of paintings about his Cork home running parallel to his Dublin *No 3* series. The long gap is explained by the necessity to support a young family through school and college, not to mention the sometimes conflicting demands of his political activism. He had far less time than he would have liked to paint purely personal paintings for which there might be no immediate buyer. *Upstairs Number 4, The Studio, The Bogman* and *Michael O'Riordan* were still unsold in his studio.

A steady flow of royalties from *Riverdance* now finally gave him the independence he needed. "To paint in the way I paint, where it can take anything up to six months to paint a picture, doesn't make financial sense whatever, particularly if there is no buyer lined up. I can now understand why many of my writer friends are so appreciative of the concept of royalties."

If *Highfield* was a work of realism, *The Orchard of Nostalgia* was more in the realm of magic realism. "The elements that make it up could not exist in the same time together. My father is 30, so it's before I was born. I think his great achievements were in

*Study for Portrait of Micheal Farrell* (2003)
*Pencil on paper.*
*Private Collection.*

sport. He played cricket and tennis for Ireland and rugby for Leinster. He also played in the Davis Cup and at Wimbledon. I felt to remember him in his prime when he was a sportsman was appropriate. The Che book resonates the 1960s, for many of us a formative period, a period of hope which young people now don't have the luxury of having. It seemed that everything was going to change for the better."

The impact of *The Orchard of Nostalgia* as a window to the soul is enhanced by the massive dark black frame. Ballagh likes to include frames in reproductions of many of his paintings. "Most artists reproduce paintings without frames. I feel that particularly if you have a complicated frame like this you just must include it. In a lot of cases the framing can be an important part of the painting."

Ballagh often wondered where his republicanism and socialism came from. "I always thought it was just me." But then he discovered after his maternal grandmother's death that she had been a member of Cumann na mBan and a personal friend of Constance Markiewicz. "My mother told me she remembered her mother pushing the pram with guns hidden under the blankets. That was kind of hard to reconcile with my memories of a nice old lady with a passion for playing cards and going horse racing."

Painting *The Orchard of Nostalgia* brought back a memory of long walks with his father and being surprised by his radicalism. "I never realised at the time that it was an influence, but now it strikes me that his middle-class Protestant background brought different values, in particular the concept of individual conscience."

Farrell was so much in his mind when he was painting his father he realised he needed to paint him too. "Micheal was best man at our wedding. I felt he deserved something. When I started thinking about it, the first thing that struck me was that he had to be in a pub. Anyone who knew Micheal knew that was the case."

When his first marriage to Pat broke up after 22 years, Farrell wanted to get as far away from Paris as he could, so he took a one-way ticket to Australia. But all the time he was there he kept painting the Paris cafés or bars he'd left behind. "Perhaps the distance brought it out," he said. "I found I had to take two steps back before I could go one forwards." Not that any of the cafés exist the way he depicts them. Paris for him was an imaginary city of personal experiences superimposed on the real. The interior of *Au Grand Pavilion,* decorations for which were painted by butchers who used to work in the nearby abattoir, becomes a jokey inventory of many of Farrell's previous preoccupations. "The butchers sometimes painted better than many so-called painters."

Through a pun on the word 'butcher' Farrell also returned to the painter Boucher whose work he parodied in his *Miss O'Murphy* paintings dealing with butchery in Ireland. Meanwhile, at the *Café Etrange* a dog lurked near a coat-stand from the earlier *Café Tristes* paintings. The same dog, smoking a Gauloise, reappeared at the *Un Chien Qui Fume* café. "If artists in the past could put wings on horses, I didn't see why I shouldn't give a cigarette to a dog."

Looking for ways to match this playfulness, Ballagh decided to seat Farrell against a partition in Ryan's of Parkgate Street, a lovely old Victorian pub where they often met for a drink. "The other thing I decided was that there was never silence around Michael, he was always loquacious, argumentative, good fun to be with. So I wanted a very busy background. It struck me that his *Pressé* series with squirts flying out – inspired by the implement used in Paris bistros for producing fruit juice – might work. It seemed appropriate to choose one from the first political *Pressé* he did about the Dublin Monaghan bombings, where he took newspaper headlines and silk-screened them on to the squidges."

Ballagh wanted the picture to connect almost in a physical sense with the viewer, somewhat in the manner of the Noël Browne portrait. He came up with the idea of a three-dimensional bar with a three-dimensional pint. He asked a man who had done wood-working for him to provide a wooden bar counter and pint glass. "When I went back to him I expected to pick up bog-standard wood. He'd actually turned them from ash.

"My intention had been to paint them, but it would be shameful to paint over such beautiful wood. So I used an ebony wood stain on the wooden pint glass, so the wood grain still percolates through giving the impression of a pint settling – the bubbly sort of thing you see in the stout. I'd being planning trompé l'oeil marble work on the counter top but it was so beautiful I just gave it a green wood stain so that the natural wood shows through."

The colours on the three-dimensional palette gripped in Farrell's thumb are the blue, white and red of France, but the colours on his brushes are green white and orange. "Even though he lived for years in France his subject matter was always from home."

Ballagh drew the legs much in Farrell's gestural style. "He used tease me incessantly about being too fussy, too detailed. He'd tell me to loosen up, so I decided to loosen up in the way I depicted his legs."

The portrait, which was exhibited at the Crawford Gallery in 2003 and bought by Dermot Desmond, is a stunning riposte by Ballagh to critics who had written both Farrell and him off. It is at once brash and affectionate, capturing the nature of the man and his art with a witty flair Farrell would have relished. The exhibition was curated by Peter Murray and included important little-seen Ballagh works from the previous twenty years, in particular *The History Lesson, Upstairs No 4 The Studio, Gerry Adams* and *The Orchard of Nostalgia*. It was, astonishingly, his first-ever exhibition in an Irish public gallery. Like it or not, he had come in from the cold.

"Farrell with the passing of years will be seen as one of the most significant Irish artists of the second half of the twentieth century," noted Murray. Brian O'Doherty's catalogue essay argued that "Ballagh's portrait unites two artists of common sympathies in an artwork that is an aggressive act of memory in a culture that suppresses memory – at times, grotesquely – as much as it exercises it…You can't speak of – or with – Robert Ballagh without engaging his opinions, beliefs, judgements. No one is more alert to the contemporary moment, and no artist has grounded his response to it so firmly in his reading of recent history."

Not everyone was – nor is – convinced. An article by Robert O'Byrne in *The Irish Arts Review* in Spring 2008 claimed – with particular reference to Ballagh and Farrell – that political art might have been all right in the 1970s, but "as our politics have become tamer, they have been judged steadily less worthy of cultural comment or assessment". He maintained that because Farrell didn't fetch big prices at auctions "his career has never lived up to its expected promise".

To Ballagh this was a fatuous verdict. "Of course Micheal didn't make it easy. He could be aggressive and rude. A nude self-portrait of him sitting at a table with his willy hanging out is not going to appeal to people at auctions as something to put over their fireplace. But there's more to art than market economics. I still think he will be seen as one of the more important artists of 20th-century Ireland."

◆

The novelist John McGahern once said he would consider it an insult to be called an Irish writer. Although art should never be limited by a label, Ballagh was happy to be called an "urban artist" early in his career. "I never had any access to the culture that many people seem to think is the genuine Irish culture, the rural Gaelic tradition," he claimed. Since landscape painting was an expression of this tradition, he rejected it. "I can't paint Connemara fishermen. My experience of Ireland is an urban one and I paint that. It would be dishonest for me to paint anything else."

But Ireland is too small an island for such rigid aesthetic polarisation. Although he was born in Dublin, he spent summers on his great-aunt's farm at Patrickswell in Limerick. Back in the 1940s all of Ireland was in a sense rural, its economy largely dependent on agriculture As the Irish proverb that frames *The Bogman* suggests, "You can take the man from the bog, but you can't take the bog from the man."

From the late 1970s landscape began to insinuate itself into Ballagh's visual vocabulary. It had a "walk-on" part in the Liffey Valley background of the Downes family portrait in 1981. His self-portrait *Highfield* reflects its growing relevance. He depicts himself looking out from his studio in Cork at the landscape while the canvas on an easel beside him is blank. But if this implied a rejection of the traditional Irish landscape, the torn Picasso poster on the floor suggested that he didn't necessarily see the fashions of international art trends as an alternative.

He took time to absorb the implications of this opening out to nature, but by the 1990s a visionary sense of landscape was clearly evident in his work. Neil Blaney and Gerry Adams are carefully posed within a wide panoramic format in order to take in the full scale of landscape beyond them. "As an artist who didn't engage with landscape, I began to think maybe it was time to give it a go."

He decided to take a year off from more or less everything else to concentrate on what he thought could be a series of paintings that would express his own response to landscape. "The funny thing is that I soon found I was starting to make pictures that didn't end up at all the way I thought they might end up."

Several things occurred to him. "When you experience a walk on the Featherbeds in the Dublin mountains or some beach there is always more to it than just the panoramic view in front of you. There are the stones under your feet on the beach or the leaves in the forest. So that convinced me that not only should I make a panoramic view but I should incorporate a physical sense of that texture of nature. Of course I'd dipped into that with the pebbles in the Noël Browne portrait. It wasn't really new. In your own work there's nothing new, art history teaches us that in art there's nothing completely new."

He devised a horizontal polytych format the lower panel of which – the predella – would contain real materials, whether stones, sand or leaves. Each of the landscapes was

painted using the *alla prima* method he had applied to the *Riverdance* back-projection images in which the final effect is achieved in a single direct wet-into-wet application of paint to the ground. "I had developed fluidity with it, using the badger brush Farrell had introduced me to – a softening brush that if you become skilled in its use you can blend colours or tone one into another, and brush out all the brush marks. That's what gives my paintings effects people often think are achieved by air brush work."

The resulting landscapes are generic rather than specific, apart from a few references to the Poolnabrone dolmen or the fort at Aileach in Donegal. They lack the aura of time and place that landscape paintings traditionally evoke. As with the *Riverdance* images their purpose is more elemental. "My intention was to engage with something more mythical and symbolic than simply the picturesque."

Remembering how in the early 19th century British cartographers had rendered Irish place names into English, robbing them of their local identity – a historical incident which Brian Friel highlighted in his play *Translations* – he decided as "a minor act

of reclamation" to give his landscapes texts that would be an organic part of the painting. "I thought that the texts should be in Irish because the landscape of Ireland predated the English language, but also that it should be anonymous rather that quotes from great poets. I used old proverbs which everyone knows but nobody knows who wrote them. They were just the words of ordinary people."

He gave the ten paintings simple Irish titles – *Oileán* (island), *Crann* (tree), *Cloch* (stone), *Cuan* (harbour), *Muir* (ocean), *Dún* (fort), *Sliabh* (mountain), *Ceo* (fog), *Oíche* (night) and *Puróga* (pebbles) – and exhibited them late in 2001 at The Ireland Institute on 27 Pearse Street, the house where Patrick Pearse once lived.

Ballagh had not only made the paintings: he helped create the space where they were shown. Early in the 1990s, when historical revisionism was rife and free discussion stifled by Section 31 censorship, a group of people got together through concern that there didn't seem to be a space – whether physical or intellectual – for discussion and debate about issues in Ireland they considered to be important. It included Declan and Damien Kiberd, the businessman Hugo Flynn and maverick writer Desmond Fennell.

Declan Kiberd was then a lecturer in Anglo-Irish literature at UCD and later to become Professor in 1997. A friend of the Palestine-born intellectual Edward Said, he gave Irish literary criticism an international dimension with *Inventing Ireland*, a major critical assessment of Anglo-Irish literature and culture in which he argued that the English in effect "invented" their own view of Ireland, "pressing it into service as a foil to set off English virtues, as a laboratory in which to conduct experiments, and as a fantasy land in which to meet fairies and monsters".

His younger brother Damien was one of the bright talents – others included Fintan O'Toole, Veronica Guerin, Gene Kerrigan, Emily O'Reilly and Orla Guerin – who were given a chance to shine by Vincent Browne at the *Sunday Tribune*, a new independent newspaper owned and run by journalists. After two years as business editor he left to set up the *Sunday Business Post* in 1989. He recruited Frank Connolly, an investigative journalist whose story about corrupt payments to former foreign minister Ray Burke ultimately led to the Flood Tribunal and whose story on Garda impropriety in Donegal resulted in the Morris Tribunal. Editorially the paper supported the Sinn Féin/Republican peace initiative, causing it to be dubbed 'The Continuity Business Post'.

Despite its nationalist ethos it established a niche as a business paper before being taken over in 1997 by the English regional press group Trinity International Holdings in 1997. Kiberd became a millionaire overnight, but continued as editor until 2001 when he started his own talk programme on Denis O'Brien's Dublin radio station Newstalk. He became station manager in 2005.

The cricket-loving republican Kiberds had been taught "everything but singing" by John McGahern at Belgrove National School in Clontarf, where their parents took part in protests when the Archbishop of Dublin John Charles McQuaid caused McGahern to be removed from the staff for marrying a divorced foreigner.

Ballagh shared with them a belief in the need to develop study and discussion of the civic republican tradition fostered by Pearse and to promote an application of republican ideas to the everyday issues in Irish society. "The revisionists, who dismissed the 1916 Rising as misguided, conveniently forgot that Patrick Pearse was an extraordinary complex man," says Ballagh. "In *The Murder Machine* he talks about education in Ireland for children in the end of the 19th century going into the 20th century, but it's still applicable today. He criticises learning by rote, unimaginative courses, and a failure to foster creativity in children – all of which is relevant today."

The group would meet in the boardroom of the *Sunday Business Post* after the paper was put to bed. "Someone suggested we should look at St Catherine's in Thomas Street as a possible venue. It was an historic building. Robert Emmet had been executed in the street outside. We got permission from Dublin Corporation to look it over. It was in scandalous condition. Kids had robbed the lead off the roof. Dry rot was hanging down in clusters like moss in the Everglades."

Geraldine Walsh, who was involved in heritage architecture with the Dublin Civic Trust, then suggested 27 Pearse Street, a Georgian three-storey over basement red-brick house where Patrick Pearse was born in 1879. He lived there for the first five years of his life – it was then Brunswick Street – before the family moved to Sandymount. He and his brother William, who studied sculpture at the Metropolitan School of Art and later in Paris, ran the family monumental sculpture business at number 27 until 1913, when it became a Workingmen's Temperance Club and later a motor car company, a bicycle shop and an upholstery company. Although the façade was still intact, the interior was in desperate condition. Walls had been knocked down. The roof was leaking.

"The challenge was to acquire the building. The only one of us around the table who had access to serious money was Hugo Flynn. His civil engineering company agreed to purchase the building in 1996 and lease it back to the Institute. We gradually put together funding for restoration, receiving grants and subsidies from the Irish Government and the EU. We even got an architectural heritage grant for restoring the timber windows."

When Bertie Ahern performed the official opening in July 2000, Damien Kiberd referred to his pleasure at hearing a "positive reference" to Pearse on RTÉ radio the previous morning, "the first time Pearse has been spoken of positively by the national broadcaster since 1966." Ahern responded that he had a "fine portrait" of Pearse above his desk. "So whatever about not talking about him, they can't dodge filming him when they come to film me." He hoped his presence at the opening would underline the fact that "republicanism is not something out there on the political fringes but that it is a mainstream political force in this State, and arguably gives it its cohesion".

*Patrick Pearse (2009)*
*Oil on canvas. Diameter 40cm.*
*Ballagh created artwork featuring the seven signatories*
*of the 1916 proclaimation for the creation*
*of silverware by Boru Jewellery.*

The Institute rents out the top floor to the HSE Drugs Treatment Section to help cover running and maintenance costs, and the first floor for meetings. Trinity Capitol Hotel, which is next door and is owned by Liam O'Dwyer, proprietor of several pubs and restaurants, sought permission to expand across number 27's derelict back yard. After protracted negotiations, it was agreed that the development could go ahead in return for a hall or theatre being built on the ground floor for the Institute's use. The 75-seat theatre, which is also equipped as a cinema, opened in 2008. The idea is that it will serve as a venue not only for arts events but for meetings and discussions.

Ballagh feels the Institute is now in a position to get back to its core idea. "The goal-posts have shifted. The peace process has resulted in power-sharing in the North and an end to violence. But it's not an end to the difficulties that face Ireland. Areas I'd be particularly interested in addressing are the effects of globalisation and neo-liberal capitalism. You can't pick up the papers where a factory hasn't closed down and moved to Poland or somewhere. These matters should be discussed and debated."

Ballagh's landscapes exhibition led to a commission to paint the Saltee islands for an English friend Mick O'Gorman, the sound designer of *Riverdance*, who lives in Wexford. "I drove down with Betty and decided on the view where you look out from Kilmore Quay. Instead of a proverb written in Irish, I put it in Yola, a dialect that flourished in Wexford well into the 19th century. It's a mixture of old English, French and Irish."

He exhibited a selection of his landscapes at the Irish Arts Centre in New York the following year, where they were introduced by the film actress Fionnuala Flanagan. He first met her when he was a speaker at a meeting of the Irish American Unity Conference in California. Another speaker was London's former mayor, Ken Livingstone. "We spent the flight to LA sitting beside each other. He never stopped talking."

Ballagh stayed in Beverly Hills with Flanagan and her husband Garret O'Connor, a brother of Ulick. "They've a lovely house they bought years ago for very little, because it was on the outskirts. But now Hollywood stars are their neighbours. It's probably worth millions." O'Connor is a psychiatrist who has done pioneering work on how alcoholism and depression affect the Irish. "He'd argue like Noël Browne that we are victims of two empires, the British and Roman."

◆

*Yola* (2001)
*Oil on canvas, stones and sand blasted glass. 40 x 60cm.*
*Private Collection.*

Larry Lenane doesn't regard himself as racist: it's just he wouldn't want a black for a son-in law. "But Phil Lynott was black, love," his wife says, trying to calm him when their daughter brings home a 'black fella'. "And," she adds, "you like Paul McGrath."

Roddy Doyle's play *Guess Who's Coming For the Dinner*, performed by Calypso Theatre Company at Andrew's Lane Theatre during the 2001 Dublin Theatre Festival – and which began life as a short story published by *Metro Ireland*, a newspaper started by two Nigerians and aimed at immigrants – was a cheeky Irish variation on Stanley Kramer's 1967 Oscar hit. By confronting a couple of regular Dub parents with the same dilemma faced by the upper-class supposedly liberal parents originally played by Spencer Tracy and Katharine Hepburn, Doyle created a topical commentary on a booming Ireland where an average growth rate of 6.8 percent and net immigration of 222,500 over a ten-year period was leading to the emergence of a vibrant multicultural society.

Much had changed since Jimmy Rabbitte famously quipped that "the Irish are the niggers of Europe" in Doyle's 1987 breakthrough novel *The Commitments*. "If I was writing that book today I wouldn't use that term," said Doyle. "It wouldn't occur to me because Ireland has become one of the wealthiest countries in Europe and the line would make no sense."

The fun of the play is watching Larry stumble from one faux pas to another. Because of the cramped space in the backstreet Andrew's Lane Theatre, Ballagh decided to create a set on several levels, each one of which was a different room in Larry's Ballymun house. It effectively captured the hilarious simultaneity of Dublin family life. "The play is obviously a light work but very entertaining. It gets the point across and was successful at a time when there had been outbreaks of racism."

The previous year newspapers reported on a Romanian restaurant being trashed by hooligans, and something similar happening to a Nigerian shop. One incident was near where Ballagh lived. He wrote to Moya Doherty saying he didn't know what to do, but he felt strongly they should take some action to deal with the threat. "*Riverdance* above all is about embracing different cultures – we've black dancers, white dancers, Spanish dancers, Russian dancers, American dancers." "Leave it with me," she told him.

Through her brother-in-law Conall O'Caoimh, who worked with the non-governmental agency Comhlámh, she arranged a meeting with Colm ÓCúanacháin, later to work for Amnesty and Africa Aid. They came up with the idea of *Le Chéile*, an organisation to bring together artists in Ireland against racism. With *Riverdance* about to open at The Point, she offered a benefit performance to raise funds and also a free afternoon performance for foreign nationals in Ireland.

"The free show was like the United Nations. Africans came with their children in national costumes. Everyone in *Riverdance* waived their royalties from the evening performance, which combined with the box-office amounted to about £65,000. Iwa Sebit, an African who worked with Comhlámh, came on stage after the show and I handed the cheque over to him."

The Calypso Theatre Company, which was established to produce plays dealing with social issues, held workshops and lectures with each production as well as issuing educational packs. Ballagh subsequently designed a set for a production of *Stolen*

*Robert Ballagh presenting a cheque to Iwa Sebit after a benefit performance of 'Riverdance' in the Point Theatre, Dublin.*

*Child*, a play about an adopted child trying to trace and meet her biological mother. "It related to a terrible fire in an orphanage in Roscommon when 35 children died because the doors had been locked. Brian O'Nolan (Myles Na Gopaleen) was the civil servant sent from Dublin to investigate. He didn't do much in terms of challenging the authorities."

◆

"Will you be coming in your car, Mr Ballagh?" "Yes." "Could you give us your registration number so that you can park within City Hall? There's room for just a few cars inside."

Ballagh was driving to Belfast to paint Alex Maskey, the city's first ever republican lord mayor. According to long-standing tradition, a portrait of each new mayor was commissioned for the City Council's collection. The election of veteran Sinn Féin councillor Maskey in 2002 with the support of Alliance Party councillors was dramatic public confirmation of the transforming effect of the power-sharing process initiated by the signing of the Belfast Agreement on Good Friday in 1998, just four years earlier.

"I presume the people I was talking to were part of the regime that up until recently had a monopoly of power at City Hall, but they were extraordinarily polite and nice to me. If I'd been driving North with a Dublin registration years ago I'd have had more chance of being attacked than allowed VIP parking in City Hall!"

Fifty-year-old Maskey was a former barman and boxer – he lost only 4 out of 75 fights – who had been interned twice in the 1970s. A key ally in Gerry Adams's strategy of engaging in the political process, he became the first member of Sinn Féin to win a seat on the City Council in 1983, declaring, "The City Hall has for too long been a bastion of loyalism". He narrowly escaped assassination in 1987 when loyalist paramilitaries attempted to gun him down in a restaurant.

"Back then whenever Sinn Féin councillors tried to speak in the chamber, Ian Paisley's DUP councillors would try to drown them out with football rattles and whistles. Sinn Féin being Sinn Féin would always say the *cúpla focal* in Irish, at which the loyalists would all shout, 'Leprechaun language!' Maskey had to put up with all that."

The new Sinn Féin lord mayor's first duty was to open the annual Presbyterian General Assembly. He then angered some nationalists by laying a wreath in memory of the many Irish soldiers who died in the First World War. "On taking office he had invoked a policy of parity of esteem for both traditions. So in the lord mayor's parlour the Union Jack and the Tricolour were both flying."

Ballagh took lots of casual photographs of Maskey in City Hall. Many of the portraits of earlier mayors hanging on the walls showed them in full regalia. He was determined his was going to be different. "I didn't want all that formality. Luckily Alex was of the same view. He saw his year in office as being mayor for all the people, so I took equality as my motif. But how do you paint

that? As I was going out I saw a small poster, Belfast: City of Equals. 'What's that?' 'Oh, it's a poster I brought out for my year in office.' So that became the background."

Some weeks later, while Ballagh was working on the portrait, Maskey called. "How's it going?" "Fine." "I've a bit of a favour. You know the people in the background of the poster? My wife Liz has been very supportive. Do you think you could put her in?" "Sure." So he painted in Mrs Maskey. A week later there was another call. "Any chance you could put my grand-daughter in?" Again Ballagh was happy to oblige.

Maskey stands to one side of the portrait wearing a tie but no jacket, and one hand in his pocket. Another image of him in a formal black suit, with his mayoral chain, is partly visible in the poster behind him – a variation on Ballagh's fascination with images within images. The word Equality is written across the poster in English, Irish, Ulster Scots, Arabic and Chinese. The faces are multicultural. "I don't know how to tell Protestant and Catholic apart, but they're both there too."

The dominant colour is blue, as in the Micheal Farrell, Gerry Adams and Neil Blaney portraits and indeed his self-portrait in *The Bogman*, not to mention *Winter in Ronda* and the branding of *Riverdance*. In his clothing Ballagh invariably opts for blue shirts and blue jeans. His Blackrock Colleges colours were blue and white. No doubt there's a psychological explanation for its recurrence. Maybe it's in his DNA. According to research published in 2008 by Hans Eiberg in Copenhagen, Charles Darwin may have got his blue eyes because of a single misplaced letter in his DNA – a mutation from A to G – thousands of years before he was born. Eiberg suggests blue-eyed people may be more prevalent in certain geographic regions simply because they happened to be more attractive to the opposite sex. To Ballagh it's simply an instinctive choice. He just likes blue.

He worked that August with local Falls Road children on an anti-sectarian mural during the West Belfast Festival or Féile na Phobail. There was a lot of debate that despite the Belfast Agreement there were even more walls dividing the two communities. Mairtín ÓMuilleóir, a former Sinn Féin councillor and CEO of the *Belfast Media Group*, wanted an image for his boardroom that would symbolise a wall being broken down. Ballagh painted a brick wall split down the middle so that another community could be glimpsed on the other side. Lilies sprout out of its crevices. Graffiti on the wall quotes a news headline NUN FIRED BY CANON, a reference to a cleric's objection to Mother Teresa coming to Belfast. Scrawled across the bottom is the signature 'Mayor Maskey'. Ballagh titled the painting *City Without Walls*.

Ballagh's proficiency in Irish improved with his many visits to West Belfast, where a disused Presbyterian Church had been converted into an Irish-speaking arts centre, An Cultúrlan. He could carry out a conversation in Irish and even took part in Irish language radio programmes. Irish references increasingly featured in his paintings. His exhibition of landscapes had Irish captions and a bilingual title, *Tír is Teanga/Land and Landscape*.

He was invited to illustrate a poem by Séan ÓTuama for *An Leabhar Mór*, a joint publishing venture by language enthusiasts

*Alex Maskey, the first Sinn Féin mayor of Belfast signing 'City Without Walls' in Robert Ballagh's Arbour Hill studio.*

in Ireland and Scotland involving Scottish and Irish poets, illustrators and calligraphers. His illustration was an action image of the legendary Cork hurler Christy Ring about to hit a ball, one of the few sporting images he has painted. "The publishers were based in Stornaway on the Isle of Lewis. When they came on the phone, they'd answer in Scots gaelic."

A leading figure in the Irish language movement Seán Mac Réamoinn, a special correspondent for RTÉ at Vatican 2 in the 1960s and later Controller of Radio Programmes and a founder of the Merriman Summer School, was in failing health but still walking about. A businessman friend commissioned a portrait. Ballagh asked Mac Réamoinn his usual question, "Is there anything in particular you'd like me to include?" "The things that have been really important to me are the Irish language, religion and socialism," Mac Réamoinn replied.

To meet this remit without cluttering the picture Ballagh chose to paint Mac Réamoinn in his eighties, against a page from James Connolly's *Labour in Irish History*. "That covered the socialism and I got a friend to translate it into Irish, even though it had never been published in Irish, which took care of the language. The religion bit is an echo from the holy pictures we used put in our prayer-books as children. I gave Seán a glow coming down on him like the halo of the Holy Spirit."

The portrait was exhibited at the Royal Hibernian Academy. Mac Réamoinn, who was by then in a wheelchair, was brought to see it by his daughters Seona and Laoise and afterwards repaired to a favourite haunt in Baggot Street, the pub Doheny & Nesbitts. He survived a few more years. President Mary McAleese attended his funeral in 2007, and Seamus Heaney was among those who spoke. His Canadian wife Pat was there but unaware of what was happening. "She was in an advanced stage of Altzheimers. She used give wonderful parties and sing Cole Porter songs with sophisticated clever lyrics, and now she was at a loss to remember anything."

◆

Betty was sitting in the kitchen sipping coffee. She heard a knock on the door. She opened it to find about thirty Germans gathered outside, one of whom politely explained they were architectural students. "We saw your house in a magazine in Germany, can we come in to have a look?"

She ushered them in. She was becoming used to such intrusions. When the people living next door at No 5 Temple Cottages decided to move a few years before, they offered the Ballaghs first option on their house and settled for £160,000, which was an indication of the accelerating rate of property inflation in Dublin's north inner city. It had cost £750 to buy out No 3 from the Dublin Artisan Dwelling Company in the early 1970s. They'd acquired No 4 from the Hyland family in 1985 for £17,500, knocking holes in the walls to turn it into one house. "We decided we couldn't burrow through this time. Having studied architecture I suppose

I felt I'd have been competent enough to design something, but I couldn't take it on because it would have taken a year out of my life."

Instead he engaged Dermot Boyd and Peter Cody, a firm of architects recommended by Niall McCullough and Valerie Mulvey, who couldn't take on the job themselves because they were too busy designing a new arts building for Trinity College. Boyd had worked in London for John Pawson, a leading minimalist. His approach appealed to Ballagh's liking for a clean look to things.

The work was expected to take five months so the Ballaghs took a six-months lease on a flat in Benburb Street, beside the National Museum. "The project almost broke my heart. It ran over-budget, it ran over time, but that's just part of building in Ireland. The whole place was gutted. We were still waiting to move back in after nine months. But it was worth it. It has won awards and medals. It keeps being featured in magazines."

Ballagh's whole idea was that from the outside you wouldn't notice anything had happened. His paintings had made their terraced cottage No 3 an icon in Irish art. "I wanted the effect to be that when you walk in the door you expect to be in a tiny little house, and then it opens up." He had in mind the concept of an inner courtyard that is a feature of buildings in Spain and North Africa. "Someone might leave a door open and passing by you would glimpse this oasis on the inside."

To achieve this Boyd and Cody retained the shell of the three houses while doing away with the extensions at the back. Two new rooms – a study and a kitchen – were created at either end to form a tall U-shaped inner courtyard. Since the building looks south, an acid-etched glass screen serves the dual purpose of shutting out overlooking flats behind while reflecting light into the house.

The building is a triumph of contemporary cool in which nothing is allowed to jar the overall effect. The doors have discreet indentions at the edge in place of the usual handles. This led to a surreal contretemps at a supper party when designer Paul Rattigan's wife Joan Burke couldn't open the bathroom door to get out. Nobody noticed she was missing. She had to use her mobile to contact Paula Burke – Moya Doherty's personal assistant – for the Ballagh's number, so she could phone downstairs and be rescued.

Ballagh felt almost guilty hanging any pictures on the walls or putting in furniture that might seem intrusive or interfere with the pristine vision of the building when it was finished. "I notice when the house is illustrated it's usually the photographs the architects took before we moved in and before it was all ruined by human beings!"

He'd come a long way from the pokey bed-sit in which he and Betty started out as a young married couple. He chose to mark his 60th birthday in September 2003 with a self-portrait placing him not in the rebuilt No 3 but in the cottage in Cork where Rachel now lived, a third painting in *The Cork Series*. "I always felt the space there was interesting, even though when you see it from the road it looks like a fairly small traditional cottage. Inside it has this enormous big room open right up to a sloping ceiling with wooden rafters. You go up a steep staircase into two bedrooms over the hall. But when you come out of the bedrooms, it's like being

*Top: New courtyard created for 3,4 and 5 Temple Cottages.*

*Above: New hallway in 3 Temple Cottages.*

up on the balcony of a little church."

To capture this sensation he opted for a fish-eye perspective which dictated the format of a circular painting set in a black frame, echoing *Upstairs No 3*. The view is a little distorted, but not as dramatically as it might be through the spy-hole of a hotel bedroom. Ballagh is stretched out below on a lush red upholstered sofa watching television, a reference to *Inside No 3*. He is wearing a white T-shirt with the provocative slogan, 'Fuck the Begrudgers'. The door behind him opening into the garden, and also the terracotta tiled floor, were featured in *Highfield*, but this time the natural light illuminating the painting comes from the side rather than 'contre jour'-. Apart from a print of *The Third of May* hanging on a wall, the only other picture is a birthday card on the television set. The furniture is from his parents' home in Elgin Road which he moved to Cork after their death, his father's empty red chair symbolising not only his death but also his absence from the artist's life. He borrowed the title of the painting – *Still Crazy After All These Years* – from a Paul Simon song.

"For years I'd been intending to do something with this space. The birthday provided the opportunity. The mood behind it is an urge to escape from the studio and to relocate in the calm of the country. I made up the slogan on the T-shirt, but since then several people have asked where they might buy one. The phrase is from Brendan Behan, who coined it 'for those who find themselves ploughing a lonely furrow, being cut out of things or treated unfairly on occasions'. I remember somebody saying, 'My God, you'll never sell that painting with those words on it.' But it sold."

◆

"I'll be back," promised Arnie Schwarzenegger as 85,000 flag-waving spectators turned Croke Park into a multi-coloured sea of flags. He'd just led a parade of 7,000 athletes with learning disabilities from 150 countries into the vast revamped stadium for the opening ceremony of the 2003 Special Olympics, the first held outside the United States since their launch in 1969.

Apparently Schwarzenegger was taken literally by a little boy from Derry chosen to receive the Olympic torch from a cross-border police motorcycle cavalcade. When he reached the top of stairs where the Flame of Hope was to be lit, he couldn't understand why Nelson Mandela was waiting for him instead of Arnie. "Who's the black guy?" he panted.

Croke Park had witnessed many astonishing days down the years but nothing quite like this. The biggest stage ever built in Ireland, designed by Ballagh, filled the whole of the historic Hill 16 end from one side of the pitch to the other. It had to be that size to allow the largest *Riverdance* troupe ever assembled to perform their iconic party piece, one hundred dancers high-kicking in unison to the soaring music of the National Symphony Orchestra backed by a five hundred-strong choir who then delivered the Games anthem with heart-stopping fervour.

"You inspire us to know that all obstacles to human achievement and progress are surmountable," Dr Mandela told the athletes. He'd been brought on stage to a standing ovation by Bono, lead singer of U2, who introduced him as "the President of everywhere and everyone who loves and fights for freedom".

Ballagh was asked to get involved by Rupert Murray, who was artistic director for the event. "I remember pointing out to him that while the Commonwealth Games, which were in Manchester the same year, had a budget of £15 million for their opening ceremony, we got around £3 million, which sounds like an awful lot of money until you realise what you have to do. The only way we made it happen was through voluntary work."

There was the idea of giving all 80,000 spectators a flag each. They were sewn by prisoners at Mountjoy and other gaols, without complaint. He persuaded Colm O'Briain, now director of the National College of Art and Design, to make the creation of the flame a project for his students. Ballagh designed an outline for the cauldron of the bowl and invited students in the college's craft department to submit maquettes and models from which he and Murray picked a winner, designed by Tracey O'Callaghan and Grainne McEvoy. The students then joined together to build a massive brutalist construction called *Celtic Warrior* which was clad in copper with a huge blue glass broach inset and strips of metal wrapped around the exterior, its whirling shapes conveying a sense of dynamism. Ballagh liked it because "while it had a modern look, it drew on the metalwork from the golden age of Celtic art".

Southern Gas, part of the Calor Gas company, agreed to provide the gas burners and a tower on top of which the cauldron would rest. "I'd to go a lot of times to Clonmel, which I remembered well from all those years ago when I was painting the *Tristram Shandy* mural. The people there cut the end off an old gas tank to provide a perfect bowl shape made out of steel with which the students could build their piece."

Unlike other sporting events, the rules for the Special Olympics prohibit not only national flags or emblems, but company logos. "When I explained this to the man from Southern Gas whose firm put up sponsorship worth probably €50,000 or more, he said, 'I don't care, my daughter is handicapped and she gets great value out of the Special Olympics, so this is my gift.'"

Although suffering from Parkinson's Disease, Muhammad Ali paraded with the American athletes. All performers and celebrities involved in the opening ceremony – including The Corrs, U2, Patrick Kielty, Jon Bon Jovi – were to give their time for nothing. "Roy Keane was incredible. He came over and said I'm yours for a week. I'll go to meet the athletes anywhere. I don't want any publicity. So he was at all the venues, whether the RDS, the Morton Stadium or the National Basketball Arena in Tallaght, a complete reversal of the celebrity thing. He didn't care whether there were cameras or not. He was there for the athletes."

*The Special Olympics flame,*
*Croke Park, 2003.*
Photo: The Irish Times

Bertie Ahern's presence was perhaps seen as a political intrusion by some, prompting a few boos – not the sort of reception he was accustomed to at Croke Park, which is just down the road from Fagan's pub where he conducted a lot of his constituency work. "The feeling was, what's he doing here? This was my first indication that the Bert was slipping."

While the threat of a global SARS epidemic didn't prevent the Chinese Olympians getting to the Games – where they were greeted by sympathetic cheers when Keane led them into the Croke Park arena – a pioneering *Riverdance* visit to China proved more of a problem. The respiratory disease SARS had been responsible for several hundred deaths since it first appeared in Guangdong province in November 2002. Chinese officials, hoping to avoid panic, initially failed to inform the World Health Organisation. The cover-up led to panic in February 2003 when an American businessman James Earl Salisbury became afflicted with pneumonia-like symptoms on a flight from China to Singapore. He was rushed to hospital in Hanoi, where he died. Medical staff treating him soon developed the same disease, and an Italian doctor who recognised the danger and reported the case to WHO also died. People were advised not to travel to China. FIFA switched the Women's World Football Cup to the US. Amid the hysteria it was deemed prudent to cancel *Riverdance's* long-awaited tour and an alternative tour to Japan was arranged.

The Chinese president Hu Juntao and prime minister Den Jiabao visited Guangdong to restore confidence, sacked the health minister and successfully set up more transparent procedures to bring the epidemic under control. The Chinese at this stage came back to *Riverdance* and said, how about now? Mary McAleese was going out to China with a trade delegation and the plan was that she would attend the opening in the Great Hall of the People in Beijing. "So that obviously was too tempting to turn down. The problem was that all the equipment and sets were in containers on the high seas on their way to Japan. There was no way they would reach China in time."

Economic reforms introduced by Deng Xiaoping in the aftermath of the Tiananmen Square massacre fifteen years before had created a rapidly growing middle-class in big cities like Beijing and Shanghai. Private property, once taboo under Mao, was the new public virtue, and there were already over three million millionaires. In the first four months of 2004, a total of 186,033 new cars came on the streets of Beijing. A splurge of capitalist investment and development of airports, motorways, railways, telecommunications, offices and housing, not to mention infrastructure for the 2008 Olympics, combined with an average income of around €100 a year – over 900 million of the population were still peasants working in near feudal conditions – had generated a double-digit growth rate that would soon push China to superpower status.

With this sudden affluence came not just a taste for Gucci and Louis Vuitton, but greater freedom of cultural expression and an eagerness to embrace Western culture. During Mao's misnamed Cultural Revolution anyone caught in possession of "imperialist" literature was liable to be exiled to a remote rural village for political re-education. Now *Lady Chatterley's Lover* was easily available in any book store, and even *Ulysses* had been translated into Chinese. "Having a copy of it was seen as a sign of being educated and cultured," Professor Ding Hongwei told me at Beijing University where he was preparing to celebrate the centenary of Bloomsday. Earlier that year reforming premier Den Jiabao had dazzled Bertie Ahern with his knowledge of *Ulysses*. "Someone made the mistake of mentioning the Joyce centenary, and 25 minutes later we were still listening to him," Ahern joked afterwards.

Whatever about literature, music was the most popular and direct expression of China's cultural love affair with the West. They'd set their hearts on *Riverdance*, and *Riverdance* had no intention of letting them down. With all the gear somewhere on the high seas, Ballagh had to come up with a quick and simple alternative way of staging it. "You couldn't build a whole new set just for a week in Beijing. I decided on a simple black box and asked the Chinese to supply the black drapes with a few colourful cloths that I could use. It wouldn't be as spectacular as the usual set, but it would pass muster. Rupert had to enter into negotiations about lights, because he uses a very sophisticated lighting system. 'Oh yes,' they said, 'we can get all that for you.' But when we arrived in Beijing, they didn't have everything they said they would. We were facing disaster."

Theatrical blacks are always made out of matte non-reflective materials like velvet or black serge, but the Chinese had provided a satiny black that picks up every bit of light and, even worse, was semi-transparent so that if there were any lights backstage you could see through the cloths. Murray then found they didn't have all the lights he wanted, which meant the entire lighting system would have to be reprogrammed.

"Time is running out," production manager Ken Binley warned the Chinese. "We're not getting the work done. We need more people." "No problem."

The next day Ballagh looked out of the lobby and saw two flat-bed trucks arriving. Dozens of men emerged wearing striped uniforms and numbers on their chest. "The Chinese had emptied the prisons to finish *Riverdance*. The most liberal capitalist regime in the world today is being run by a totalitarian Communist government, where there are no trade unions and workers have no protection and no rights. There's an inherent contradiction in that which is hard to see lasting."

Because *Riverdance* was being staged in the Great Hall of the People where the Communist Party held its Congresses, security couldn't have been tighter. "Everyone and everything going in had to be X-rayed – every instrument, every amplifier, every light, every tool. They only turned on the X-ray machine at 8am, 12 and 6pm so if you went in at 8am and suddenly discovered you'd

forgotten your glasses and went out to fetch them, you couldn't get back in until 12 or 6."

The cheapest *Riverdance* seats were $30-35, the highest $70-90. "With wages so low, I remember wondering how people could afford this. It was the first time Irish dancing was seen in China. Would anyone show up? Would they get it? But I'd failed to take into account the changing capitalist nature of the new China. It packed out every night. They just went crazy. I remember I was down near the stage and as it started there was a funny glow. They all had camera phones out, taking pictures." Among the audience was Professor Ding. "Ah yes," he told me. "I watched it to please my daughter, but was completely won over."

After ten years touring, *Riverdance* had been seen in 241 cities in 29 countries throughout the world. All of this was master-minded by Maurice Cassidy, its publicity-shy international promoter. Ballagh remembers seeing him front-of-house after the New York opening. "What are you doing?" he asked. "Hoovering the till," Cassidy joked.

A contemporary of Noel Pearson (manager of Ballagh's band The Chessmen in the 1960s), he learned the business as an impresario in the show-band era and later looked after The Chieftains, Clannad, De Danann, Colm Wilkinson and Phil Coulter. Together with director Joe Dowling he brought leading Irish theatre productions to London's West End and Hugh Leonard's *Da* to Broadway, where it won a Tony Award. He took FM 104 from being a loss-maker to number one in the Dublin commercial radio market. "He knows everyone and has seen it all. The thing that struck me about Maurice is that he's been enormously successful, yet jealously guards his privacy. So when he approached me about doing a portrait, I jumped at it."

Ballagh pictures Cassidy standing in the wings, behind a theatrical flat, a pensive bespectacled man wearing a loosely-knotted woollen scarf, his hands in the pockets of a beautifully tailored brown overcoat. It's as if he has just dropped into the theatre inconspicuously to check out how the show is going. Behind him out of his sight floodlights illuminate part of the front row of a smartly dressed audience in tuxedos and low-cut designer dresses. They gaze intently at a performance on stage which is invisible to us but not to him. It's a virtual audience which Ballagh built up digitally from photographs with the help of graphic designer Paul Rattigan. "If you look carefully you'll see Paul put himself in and his wife Joan Burke, and also executive producer Julian Erskine, who keeps *Riverdance* on the road. Tony Barnes, husband of Liz Reeves who works for Maurice, is there too. So the audience is full of people Maurice knows."

◆

*Maurice Cassidy (2005)*
*Pencil on paper.*
*Private Collection.*

The National Portrait Gallery in London was looking for Charles Haughey. They had difficulty sourcing a reproduction of Ballagh's 1980 portrait of the now former Taoiseach which they needed for *The Irish Face*, a history of Irish portraiture. When Ballagh went to check his files he couldn't find one for them, which was embarrassing.

He'd met Haughey a few times since their disagreement over the decision to house the Irish Museum of Modern Art in the Royal Hospital Kilmainham instead of Stack A on the docks, but they were no longer on calling terms. "If you criticised Charlie Haughey, he didn't talk to you. That was all forgotten with time. But I still felt strongly about the Kilmainham decision. I think it was a catastrophe. With the best will in the world they're still struggling to make the Royal Hospital into a satisfactory museum of modern art. I saw an exhibition in just one section of what was Stack A in the docklands by an artist who spent time in Cuba, and it was magnificent, a big open space full of light, right in the middle of the city, a perfect place for a modern gallery."

He spoke to a friend of Haughey, who suggested making a call. When he looked through his phone book he found he still had the private Kinsealy number. He phoned up. Haughey came on the line. "Ballagh," Haughey exclaimed – he always addressed him by surname, never as Bobby or Robert. "I need to take a photograph of your portrait." "What are you doing today?" "Nothing in particular." "Come on out. Make sure you bring some film for the camera."

This was a joke about a slip-up when Ballagh was doing the portrait and discovered in the middle of a photographic session he had no film in his camera, prompting Haughey to tease, "Isn't it a good job you don't earn your living as a photographer." He never forgot little things like that, and took delight in catching people out.

Haughey had been forced to sell off his Abbeville estate in Kinsealy to private developers in 2003 to pay a €5 million settlement to Revenue over secret gifts he'd been caught out accepting to finance his regal life style as Taoiseach, the largest of which was £1.3 million from the supermarket tycoon Ben Dunne. All of this was during a period of economic crisis when he was calling for a collective tightening of economic belts and warning against living "beyond our means". The Moriarty Tribunal, set up to investigate political corruption, ruled he was too ill to give evidence after he was diagnosed with prostate cancer.

"At this stage everyone said he was dying. When I arrived out at the Georgian mansion at Kinsealy, which he had managed to hold on to, I found him frail but in great form. The painting was hanging upstairs on the mezzanine level, where the light was a bit gloomy. 'Can we take it down?' 'Yeah, sure.' So I took it down and set up the tripod. 'Can you possible hold it while I take some shots?' So he did and I took the photographs. I was tempted when I sent them to the National Portrait Gallery to say, 'Do you see that hand in the top left corner. That's actually his hand.'"

It was the last time Ballagh met Haughey. He died a year later on 13 June, 2006. "I was glad I met him again before he died. There are so many aspects of his personality and politics I would have disagreed with. He was a likable old rogue as a person. I must say he was one of the few who ever used their political power to advance the arts."

With Haughey in disgrace and dying, everything he touched came under scrutiny. An easy target was the tax break for artists he introduced in 1969. Ballagh met with the Minister for the Arts John O'Donoghue in May 2005 to argue for its retention. "Although he assured me he didn't want to see any change, the government eventually put a €250,000 cap on what an artist could earn before paying tax, an utterly pointless gesture. There was no public outcry. It was a controversy generated by tabloids and Bono envy. A sad consequence was that fewer international artists will come to Ireland to live, and soon afterwards U2 moved their business to Amsterdam."

The meeting with O'Donoghue provided an opportunity to ask whether the government was doing anything to implement an EU directive giving member states five years to put in place the necessary legislation to introduce a resale right (*droit de suite*) for visual artists. "From his response I knew they'd done nothing. I reminded him that the directive was due to come into force on 1 January 2006 and if nothing was done by then there could be a huge legal and financial mess. I just left it at that. He took on board my concerns but made it clear that the Department of Enterprise, Trade and Employment had responsibility for introducing the legislation."

Ballagh had been badgering politicians for years about the resale right, particularly Garret Fitzgerald when he was Taoiseach. It was one of the aims of the Association of Artists in Ireland, which he helped set up in 1980, serving for six years as its first chairman. "Every time we lobbied government or met ministers it was always one of our demands, but I never thought I would see it happen."

When he got involved with the International Association of Art, he made contact with the cultural section of the EEC, as it was then, and discovered that it supported the resale right – which was first established in France after the First World War in order to help the widows of the many artists who perished – and was lobbying for its implementation. "Much to my surprise they finally adopted it as a directive in 2001. But nothing was done in Ireland. The 1 January 2006 deadline came and went."

By that stage the Irish Visual Artists Rights Organisation (IVARO) had been formed – with Ballagh as its chairman – to inform artists about their rights and serve as an agency for collecting the royalties they were entitled to under the EU directive. "We decided to take a test case at the first opportunity. A painting of mine was sold at auction on 5 February. I had my solicitor John

Gore-Grimes in place, and we got Pauline Whalley as our senior counsel and Caroline Costello – Declan's daughter – as her junior. We secured leave in the High Court in April to bring judicial review proceedings to have the directive implemented in Ireland."

Ballagh claimed that he was incurring financial loses because of the delay and sought damages from the State for its failure to vindicate his property rights under both the Irish Constitution and the European Convention on Human Rights. "We ended up finally getting our time in court in June – in the same week Haughey died – but just after the government rushed through legislation so they wouldn't be totally embarrassed. They still lost the case, but at least they were compliant with Europe."

The High Court agreed Ballagh was wronged and awarded him €5,000 damages, plus costs. "Our senior counsel Pauline Whalley tempered me quite a bit. I'd been commissioned to write a piece for the *Sunday Business Post* a week before the trial. You'll have to pull it, she said. Judges don't like that. She said you don't want to appear greedy in this. Leave it to the judge. You want to appear as a principled artist, not looking out for yourself but for others. Do you want headlines in the *Sunday World*, Greedy Irish Artist? Her advice was spot on."

It was a complicated legal affair. The only way the State could act quickly was by what is called a statuary instrument. This is where the relevant minister can introduce minimal legislation by dictate. But this can only be done if no choice is involved. If there is a choice to be made, then the issue has to be processed through parliament like most normal legislation, and this takes time. "They went for an exemption on things we wanted in, such as that the estates of artists would benefit. We wanted the threshold for it to operate to be €1,000. They went for €3,000. We wanted compulsory collective management, like they have in the UK, but unfortunately the Irish government decided on little or no regulation. They went for what would least benefit artists. But it is law now. Painters and sculptors will get 4 per cent of the hammer price on works sold for €3,000 or more and although auctioneers have not been as cooperative as you'd like – and some sought to impose a charge of €50 for every royalty they collected – slowly but surely they're coming on board."

The next stage will be to bring in galleries who deal in the secondary market, which is more difficult because much of their business is done in private. Auction houses publish their results, so it's easy to keep track of sales that are happening, but getting information about gallery sales is more complicated.

In the first two years of the scheme, IVARO collected and distributed to artists between €100,000 and €200,000. "But unfortunately the Government has produced regulations that are difficult to operate and tend to benefit rich and successful artists rather than struggling ones, which hardly represents the spirit of the directive."

❖

*The Artist's Lot (1984)*
*Mixed media on board. 46 x 36cm.*
*Private Collection.*

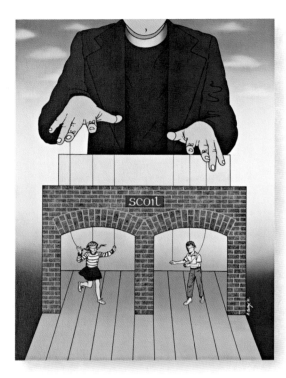

"Sure I'm a writer, and you're a writer too," Brendan Behan assured JP Donleavy. Having served in the US Navy during the Second World War, Donleavy had come to Trinity College courtesy of the GI Bill "to take his degree in drinking and harlotry in the Dublin pubs". With Behan's help he proved a good student in both pursuits, and a few others as well. Impressed by the prices and delighted by the whorls of colours of a Jack B Yeats exhibition at the Victor Waddington Gallery, he rushed out to buy paints, brush and canvas, undaunted by the fact that he'd never painted before. With John Ryan's help he was soon exhibiting at the Dublin Painters' Gallery. "Semi-abstract stuff, not half-bad," he says. Writing catalogues for his exhibitions was the part he enjoyed the most, so much so that he began having exhibitions so that he could write catalogues. "I became famous as it were, but of course in Dublin if three people in the same room know who you are, you're famous."

His rumbustious experiences as an American on the loose in the alcoholic Dublin of Anthony Cronin's *Dead as Doornails* inspired *The Ginger Man*, the first 120 pages of which Behan read and corrected before urging him to despatch it to Maurice Girodias at the Olympia Press in Paris, a publisher who got away with the most outrageous porn by also including serious writers like Genet, Beckett and Nabokov on his lists. "This book is going to go around the world and beat the bejaysus out of the Bible," Behan shrewdly predicted. Its iconic literary status enabled Donleavy to live the life of a country squire on a 180-acre estate on the shores of Lough Owel, along with "an enormous reservoir" of his paintings. A number of these were exhibited in his first retrospective at The Molesworth Gallery in Dublin in 2006 and later at the National Arts Club in New York. "I'm the painter who became the writer who's been rediscovered as a painter," he claims. His work was described by Enrique Juncosa, director of IMMA, who opened the exhibition, as "wildly funny, being sometimes dirty, violent, satirical, charming and even lyrical, characteristics that have been given to his literary style."

To celebrate his 80th birthday that year, the dealer Damien Matthews commissioned a portrait by Ballagh, who found Donleavy's domain on Lough Owel overgrown with the wildflower montbretia. "They were brought to Ireland and England from South Africa for putting in gardens, but decided to move out and they're now all over the place, particularly in the hedgerows in Cork. They're like a plague, but a pleasant-looking plague and they're harmless."

Ballagh spent a day with Donleavy taking photographs. "When I was going he ran out to the gate to open it and let me out. He's fairly fit for his age." Despite his student days cavorting, one-time boxer Donleavy lives a relatively healthy life. He welcomes the chance to scythe thistles and cut hedgerows or to build dry stone walls on his estate. "The dangerous think about writing is that it's so sedentary," he told me. "Having been an athlete I'm very conscious of the need to keep the body moving all day long."

Ballagh portrays him blue-shirted in a squire-like tweed suit and waistcoat, glasses dangling round his neck, a silk handkerchief in his lapel pocket. He is seated on a blue cushion on an upright wooden chair, placed left-of-centre. He leans his left shoulder on an arm of the chair so that his face is in the upper centre of the picture, framed by the centre-pane of a Georgian window:

the house was built in 1742, and was once visited by James Joyce. He looks directly at the viewer, but the iris of his right eye steals a glance to the side, giving his white-bearded face the look of an old devil. On top of a pile of books on the wooden floor is a first edition of *The Ginger Man*, and through the window behind him the Montbretia are bursting into bloom.

The JP Donleavy portrait and Ballagh's *Self-Portrait in the Italian Style*, a mock painted version of Michelangelo's iconic statue of David, were the most recent paintings in a major retrospective of Ballagh's work at the Royal Hibernian Academy in September 2006, suggesting perhaps that in terms of irreverence he and Donleavy are natural soul-mates.

He got the idea for the nude David self-portrait from a pair of underpants given to him as a joke by artist friends Campbell Bruce and Jackie Stanley, who spotted them in a street stall in Venice. Printed on the flesh-coloured underpants was a reproduction of the David figure's impressively sculpted genitals. When worn they give a *trompe l'oeil* illusion of nudity. "I thought it might be a bit of fun to do a nude self-portrait that wasn't a nude. I'd been struck some years before at a Lucien Freud retrospective by a marvellous self-portrait showing him standing naked except for a pair of boots, holding a palette and brush, as if to say 'I may be an old guy, but I'm still up for it.'"

He was reticent at first about doing the painting because whenever he's done a nude self-portrait before he's got into trouble, most famously with the *Kilkenny Kite* but also with *Upstairs No 3*, a print of which had been removed from a gallery in Galway by the Gardaí following protests. "The first I knew about this was when I got a call from *Morning Ireland* looking for a comment. I had to scratch my head. I didn't know what they were talking about."

He went ahead with the David anyway because once he gets an idea it's hard for him to abandon it. "My physique doesn't resemble David as sculpted by Michelangelo, which is an idealised portrayal of a beautiful young man. But I thought there was a certain irony in replacing the beautiful young man with a pot-bellied ould fellow, and the sling-shot, which was David's weapon of choice, with paint brushes." He poses as if in a classic architectural niche, standing on exactly the same plinth as David stands on in Florence. Placed at the top of the majestic marble stairway leading up to the main exhibition hall of the Royal Hibernian Academy in Ely Place, the portrait proved an eye-riveting way to lead people into the retrospective.

The retrospective was conceived to create the illusion of walking through a gallery within a gallery. It took the form of an installation of interconnecting rooms the entrance to which was through a doorway in a pseudo Palladian-style façade printed on cloth and stretched out on frames emblazoned in chiselled lettering with the Latin phrase, *Pitura veritatis revelatio* (Painting Reveals the Truth). It replicated an experience common in Ballagh imagery of being drawn into endlessly repetitive rooms within rooms and windows within windows as if reaching into the soul. A similar sensation was evoked on the cover painted for his 1986 biography

*Kilkenny Kite (1975)*
*Acrylic on cotton. Life size.*
*A supposedly humorous entry for an exhibition*
*entitled 'Artists Make Kites'.*
*After it's unilateral removal by the Dean of Kilkenny,*
*an unholy row about censorship ensued.*
*The photo shows the kite on display in the*
*David Hendriks Gallery, Dublin.*

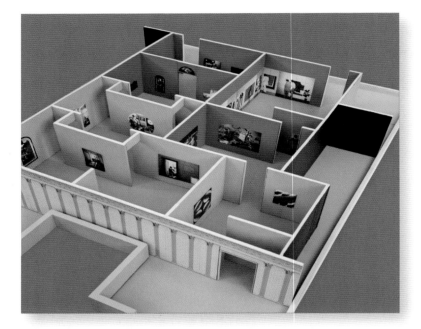

which shows him sitting on a chair as in *Winter in Ronda*, but the book he is reading is the biography itself rather than about Velazquez, so that the image keeps recurring.

The gallery-within-a-gallery concept was not an indulgence. It served the practical purpose of reducing the RHA interior to the human scale of a domestic dwelling in which paintings hang naturally on walls. "Otherwise the RHA is a huge space. Pictures on the big gallery walls can look like postage stamps." It was also a way of locking the viewer into the chronology of the work, creating the effect of a narrative through time as the viewer moves from room to room, each coloured green, grey or beige but never white because he wanted to get away from the contemporary art aesthetic of the white cube.

After passing through the early rooms showing the 1968-69 silkscreens, the early 1970s versions of Goya, David and Delacroix masterworks and the *People Looking at Paintings* series, visitors were obliged to exit temporarily into the gallery proper to explore Ballagh's design work, ranging from his stage sets to postage stamps and banknotes, and also his landscape series shown at the Ireland Institute in 2001. A second door then led back into the inner gallery and the portraits and self-portraits, culminating with the autobiographical Cork paintings.

The director of the RHA gallery Patrick T Murphy had been astonished when he returned after some years in the US as a curator to discover that there had been no big Ballagh show in Ireland. Before he left Ireland he'd collaborated with Declan McGonagle at the Orchard Gallery in Derry to put on a show of Ballagh's work from the 1970s. "No other artist at the time was making work that directly addressed the Troubles in Northern Ireland," said Murphy. "Ballagh cast his art in the tradition of public history painting from the triumphalism of Delacroix through to the neo-classicism of David and the humanity of Goya. His insistence on commenting on the political and the topical placed him firmly within the chronology of history itself."

In a catalogue essay putting Ballagh's work within a social and political context, Professor Declan Kiberd contrasted his outspoken espousal of the causes of socialism, republicanism and civil liberties and a whole range of other issues of the day – whether on the airwaves or in opinion columns and letters pages – with the restraint of his art. "His is an art which does not preach revolution but seeks instead to heighten the awareness of its viewers, so that they can make their own analysis. For him there can be no more radical or beautiful an art than a detailed and honest description of things as they really are."

The wide coverage the retrospective received – ranging from extensive interviews and profiles, to a special edition of RTÉ's arts programme *The View* – was in inverse proportion to the lack of enthusiasm of some reviewers, who seemed inclined to judge Ballagh the artist in terms of their opinion of Ballagh the citizen. A blog review on the Saatchi Gallery web-site, for instance,

complained that "you don't have to be a Northern Protestant or English victim of the IRA to feel utter revulsion at Ballagh's portrait of Gerry Adams astride a mountain (yet another plagiaristic rip off, this time of Casper David Friedrich). But look closer – is Gerry Adams just happy to see us or is that a gun in his pocket? In fact I think it's just one of many clumsy anatomical aspects of Ballagh's art."

Cristin Leach in *The Sunday Times* noted that "Ballagh is probably the closest thing Ireland has to a state artist, and yet he has been one of the least celebrated...Whether his artistic merit has matched his high visibility, however is a subject of debate... It's not that Ballagh isn't passionate about what he has to say, but his paintings are peculiarly restrained, his concepts contained and exceptionally controlled...Love him or hate him, Ballagh has become part of the fabric of Irish art, as iconic a figure as he could imagine himself." Billy Leahy in *The Village* while acknowledging that the retrospective "sums up Ballagh's career brilliantly and is sure to divide visitors down the middle", concluded by dismissing him as "an unfunny cartoonist".

More perceptively, Eimear McKeith in the *Sunday Tribune* believed that "perhaps one of the reasons for Ballagh's enduring popularity is his ability to combine an appealing accessibility with multi-layered complexity, as well as integrating technical skills with conceptual inventiveness...rather than reveal truth, his paintings play with shifting levels of reality and a slippery indefinable truth."

This divergence of opinion confirms Kiberd's judgement that Ballagh's work "is based on the idea that all good art – like every democratic society – should contain within itself the essential criticisms of the code to which it finally adheres".

A comprehensive exhibition of Ballagh's stamps was organised by An Post to run at the GPO concurrently with the retrospective. He had signed off from designing stamps in 2003 with a series of portraits of three figures from the 1803 rebellion, Robert Emmet, Thomas Russell and Anne Devlin. "I thought it was only right and proper to retire. I'd done 66 stamps in the thirty years since I received a phone call from the Department of Post and Telegraphs in 1973 asking me to design a stamp to commemorate The World Meteorological Year. I'd only being an artist for six years at that stage. It was like suddenly being picked to play sport for your country."

The Stamp Design Advisory Committee under Arts Council director Fr Donal O'Sullivan had been given a brief to modernise the image of Ireland projected by its stamps, which up to then had a dowdy provincial look. It was decided to provide more space for design by adopting the new larger Gentleman format, called after a leading British designer of that name. Ballagh's dramatic photo-realist iconic style made him an obvious choice. His simple uncluttered concept of stylised weather maps of Europe in bright

*Top: The 2006 exhibition layout under construction.*
Photo: Robert Ballagh

*Above: One of the spaces in the exhibition.*
Photo: Davison and Associates

119

solid colours brilliantly exploited the full range of the photogravure printing process, although someone wrote in complaining that he had put a depression over Cork. His stamp in 1979 marking the centenary of the birth of Patrick Pearse, referring again – as he had in his painting – to Delacroix's *Liberty at the Barricades*, but this time with the Irish rather then the French Tricolour, was the finest of his photogravure stamps.

The switch in the late 1970s to offset litho printing opened up even more possibilities, allowing the accurate reproduction in stamp format of drawings, photographs and paintings. "Many of my stamps were submitted as little oil paintings. Perhaps I was prompted in this by an international survey which found that the majority of the public wanted stamps that resemble miniature paintings."

While developments in printing offered more freedom to designers, this was sometimes counteracted by bureaucracy and political interference. All stamps were subject to cabinet approval, as he found out when his idea of a triangular format for An Óige stamps was turned down and his 1989 stamp for the Bicentenary of the French Revolution was shredded.

An Post retains all the art work for its stamps. "They've a wonderful archive by now, and were able to draw on it for the exhibition. Being in the GPO, I think it attracted far more visitors than my RHA retrospective" – a fulfilment perhaps of his joking prediction back in his 1986 biography, now much-quoted, that he could well end up better known for his stamps than his paintings.

He was horrified in 2007 when Bertie Ahern's brother Noel flew a kite suggesting that An Post were no longer going to need all of the GPO, so there should be discussions about the viability of converting it for retail use. "I wrote to Bertie saying it was a ridiculous idea, and that what was needed was a museum for both the Irish people and the visitor showing the historic events that took place in the building. There could also be a philatelic museum to record the Post Office's involvement, and perhaps also a theatrical museum, since The Gate was just up the street, and The Abbey over the other side."

All he heard back was a letter expressing interest in his suggestions and saying somebody would get back to him. "Nobody did. Then I saw an announcement around Easter saying the Government was seriously considering a museum dealing with the GPO's historical associations and also a philatelic museum."

Seeing again the early Ballagh stamps from the 1970s – but with an awareness of his work since – is to glimpse hints of the stage designer he was to become. He treats the space of a stamp as a stage on which a few key minimalist props imply a narrative or drama of the event marked by the stamp, a window of understanding: indeed with the 1990 Theatre series they actually become a stage for *Waiting for Godot, The Field, Juno and the Paycock* and *The Playboy of the Western World*.

The art of hand-painted stamps now seems more or less to have had its day. Designers avail of the manipulative power of computer-generated graphics and digitally-enhanced photographs. Ballagh is not just a redundant designer of currency. "I'm a retired stamp designer."

There is no mistaking the tall man sitting near the revolving entrance to the foyer of the Shelbourne Hotel. It's all in his smile. Ballagh spent weeks working the paint to capture the tiny detail of the slightly crooked upper lip that makes it so distinctive. "Professor Watson?"

He stands up, reaching out his hand to shake mine, a tall man with the bearing of a professor. "Ah," he says, his smile widening. It's the morning after the unveiling of his portrait at a dinner in Trinity to celebrate the anniversary of the establishment of the Department of Genetics in 1958 – his first glimpse of the actual painting, although a photograph had been sent to him. After the black drape was theatrically lifted away, he'd remarked to Ballagh, "This is marvellous. It is the beginning of a wonderful friendship." Some guests thought he looked Christ-like in the way he was depicted, reaching out for the ethereal double helix shimmering in the glass frame. "I'm not sure I ever used my hands that way," he chuckles.

What about the smile? "It's extremely accurate. I had a skin cancer taken out fifty years ago, and my lip is asymmetrical. And Bobby caught it. I'm not sure anyone would notice it except me."

Just as Darwin's theory of natural selection gave biology the governing law that explains all of life, Watson and Crick's discovery of the molecular structure of nucleic acids opened the way for understanding the information transfer in living material and the DNA genetic code that determines our individuality. "The trouble about DNA is that it is not always kind," Watson says. "Some people lead healthy lives and other people get DNA which leads to diminished lives. So there's fear of DNA. If your message is cursed, how do you take the curse away?"

Perhaps by understanding it? "That's the beginning of it," he agrees. Hence the Human Genome Project which he headed from 1988 until 1992, a massively funded programme designed eventually to sequence the entire human genome and provide knowledge for an emerging era of personalised medicine, in which information contained in each person's DNA code can be used to identify and prevent disease and to create individualised therapies. Inevitably this will have profound social and political implications. "Should money be redistributed from those who are better off to those who aren't?" he asks. "Should you work hard in order to pass it on to people who don't? Well, it's not that simple if people aren't equal. Our DNA – and people don't like to admit this at all – makes us unequal."

He's found redistribution is an evil word in the US, particularly with Republicans. "We wouldn't have survived as a social species unless we cared for other people in life. Man's morality comes out of his dreams. We want to redistribute because we don't like to see people in the gutter." This raises the question of how much to redistribute and what to redistribute. "I certainly would redistribute education so no one from a poor background would ever be denied an opportunity to reach the top because their parents weren't successful. And it's the same with health. You can't really make a dumb person an interesting person, but you can't let him starve either."

Watson is a patently humane man but has an uncompromising way of thinking outloud about genetics that can get him into trouble. An interview published in *The Sunday Times* in 2007 by a former intern, who had visited him at Cold Spring Harbour, purported to summarise his views on DNA as if quoting him directly. The reporter noted that Watson says "he is inherently gloomy about the prospect for Africa because all our social policies are based on the fact that their intelligence is the same as ours – whereas all the testing says not really, and I know that this hot potato is going to be difficult to address. His hope is that everyone is equal, but he counters that people who have to deal with black employees find this not true." Not surprisingly this led to accusations of racism, despite the fact that Watson immediately issued a statement saying, "That is not what I meant. More importantly, there is no scientific basis for such a belief. I cannot understand how I could have said what I am quoted as having said. I can certainly understand why people reading those words have reacted in the ways they have."

DNA may be a given in life, but how you play the genetic hand you have been dealt can be as much subject to luck and circumstance as any predetermined biological condition. Ballagh's potential talent is perhaps encoded in his genes but what he made of that potential is his own doing, just as Watson's intuitive leap of discovery didn't just come from his genius but from a chain of random connections that put him in a situation in the laboratory in Cambridge in 1953 to do what he did. Similarly it was coincidence that brought Watson to Dublin in 2001 to receive an honorary degree from Trinity College and led to him walking past the Adam's showrooms in St Stephen's Green where he saw a painting by Robert Gregory in the window that hadn't sold. He promptly went inside and purchased it.

The fine arts showroom followed up by sending him its auction books, in one of which he saw Ballagh's *The History Lesson*. "I thought it was an interesting painting, without knowing who Ballagh was or who the people in the painting were. I called up and found out Ballagh was well-known and the people he portrayed were Connolly and Pearse. So that intrigued me. But I think I would still have bought it without knowing who they were. I wanted paintings to make the lab in Cold Spring Harbour look more than a place where we turned out scientific data. Everyone who walks into our auditorium now walks under *The History Lesson*."

Watson continued to keep in touch with Irish art through Adam's. "That's how I saw Ballagh's extraordinary portrait of Micheal Farrell. It made me want to be painted by him. But I'd no idea he'd be so imaginative with the DNA in the glass. The painting is a great labour of love. Years from now I'll be known from the painting."

It could be argued that Watson looking in the window at Adam's wasn't altogether accidental. His DNA may have had something to do with it. He'd been interested in art since his childhood in Chicago during the Great Depression. "Our family was too poor to have any paintings in the house except a portrait of my mother's father which was done for the World Trade Fair of 1893."

This grandfather was a tailor from Scotland and his wife was Lizzie Gleeson, the child of Irish immigrants from Tipperary. On his father's side there was an uncle who was involved in art and had been director of the Milwaukee Museum when he was young. "He said he taught 100,000 people how to draw at the Art Institute in Chicago, including Walt Disney. He took me there when I was 12 or 13 and I saw the French paintings."

When Watson got to Cambridge a Swiss friend had a tiny Picasso. "It made me want to have something myself, so I bought an unsigned Picasso lithograph. In 1957 I got a $15,000 prize and bought an Andre Derain drawing of two nudes for $1,000. That started me off." By the early 1960s when he was married and his salary was approaching $15,000 a year, he was spending 20% of it on art. "I bought a very good Degas for $4,000. I was tempted to buy a Bacon for $10,000, but my limit was $5,000. That was stupid."

After the unveiling of the Ballagh portrait, there was talk about where it should be hung. Watson isn't happy about a suggestion that it might hang in the Dining Hall. "That's no place for it. I'm not a Trinity man. My intention was that it should hang in the Department of Genetics so students there could see it."
He's going back to Trinity in the afternoon to see the painting again. "It's a big work. You'd need a big wall for it. There's a very good sculpture of the double helix by Brian King outside the Department, and I was there when it was dedicated in 2003. I hope Bobby's painting will not be too far away from that."

His ambition is eventually to return *The History Lesson* and his Robert Gregory painting to Ireland, if he can find somewhere suitable for them to hang. He checked out the National Gallery, but wasn't impressed. "I have the idea that since there isn't really a good place for me to give *The History Lesson* and the Gregory to hang I should persuade maybe Chuck Feeney to help fund a new Museum of Irish Culture down on the docks, perhaps next to the new Calatrava bridge. It would embrace the whole Irish imagination, bringing literature, the visual arts, drama, music and the sciences together in the one place. You'd have to get a landmark building – I'd say it would cost about $250 million – which in itself would have the impact to attract people to Ireland from all over the world."

Dermot Desmond, who helped transform the docklands into the International Financial Services Centre, had in mind a somewhat similar project as a way of rooting the IFSC more deeply in the wider life of the community. He unsuccessfully proposed as a millennium project an Ecosphere to house an aquarium and simulate a tropical forest habitat. "If supported, what an engaging learning experience that could now be for young and old alike, particularly with the world's focus on climate change," he argues in an introduction to *Capitalisation and Culture: Competing on Difference* by Finbar Bradley and James J Kennelly.

Watson dislikes the way the different arts and sciences tend to be segregated rather than feed off each other, because imagination can have no boundaries. His own creative vision originally found expression in pure science. "Now the only way I can use my imagination is when I try and write a sentence. You might have one idea a year as a scientist, but if you're a writer you're constantly

*James D Watson and Robert Ballagh after the unveiling of the Watson portrait at a dinner to celebrate the 50th anniversary of the founding of the Genetics Department in Trinity College, Dublin.*

forced to imagine. It's a way of thinking."

He's curious about three paintings he's noticed in the Adam's window just across the street from the Shelbourne. He wants to check out them out. They're by the Irish artist Colin Middleton. As with *The History Lesson*, it's the painting rather than the artist that first attracts him. He doesn't know anything about Middleton but he trusts his gut instinct.

So standing there in the wind, we talk about Middleton and how when I visited him at his home in Bangor before his death he talked about the wonderful craft of damask he encountered as a child. It perhaps accounts for the beautiful texture and deep glazed colours of his paintings that give reality to his strangely surreal juxtaposed figures and objects.

Watson is drawn to painting by the same curiosity and thrill of discovery that pushed him to nail down the double helix. He doesn't give up easily. Some years ago David Hockney was to paint a portrait of him with Francis Crick. Crick got ill and nothing came of it. Time passed and Watson found himself in London again for a television programme. One of the producers put him in touch with Hockney, who agreed to do a drawing.

"We talked for about 45 minutes about Iceland. Then he made a quick drawing of me. He looked at it, and went into another room. He returned with two colour Xeroxes of the drawing and gave them to me. Six months later I get a catalogue for the Annely Juda gallery and I'm for sale for $20.000. So I bought the drawing myself. The difference between the Xeroxes and the original was slight."

We part outside the Shelbourne. 'I think Hockney makes me look like an English bishop, but that's fine," he says. "But with Bobby, it's really me, for better or worse."

*Louis le Brocquy at 90,
painting in his Dublin studio.*
Photo: Robert Ballagh

The art dealer Damien Matthews had been an intermediary in setting up the JP Donleavy commission. Now he was back on the phone again. "I've a client who'd like to commission a portrait of Louis le Brocquy," he said.

Of course Ballagh was interested. As a schoolboy he'd painted pastiches of le Brocquy, which his mother had shown proudly to friends. "I've always got on well with Louis. I find him an extraordinarily decent man." So he told Matthews he'd only take on the challenge if le Brocquy was happy to cooperate. This didn't seem likely. When he sounded him out, the painter said, "At my age I don't have a lot of time and I want to spend it doing my own work."

It was early 2006. Louis le Brocquy was approaching 90, but still painting. He was born in the year of the Easter Rising into a family that was originally from Belgium. His great-grandfather came to Ireland to buy horses for the Belgian army, fell in love with a Kilkenny girl and never returned. Louis trained as a chemist to work in the family oil business at Harold's Cross but soon quit and left Ireland to become a painter, teaching himself by studying the work of great masters like Velazquez, Rembrandt, Manet and Goya on visits to public galleries in Paris, London and Geneva. Much of his life was spent in the South of France, although he and his painter wife Anne Madden now lived in an inner-city cottage near Portobello.

He made his international reputation painting heads, trying to evoke from the depths of the canvas or paper vestiges of cultural figures like Joyce, Yeats, Beckett, Lorca and Heaney. The concept of the disembodied head as an image of human consciousness was inspired by Polynesian heads he found in a Paris museum in the early 1960s. "Horrifying, really, skulls of ancestors which had been over-modelled in clay and then painted in a decorative way, often with coral shells for eyes," he explained to me. "It gave me the idea of the head as a magic box that contains a spirit. And I began painting in that way, concentrating on the head not as part of a body, but in isolation."

Francis Bacon, who was one of his subjects, said that "Louis le Brocquy belongs to a category of artists who have always existed – obsessed by figuration outside and on the other side of illustration – who are aware of the vast and potent possibilities of inventing ways by which fact and appearance can be reconfigured."

By contrast Ballagh's preoccupation has always been with the surface of reality. His portraits attempt to reveal the subject through a meticulously observed inventory of their life or circumstances. They are iconic rather than revealing: it's up to the viewer to read them as they wish. Yet his recurring references to windows within windows and doors within doors have some affinity with le Brocquy's probing beyond the palpable physical appearance of man into his invisible reality in the conviction that "there lies behind the face an interior landscape which the painter tries to discover, but I know too that this landscape may also be a reflection from within the painter himself."

Both painters are minimalist in their approach and clearly belong in a photographic age. "Long conditioned by photographs, the cinema and psychology, we now perceive the human individual as faceted, kinetic," said le Brocquy, one of whose most loved paintings of Dublin schoolgirls after the blessing of the lilies was inspired by a photograph published in the *Evening Herald* on Bloomsday, 1939. "I often wonder what became of those little girls whose childhood has been frozen in this moment of time."

About seven weeks after Ballagh approached him, le Brocquy phoned back. "Can you work with photographs, as I do?" Ballagh assured him he could, that this was the way he always worked. "Oh well, then there's no problem at all." Apparently he'd been afraid he'd have Ballagh turning up for hours every day, or that he might have to go to his studio for sittings.

All Ballagh needed was two photo sessions. Afterwards he showed the contact prints to le Brocquy, who picked out a photograph in which he is standing at his easel looking out. Ballagh sent him a watercolour based on this shot to make sure he liked it. Louis phoned back. "I don't think I like myself looking away. I should be looking at the canvas I'm working on." Ballagh changed it. This became the final composition.

Ballagh conceived the portrait partly in homage to Velazquez. "I'm well aware Louis is very much a fan of Velazquez, as are many other artists. Any artist worth their salt has to admire Velazquez."

One aspect of the portrait is that – as in *Las Meninas*, one of the few self-portraits of Velazquez – the artist is partly obscured by the back of the canvas. Whereas Louis is looking at the canvas, Velazquez looks out either at the observer or the Spanish King and Queen, who are looking in on the scene. As a further touch, Ballagh decided to put in a mirror image in the background which has a reflection of him taking a photograph of Louis. It's a quote from his own 1977 painting *Winter in Ronda* which was also an homage to Velzaquez. "So things go round in circles. Life is full of repetitions."

In many of the shots taken of Louis working in his studio he had a big palette on a stool beside him. It assumed a dominant role in the photographs. The question was what to do with it in the painting. "I thought of getting rid of it but then decided to use it. I had this idea of it bursting out so that one half of the palette physically exists beyond the picture plane. I seem to have a predilection for that sort of thing. Whether it's the stones falling out of the Noël Browne portrait, or Micheal Farrell's thumb, there's this 3-D element that's part of a 2-D art piece."

The cubist collages of Picasso could be considered a precedent for this, but an even greater influence is perhaps the Renaissance painter Carlo Crivelli, many of whose altar pieces Ballagh admired at the National Gallery in London. "He obviously had a thing for gourds and melons and squashes. There's 3-D fruit all over the place. They almost look like a Salvador Dali, but painted hundreds of years ago. I think they're fascinating."

Apart from being jailed for an adulterous affair, little is known of Crivelli's life. He was of Venetian origin, and lived most of his career in that area. Vasari didn't consider him important enough to include in his *Lives of the Artists*, and his ultra-realist style and predilection for *trompe l'oeil* and working only in tempera fell out of favour after his death circa 1495. The Pre-Raphaelites admired him, particularly Edward Burne-Jones.

"Crivelli has a picture of St Peter with a big bunch of keys sticking out of the picture plane and he also did a famous Annunciation that's very dramatic in terms of perspective and detail, but it's his pictures with lumpy pomegranates and things that play around with perception that I find most interesting. You look at them and wonder is it part of the flat surface or is it added on."

The le Brocquy painting has the same effect. The palette sticks out and there's actually a real brush lying on it. He is holding a bunch on brushes in his left hand. At first glance it is hard to tell which brushes are real and which are painted. Crivelli would have approved.

The apron le Brocquy wears is unsmudged by paint. Here is a man of refinement and wonderful technique, quietly at work, still searching for a truth that can only be found in the act of painting. "People at one stage used compare him to Bacon or Freud. But Louis very definitely belongs to the situation described by Matisse that art should be like a nice armchair, whereas when you're dealing with Freud and Bacon, art is a hard bench. I wonder whether his background made him that kind of artist."

Le Brocquy isn't a political artist, but as a citizen he and his wife Anne Madden have spoken out on civil rights issues. "His heart is always in the right place. I remember years ago when I did a poster for the Irish Nicaragua Support Group and got a little bit of publicity, the next day Louis phoned me and said, I want to give them a print. Nobody had been knocking on his door. More recently he and Anne had two letters in the papers criticising the decision to drive a motorway through the historic Hill of Tara. There's no need for him to be doing anything like that, but he does."

◆

It's an impossible view. Look to the right and you see the Custom House and Liberty Hall and, across the Liffey, the Ulster Bank with its odd structure of glass-like cubes. Turn the other way and the Liffey forks out to the sea. Tree-lined walkways on either bank humanise the ever-expanding office developments, engine room for Ireland's sudden economic surge in the 1990s.

In the foreground of this astonishing backdrop – the brash new face of Dublin – is the man who helped bring it about. Dermot Desmond is at the window of his office in the International Financial Services Centre, an audacious project that transformed Dublin in the same way the Docklands reinvented London. Yet no politician would touch Desmond's inspired feasibility study until he persuaded Charles Haughey to put it in Fianna Fáil's 1987 election manifesto. Seven years later 443 international financial service firms were operating out of Dublin, and the centre had generated nearly 11,000 new jobs. A derelict area of Dublin was dramatically regenerated.

A dapper man with a trim grey moustache and a quizzical smile, Desmond became a billionaire by following his hunches. He bought London City Airport for £23.5 million in 1995 when London's Docklands was in recession, and sold it for £1.2 billion

*Portrait of Dermot Desmond showing the curved format.*

*The Four Courts at Night* (2007)
*Oil on canvas. 51 x 76cm.*
*Private Collection.*

in October 2006 before the global economy went into a tailspin. He is co-owner with John Magnier and JP McManus of the Sandy Lane Hotel in Barbados and has stakes in his favourite football clubs Glasgow Celtic and Manchester United.

With several homes – a restored Georgian house in Merrion Square that used be fashion designer Sybil Connolly's salon, another house at the K Club, a villa in Marbella, a Palladian property in London's Belgravia – he had lots of wall space for art, which he bought by trusting his own eye.

"I thought I'd have the Micheal Farrell portrait on my hands a long time," Ballagh remembers. "But at the first outing he bought it. He also bought lots of works from my landscape show."

When it looked as if Ballagh's 2006 RHA retrospective might have to be cancelled because there was insufficient funds to accommodate the ambitious installation concept of creating a gallery within the gallery, Desmond came to the rescue. "I decided – something I'm not good at – to ask to see him to consider sponsoring it. To my great surprise he said it was no problem at all. I was so thrilled that when I was leaving his office, I turned round and said I'll do your portrait as a thank-you. Desmond said there's no need for that. No, no, I will. And that's how the portrait came about. It wasn't commissioned. It was a voluntary project."

The concept for the picture stemmed from the fact that every meeting Ballagh had with Desmond was in his office at the top of the Financial Services Centre. "So I went up there one spring day with my Rolleiflex and took twelve shots, right around a 180-degree arc. I brought them to Paul Rattigan and we scanned them. Because of the laws of parallax, each picture had a different vanishing point which meant they didn't actually join up. Paul being the genius he is with computers managed to straighten and join things up to create this vista in which – if you look carefully – the Liffey is almost straight, a view that couldn't exist but looks as if it does because the awkward join that makes it possible is covered by the portrait of Desmond."

Ballagh finished the image by ink-jet printing it on canvas using archival inks. When that was done he went over it with paint and glazes, and then painted the portrait based on the photographs he took.

"I did something I'd never done before – or ever seen done – which was to stretch the canvas on a curved ground, which is contradictory because if you pull it up tight it should go straight across the curve. I didn't know whether it would work or not, so I had to plan it out very carefully. I marked the canvas at every inch or so and I marked the stretcher the same, because the stretcher was bow-shaped. I started right at the middle, stretching it tight front to back, and moved on just a little bit and pulled it out, stretched it and shifted it, and then moved on and on. For a while I could see buckles coming in, and thought it wouldn't work. I don't know whether it's geometry or luck but whatever happened, it suddenly took up the shape." A comparison would be when an umbrella blows inside out and you try to push it back: if you do it right it'll suddenly snap back into shape. Art is all about having the courage to take chances, rather than just do what has already been done before.

Ballagh remembers standing with Desmond at the window of his office one day in 2007. Two years before at an IFSC annual lunch, Charlie McCreevy, Ireland's European commissioner, famously advised the Irish financial regulator, "Don't try to protect everyone from every possible accident...Leave industry with the space to breathe and investors with the freedom to learn from their mistakes."

But such lack of regulation would eventually be to the detriment of the IFSC when the global credit crisis plunged Ireland into recession, something Desmond seemed to see coming. "The financial services industry has been good for Ireland," Desmond said, looking out over the revitalised docklands, "but like all things it will run its course. We should be prepared to find something to replace it, culture could be that something."

Anthony Coughlan is in many ways the political opposite to Dermot Desmond. He views the European Union with scepticism and has opposed every stage of its expansion. His National Platform helped defeat the Nice Treaty in its original form and it became part of an unlikely coalition of far-right Catholic pro-life activists, left-wing groups and Sinn Féin to defeat the Lisbon referendum. Ballagh first got to know him in the early 1990s during the debate on amending Articles 2 and 3 of the Irish Constitution, and attended meetings in his rooms in Trinity College where he was Emeritus lecturer on Social Policy. Now he was 70. His partner Muriel Saidléar called Ballagh. "I'd love you to paint his portrait."

Coughlan was bemused when Ballagh asked him the usual question about anything particular he'd like to feature in the portrait. "Quite honestly I don't care about myself at all, I just want something about the campaigns and my political interests," he said. Ballagh found a simple solution to the challenge of presenting political ideas visually. He pictured Coughlan against a green baize college notice-board to which were attached various anti-EU slogans and posters and a copy of *The Irish Democrat*.

It worked so well that Ballagh tried something similar for a portrait of Mary Cullen commissioned by her son Finbar, the administrator of the Ireland Institute. "Mary has been hugely important in terms of women's history through her work at Maynooth College. So I asked her about her favourite authors and writers who have influenced her. This enabled me to show her in front of a bookcase where you can read their titles." She wrote him a note afterwards: "I really do like the woman you painted. I hope someday I may live up to her."

◆

Gerry Adams is looking back on his childhood over a bowl of soup in An Cultúrlan on the Falls Road, an Irish-language cultural centre in what is now an officially designated Gaeltacht area.

"We'd go to the pictures at the Broadway just a hundred yards from here, and sometimes the Diamond which was a fleapit.

*Top: Mary Cullen (2007)*
*Oil on canvas, 46 x 60cm.*
*Private Collection.*

*Above: Anthony Coughlan (2007)*
*Oil on canvas, 46 x 60cm.*
*Private Collection.*

But I suppose I've more memories of the Clonard opposite the Falls Library because my granny would bring me there. As we got older we used go into the city to see films which was good craic, but we'd leave before the Queen was played."

The red-brick building, which is bustling with people talking *as gaelige*, was formerly a Presbyterian Church and is named in honour of Roibeard McAdam, a Presbyterian businessman who pioneered the revival of the Irish language in 19th-century Belfast and Cardinal Tomas ÓFiaich, a stalwart of the Irish language in the twentieth century. Its tower is used for the local Irish-language radio station's transmissions.

Adam loved going to the cinema as a boy, but rarely gets an opportunity any more. "I haven't been to see a film in ages," he shrugs, breaking off to take a call on his mobile. "Sorry, I have to answer this."

He hadn't yet seen Steve McQueen's *Hunger*, the Cannes Award-winning film about Bobby Sands, leader of the 1981 hunger strike and one of the ten prisoners who starved to death in pursuit of the political status refused to them by the British authorities. "But Danny Morrison and others on the Bobby Sands Trust have seen it. By all accounts it's a very good piece of film-making."

The West Belfast Festival, Féile an Phobail, launched twenty years ago in 1988 in the aftermath of some of the worst violence of the Troubles and now one of the biggest community events of its kind, is celebrating its anniversary with a wide-ranging programme of events including drive-in movies on a giant screen at the back of the Andersonstown Leisure Centre. Those without a car can watch from a double-decker bus. The programme includes *Pulp Fiction, Dirty Dancing* and *The Exorcist*.

The popular success of the festival and the very fact that Adams can sit around in public like this within sight of Divis Flats, the top floors of which were once a sniper post for British Army marksmen, and just up the Falls road from Milltown cemetery where the loyalist gunman Michael Stone ran amok, shooting dead three Republican mourners, is an indication of the astonishing normalcy of Belfast since power-sharing came into operation following a joint decision by Sinn Féin and Ian Paisley's DUP on 26 March 2007 to restore the political institutions of the Good Friday Agreement. The day after the decision was reached Adams wrote to Ballagh thanking him for his "help and support through many difficult times. Significant progress has been made, and initiatives and developments have occurred which many would have thought impossible. Of course, there is still a long way to go and much work has to be done but I believe it is right and proper that we take this time to thank all of those far-sighted people, like yourself, from all walks of life, who helped create this opportunity; and who stayed with this process even in times of deepest crisis and despondency."

The power-sharing executive formed on 8 May with Ian Paisley as First Minister and Martin McGuinness as Deputy First Minister, is now in its second year. The North, it seems, is finally at peace.

Ballagh is at the Féile to give a talk on *The Visual Arts in Ireland after the Flight of the Earls*. On the drive up in his BMW – unlike when he made the journey in his Lada twenty years before – there was nothing to indicate we were crossing the Border. We didn't encounter a single check-point or surveillance helicopter along the way. Not a British soldier, nor even a PSNI policeman – the RUC is no more – was in sight.

Adams leads us across the road to St Mary's College where the event is taking place, stopping to chat and joke with people in Irish and in English. This is his territory, the place he belongs and from where he sees Ireland. He stays for the lecture and an animated discussion afterwards in which writer and broadcaster Eamonn Mallie is in full flow on the role of women in art. Then he and I find an empty classroom to talk without been interrupted, sitting at a desk.

"I don't want to exaggerate the Féile, but its strength is that it genuinely is a people's festival," he said. "A bit of madness had happened here. It started off with the killings in Gibraltar, and then the funerals – a whole horrendous week of trying to get the bodies home, the journey from Dublin airport up to West Belfast running the gauntlet overnight. And then the attacks on the funeral at Milltown cemetery, where the mourners were praised for their restraint but when two British soldiers were killed at the funeral for victims they were described as 'savages'. The Féile was a response to this enormous deluge of abuse. August was traditionally a month of bonfires with a lot of drink taken. The RUC would come in, the British Army would come in and things would get messy. The Féile would not have been possible if people like Bobby had not come up and actually created an alternative trajectory."

The strategy of the Féile was to get people off the streets by drawing on the cultural traditions of the Falls Road, not just the music and the songs but the visual arts and literature. After all, the painter Gerard Dillon came from there, and so did Micheal McLaverty. And Seamus Heaney worked there as a teacher. Adams' idea was to allow young people to see other possibilities and get a sense of their own dignity. "I'm more than struck by the fact that a happening or an event or a development will get maybe one paragraph in a history book but may have been 15 or 20 years in the making. That's probably how history is actually made. It's about people putting their heads above the barricade saying, I'm prepared to contribute in a positive way to a different view of the situation."

In 1988 Adams was in the middle of secret talks with John Hume, following through on the argument of *Pathways to Peace* – which he wrote while he was in prison – that a way had to be found out of the violence. The British Army was privately admitting it couldn't defeat the IRA, and the IRA knew it couldn't beat the British Army. The logic was that there had to be a political solution. "We were trying to piece things together. The Féile played a role in that. When Mary Robinson was President, one of her people thought that as part of the notion of inclusivity she should make a presidential visit to Belfast, and in the course of that she should meet me. I was MP for the area at the time. So Féile became part of the sponsorship of a local event which she attended involving the fiddler Sean Maguire. He played a bit of music and St Agnes Choral Society sang some arias."

The President's decision caused consternation at the time. "The British Government tried to block it and told the President she couldn't get RUC protection coming into this area, she wouldn't be safe. The government in Dublin tried at the last moment to

*The seal of the United Irishmen redrawn by Ballagh in 2008.*

intervene and to have it put off. Those things now, looking back, seem so childish and infantile. The President in my opinion never got proper credit for that."

The Falls Road murals back then were an outlet for rage and defiance, but have long since developed into a colourful commentary on society in general and also – taking a cue from the Nelson Mandela image painted under Ballagh's supervision – an expression of solidarity with champions of civil rights throughout the world. So many tourists are coming in bus-loads to see what has become known as the International Wall – a site on the Falls Road where some of the most striking murals can be seen – that Belfast City Council is planning to sponsor a mural trail.

As the sun begins to set over Black Mountain, there is a continental buzz about the Falls Road. Sitting at a table outside An Cultúrlan sipping coffee are Mark Ervine and Danny Devenny. They come from opposite sides of the political divide but work together on murals that look beyond tribalism. Their joint work this year is a recreation of Picasso's *Guernica* on the International Wall which *The Guardian* described as "spectacular". They'd been invited to mark Liverpool's year as European Capital of Culture by painting Beatles murals in working-class areas of the city.

Ervine is son of the charismatic loyalist leader David Ervine, an active member of the paramilitary UVF, who turned from violence after serving time in the 1970s for possession of explosions with intent to endanger life and, as leader of the Progressive Unionist Party, played a pivotal role in bringing about a loyalist ceasefire in 1994. Gerry Adams, Peter Hain, Hugh Orde and David Trimble were among the attendance at his funeral in 2007. "His legacy is that he led loyalism out of the dark ages," said US peace broker George Mitchell.

Mark Ervine got involved in community art as a boy and caught the public eye with his striking mural *New Dawn* for the Progressive Unionist Party. Danny Devenny is a veteran Republican who started painting as a prisoner in Long Kesh in the 1970s. He's best known for his mural of Bobby Sands. To celebrate the anniversary of Féile he has created a wall painting on Rockville Street that replicates Ballagh's iconic image of a flower shaped like a dove bursting out through a crack in a block of cement. "That's the Ballagh poster that most caught the imagination," said Adams. "It would be gimmicky if it wasn't done so tastefully. Bobby really can turn an image. I've always been taken by that quirkiness in his work. He mirrors the mood of the moment."

*Danny Devenny and Mark Ervine with the Guernica mural on the Falls Road, Belfast.*

Robert Ballagh looks himself in the eye. There's no dodging the look. The face he has painted stares back at him as in a mirror, grey-haired, grey-bearded and sixty-five. "Somebody said, My God, you're not as grey as that," he says, turning away. But painting is not a replication of life; it is its own reality. The truth is in the difference.

Every grey hair has been meticulously rendered. "Because oil paint has to dry, you do just a bit every day and then come back the next day and overlay it. You can keep on going for ever, but there comes a time when you say that's enough."

Patience is a hallmark of Ballagh's approach to painting. No detail is too small not to justify hours of careful attention. Michael Farrell kept urging him to loosen up, but he takes a craftsman's pleasure in getting everything right. The effect in his birthday portrait – a gift to himself – is hyper-real, much as in an early Chuck Close portrait, but smaller in scale. The self-image is direct and challengingly immediate. It's almost as if you're inside his skin.

Throughout his life, starting with a surprisingly confident self-portrait drawn as a 16-year-old in which he holds a freshly sharpened pencil and wears a jacket and tie, Ballagh has made a practice of appearing in his paintings in supporting roles, perhaps taking a cue from Rembrandt ('an actor painter', to quote critic Laura Cumming). His life is an ongoing study of himself and those around him, caught in unflinching detail, sometimes nude, as if by making sense of his circumstances he can begin to understand the world – finding in the particular the universal, as Joyce would maintain.

Apart from the greying hair and the sense of ageing, there has been surprisingly little change in how he looks. A photograph taken by David Davison forty years ago captures him hurrying somewhere, dressed in a duffel coat with long black hair and black-rimmed glasses, but he's easily recognisable as he eyes the camera in that defiantly aware way of his, taking everything in.

Although one of the most radical figures in Irish art and in the wider socio-political circumstances of Ireland, he is surprisingly conservative in his way of living and working. He lives in the same house he moved into when he married Betty, although they have gradually improved and modernised it. He goes each day to his studio in Arbour Hill – just as he did to his original studio in Parliament Street – like any other 9 to 5 office worker. He still has close friends from his days as a rock musician – braving the winter snows a few days ago to attend the funeral of 94-year-old musician Johnny Devlin, who helped him play the guitar – while continuing to accumulate friends with his easy gregarious manner and articulate way of making even the most complicated issues seem comprehensible.

He rarely loses his cool although he never hesitates to argue a point with anyone with whose ideas he disagrees. His political opinions have remained unapologetically consistent throughout his life, never shifting to suit the fashion of the moment or when it might have been more to his advantage to have kept quiet and said nothing.

Time and again the stubborn political positions he has taken and been denounced for – in particular his scepticism of free market capitalism, his early support for the peace process in the North and advocacy of dialogue with Sinn Féin, and his rejection

*Jens Peter Bonde* (2008)
*Oil on canvas. 76 x 50cm.*
*Private Collection.*

of the cult of the latest art isms – have been proved prescient by events although the jury is still out on his stance against the Lisbon Treaty, for which he received an award in Jutland before Christmas from the People's Movement of Denmark and later was invited back to elaborate on his views in the Danish Parliment. It could be argued that without the euro, Ireland would have been even more vulnerable to the catastrophic global repercussions triggered by Wall Street's collapse in October 2008.

With the re-running of the referendum due later in 2009 in an attempt by Bruxelles to reverse the 'No' verdict last June, politicians opposed to Lisbon are regular visitors to Ireland, among them the Danish MEP Jens Peter Bonde. After seeing Ballagh's portrait of Anthony Coughlan on a visit to the veteran campaigner's house, he contacted him for a portrait. Ballagh took lots of photographs and gathered together all of Bonde's books on the EU. "The idea for the portrait is to have him leaning on a pile of them."

He started *The Illustrator* self-portrait over a year ago, but it is still unfinished. It depicts him in typically defiant mood, flaunting a white T-shirt with the slogan 'Fuck the Begrudgers'. Although *Riverdance* has brought him international prestige and financial security – and with that success, much carping criticism – he still sees himself as someone outside the system, an artist for the people rather than the elite, speaking for the marginalised and the dispossessed.

"There is a bewildering democracy surrounding Ballagh," Patrick T Murphy noted in the RHA Retrospective catalogue. "Although he has regularly been at odds with the State on the rights of artists (tax exemption also a notable case) he has also been as near as one can be to being an official state artist... [while] his portraits show a similar diversity, from the celebration of Noël Browne who took on the church and the medical profession in the 1950s, to Michael O'Riordan, the recently deceased leader of the Communist Party in Ireland and the leader of Fianna Fáil Charles J Haughey."

But this is a contradiction common to many artists. From Renaissance Italy and the patronage of the Medicis through to today's state-subsidised art it could be argued that the role of artists is to bite the hand that feeds them. Goya was a court painter who spent much of his career portraying the Spanish royal family and other members of the court, but this didn't stop him painting *The Third of May* and other startling images of inhumanity. "The sleep of reason produces monsters," he said. He paid for his independence by ending his days an exile in Bordeaux. "All talent has a propensity to attack the strong," proclaimed the Romantic poet, Lord Byron. For all his fame, Delacroix was only admitted to the Académie des Beaux-Arts near the end of his life. He like Ballagh was inspired by Géricault, whose *Raft of the Medusa* was initially turned down by the Louvre following right-wing political pressure: the sale didn't go through until after his death in 1824, aged 33. Undaunted, he was by then planning paintings on the slave trade and the Inquisition. "Neither poetry nor painting can ever do justice to the horror and the anguish of the men on the raft," he said.

*The Illustrator* is complete apart from the arms and hands, which Ballagh has left blank. He's hoping to complete it for the RHA exhibition in May, at which he has been invited to show – although, perhaps typically, in advance publicity for the show no mention is made of Ballagh in a list of prominent painters exhibiting. "It's all I have, because the work has to be for sale and all my other works are commissions." He has detailed drawings and photographs for the arms and hands, but will have to leave them to one side. Commissions come first. *The Illustrator* had to give way to the Watson portrait, and then again to the *Medusa*. "I'd love to finish the rest of it now, but I can't."

That's because he's now working on a portrait of Fidel Castro. He has already painted a small preparatory version on paper, working from existing photographs: it wasn't possible to take any shots of his own. Since handing over power to his brother Raul in 2006, the 82-year-old Cuban leader hasn't been available to anyone outside his immediate circle – although he is an admirer of Ballagh's work and has a copy of *Legacy,* a print done to mark the 20th anniversary of the hunger strikes, hanging in his office. It was given to him by Gerry Adams on a visit to Cuba in December 2007. "This is a wonderful artist," Castro told Adams. "He has captured the spirit of those young Irish heroes."

The portrait is minimalist and avoids the usual pop art iconography commonly used to represent the Cuban Revolution. Castro is shown standing alone – "because in the end, you are alone" – as if caught by a spotlight on an empty stage. He is bare-footed and clasps a toga-like red flag around his otherwise naked body. He is facing into the wings, perhaps about to make an exit – "It's unlikely I'll be around to see Obama complete his first term in office," Castro said on welcoming the black American senator's election as 44th President of the United States of America.

The portrait is a deliberate deviation from Ballagh's normal approach of revealing someone through an inventory of their life: by depriving Castro of the familiar props associated with his image – the military fatigues, the Cuban flag, Che Guevara – it becomes possible to see the man rather than the myth. The influence is Velazquez's series of portraits of classical or mythological figures, using ordinary people as models. "He did a really fine one of Aesop," says Ballagh, "an old man who is clutching his fables." The eventual portrait will be slightly smaller than life-size, a proportion Ballagh likes. He's also using it for his *The Illustrator* self-portrait. "It looks life-size but if you measure it, it's smaller. Life-size looks bigger than life-size in a painting, and bigger-than-life looks gargantuan."

The final portrait will be somewhat different to the preparatory painting. "The client has seen it, loves it, but would like Castro to look a bit older. He said he'd search for some recent photos. But I quite like that head. I think if I just make the hair a little greyer, the skin a little paler and if I can get that tanned look out, it might go a long way to achieving the required result."

It's early January, a few days before Obama's inauguration. Obama has indicated on taking office he would begin to ease the blockade on Cuba, a first step toward normalising relationships between the two countries. With Raul Castro also adopting a pragmatic approach, allowing limited private enterprise and opening up society by lifting the ban on mobile phones, a peaceful transition from Cuba's isolation is conceivable.

"The position the Cubans are in is unsustainable. You can't have a socialist economy just in one island in the world. When

*Legacy* (2001)
*Limited edition print produced to mark the 20th anniversary of the 1981 hunger strikes.*

135

the Soviet Union collapsed, Cubans found themselves in what Castro called "the Special Period". It was a dire period. I don't know how they survived, but they did and they did it through imagination, creativity and determination, like devising different ways of making energy. Every vacant lot was turned into a vegetable patch. With miniscule resources and despite the US blockade they have created self-sufficiency in food and energy.

"The challenge now is to strike a balance – to provide the kind of freedom the people deserve and yet ensure that the people are served by society, not by the interests of the few. If they can strike that balance, they have every right to survive."

If Cuba is sailing into uncharted waters, so is Ireland – and indeed the entire global economy. Ballagh's homage to Géricault's *Raft of the Medusa* has taken on a chilling topicality with the meltdown of Wall Street, the failure of banks and the exposure of the deregulated free market economy as little more than an unregulated casino where an inept and unaccountable financial ruling elite gambled freely with other people's money on short-sold hedge funds and valueless sub-prime mortgages.

"We sit on the raft and wait, as Géricault's wretched crew and passengers did when their aristocratic captain and the army officers and their families commandeered the lifeboats and left them to drown," says Ballagh. "The Celtic Tiger bubble has burst. Our banks lent recklessly, allowing bankers to take out huge bonuses, and builders and developers borrowed recklessly. Most have now been caught out. Yet those who benefited little or not at all are being forced to pay the bill run up by others during those years of excess. The government thinks that the best way forward is to reward this incompetence by offering the banks an extraordinarily generous bailout with taxpayers' money."

Ballagh's *Raft of the Medusa* is to be exhibited in the Gorry Gallery in February, along with prints of *Liberty on the Barricades after Delacroix*, *The Third of May after Goya*, *The Rape of the Sabines after David*, and *Death of Marat after David* which inspired the new work. He has framed the painting in the manner of Géricault's time with a weighty gold-leaf border. The idea of putting on show a single large painting is also borrowed from the period. Paintings in the 18th and 19th century were often given gala premieres much like movies are today. Géricault's *Raft of the Medusa* opened at the Salon in the Louvre in August 1819 to controversial reviews. A London showing followed in June 1820 at William Bullock's Egyptian Hall in Piccadilly, and it reached Dublin a year later, attracting queues at the Rotunda.

"Bobby has a lot in common with Géricault," says Damian Mathews on a visit to the studio with a copy of the catalogue. "He has painted *Raft of the Medusa* in a style people can easily read, yet it is also a painting of quality." Several newspapers are to run articles on the painting, and Ballagh has been invited to appear with it on Pat Kenny's Late Late Show. "It's grabbed their attention. It's so topical, although it was conceived and painted long before the recession broke."

While even Gordon Brown, the British Prime Minister, now lectures on "the collapse of a failed laissez-faire dogma" and Barack Obama has forcefully rejected the "old theory that says we should give more to billionaires and big corporations and hope that prosperity trickles down to everyone else", Ballagh has argued this all along and been dismissed as a Marxist for doing so. He takes no pleasure in being proved right.

Paul Krugman, who won the Nobel Prize for economics in 2008, has argued in the *The New York Times* that America is not going to have a second Great Depression after all, even though the economic situation remains terrible. This is because the Obama administration responded to the crisis, not by slashing federal expenditure as its income from taxes fell drastically, but by pumping the economy and by stepping in to rescue the financial sector. Ireland, on the contrary, has committed itself to massive spending cuts, particularly in social welfare but also in the arts sector. "In the arts sector, we never had anything so perhaps the pain will not be as acute as in other sectors," says Ballagh, although an early casualty is the innovative Calypso Theatre Company, forced to close when it was unable to get an advance to pay wages. Never having had a bank loan or a mortgage – "because banks don't consider artists to be good risks" – Ballagh finds himself relatively immune to the consequences of the unregulated financial hubris he has been so articulate in denouncing.

It's not the best time to put *Medusa* up for sale, still less the prints and other works that are also on offer. "Whatever about its chances, I think we're in for a hiding. It'll certainly test the market." Up to now, prices for his paintings have been holding up. While shares were plummeting and banks collapsing on Wall Street in November, his painting *Girl Looking at a Patrick Scott* sold at a de Vere's auction for €36,000. Although Russian oligarchs like Chelsea football club's Roman Abramovich squandered £43 million on Francis Bacon's *Triptych 1976* and £17 million on Lucien Freud's *Benefits Supervisor Sleeping* last summer, and Damien Hirst, by-passing galleries and selling new works direct through Sothebys, picked up £98 million in September, art markets globally are slumping. November sales at Sothebys were down to $160 million from $418 million for the same month in 2007.

Investment money traditionally runs for cover to the art market during a slump, but art prices had become so inflated that trust in the worth of contemporary art in particular began to dissipate. Like sub-prime mortgages and derivatives and various other Wall Street concoctions that had no reality other than the hype with which they were marketed – typified by Bernie Madoff's $70 billion pyramid scam which had no cash behind it other than what he kept taking from fresh investors to pay off earlier investors – too much of it was based solely on talk and the spurious fame of its purveyors. Art prices and the stock exchange became two sides of the same worthless coin. Much of the money driving art sales came from hedge funds that speculated in spurious stocks and helped fuel the Wall Street slump by selling short otherwise solvent companies.

Conceptualism had its roots in Marcel Duchamp's idea that putting a urinal in a gallery made it art. It soon became apparent that there didn't even need to be a urinal – the idea of it being art was in itself art or as Tom Wolfe quipped, "seeing is believing has given way to believing is seeing". This rejection of the art object came partly out of an understandable urge to liberate art from the market, which in the 20th century exploited the scarcity value of major and even lesser works to inflate their commercial auction price to ludicrous levels. As my essay in the catalogue for Ballagh's 2006 retrospective argued, the "conceptualist attempt

*D J Carey's Hurley (2007)*
*Oil on canvas. 122 x 46cm.*
*Private Collection.*

to reinvent art as something purely intellectual and intangible instead of a concrete object didn't stop its commodification. All that changed was that the person of the artist became commodified instead, leading to a form of celebrity art that had no substance other than the fame of the artist, fed by the voracious appetite of the global media for the sensation of the moment. Life is a reality TV show, suicide bombing the ultimate performance art. When the loyalist gun-man Michael Stone attempted to break into Stormont and assassinate members of the Executive, he claimed he was in fact creating a performance art work.

Political spin operates in a parallel world where the idea of things matters more than the things themselves. Prime ministers and presidents are elected on the basis of how they're put across on TV rather than any actual ability to govern. Embedded reporters provide commentary on push-button warfare in which the horrific actuality of death and destruction is hidden behind self-serving double-speak such as Bush's "war on terror" and Blair's "defence of democracy". Conceptualism is the institutionalised avant-garde of an era that is all about presentation rather than substance.

Although Ballagh rejected conceptualism when he broke with modernism in the mid-1970s, he has always been a conceptualist. One of his most striking political works was a completely conceptual gesture – chalking the outline of the bodies of people gunned down by the British Army on Bloody Sunday on the floor of the Project Arts Centre in 1972, making it the scene of a crime. His work is about thinking and reading. Critic Liam Kelly argues that it "is primarily about ideas rather than feelings. It is cerebral rather than intuitive". But the concept is nothing until it is realised in an object. The object of art for Ballagh is the object itself, the handmade thing. "To deny the physical connection between the viewer and the artist that an original work provides is irrational. I absolutely believe that it is part of the human condition to appreciate the well-made object."

Earlier in his career he sought to eliminate all trace of brush marks from his paintings, inspired by Walter Benjamin's argument that in the age of mechanical reproduction the fact that countless prints could be made from a photographic negative rendered meaningless the idea than any one print was 'authentic'. Yet while an image can exist apart from a painting, there is a yearning in people who see and admire its reproduction to go to the Louvre or the Prado – as Ballagh did as a young painter – to see the original in all its uniqueness. "To me art is a sensuous engagement with materials," he says. "It's going back to the primitive thing from the cave man onwards. It's taking something and making it. When you're face to face with a painting or a sculpture, you're actually coming face to face with the marks that were made by the artist and have survived through many centuries. You look at a painting by Velazquez and his fingerprint is on the canvas, so he's alive for you at that moment." Or as James Watson might say, it has the DNA of the artist all over it.

◆

*Bloody Sunday* (1972)
*Chalk outlines and blood.*

Architectural plans are spread out on Ballagh's work-table. They outline a community landmark to signify the entrance to the new Gaeltacht quarter on the Falls Road in Belfast. It's derived from a series of labyrinths already exhibited by Brian O'Doherty in plywood form in several museums in the US. O'Doherty is collaborating with Ballagh to fashion a stone version as the centrepiece of a little pocket park to be situated in line with An Cultúrlan. The park is inspired by a small space nestling amid skyscrapers on 5th and 6th Avenue in New York, close to the Museum of Modern Art.

"We want it to be a small urban oasis where people can sit down, or just walk through," says Ballagh. "Sometimes urban spaces appear to be closed off, but this invites you in. It's a sort of metaphor for the two communities in Belfast, where one community feels the other one is closed off from it. The labyrinth, although appearing closed off, in fact has a way through it."

The plan of the labyrinth creates a version of St Bridget's Cross, Ireland's iconic symbol of peace. "So we're going to set in the paving an actual bronze relief of a real St Bridget's Cross, almost like a bit of treasure to be discovered by the visitor." The £200,000 commission is jointly funded by Belfast City Council and the Northern Ireland Arts Council, as well as local groups.

Ballagh is just back from quarries on Black Mountain where amid snowstorms he checked out suitable stone. "If you look at Black Mountain from Lisburn rather than from Belfast you'll discover that the whole mountain has been hollowed out. But this hasn't been allowed to affect the skyline. So it's like a set on a film lot."

Although O'Doherty and Ballagh are eager to use local materials connected to the community, this may not be possible. "The stone I saw looked a bit shale-like, which means it would chip. We may not be able to get out the 18-inch blocks we need." If this is the case, they may have to import the stone – which Ballagh had to do when he created a black marble monolith in Leitrim to commemorate John Joe McGirl, the Sinn Féin TD.

As always with a commission, Ballagh has immersed himself in researching the nature of the new materials he is unaccustomed to working with. "My knowledge of geology goes back to school. What I do remember is that basalt is an igneous rock, in other words a molten rock which came up millions of years ago and then cooled to form the Giant's Causeway. True basalt is an igneous rock but I suspect the Black Mountain is metamorphic or rock that was originally formed through sedimentation, a kind of layering over the millennia. When the magma came up it transformed the sedimentary rock into a harder metamorphic rock, but it was still not an igneous rock. If the Black Mountain rock is in any way layered, it's no use to us. Kids will have it hacked to bits."

The James Watson portrait meanwhile is now hanging in the new Trinity College genetics building designed by Scott, Tallon & Walker. It's in a spot chosen by Ballagh on the first landing of the central glass-roofed atrium. "Facing the staircase on each landing is a large wall, but this is just right for it because it's a big picture and needs a lot of white space. It's in good company. George Dawson, who founded the department fifty years ago, was a great art collector, so there's art all over the place." Back when Ballagh

*Architectural model for public art work on the Falls Road, Belfast.*

was studying architecture at Bolton Street Technical College, he learned from Robin Walker, a disciple of the minimalist Mies van der Rohe in Chicago and until his death a partner in Scott, Tallon & Walker, that there had to be a reason behind everything you did, that form follows function. "Everything turns full circle. The same names keep recurring in my life."

Having drawn on his early 1970s paintings for *Medusa*, he's now taking photographs for an updated version of his personal and quirky long-out-of-print 1981 book, *Dublin*. "The only copy I have is my parent's copy. Someone I know who couldn't even find it on Amazon eventually saw a copy in a second-hand bookshop in New York, which he bought for $50."

The idea to re-photo Dublin was put to him by designer Conor Gallagher, who he met at an art show. A couple of weeks later Gallagher rang to ask what he'd need to get him going. Ballagh explained that when Philip McDermott approached him about the original book, they hadn't discussed a fee. It was enough for McDermott to cover the photographic expenses. Later if they thought they had a book they could decide what they'd do. "Well if you're happy with that, I'll do the same," said Gallagher. Next day he called to the studio with 40 rolls of film. "Suddenly I was obliged to take the whole thing seriously."

Michael Scott's Busarus was the only modern building to feature in the original book. "Dublin at that stage hadn't really changed from Joyce's time. But now it's almost totally changed." The Luas has transformed suburban villages like Dundrum into cosmopolitan towns, bustling with supermarkets, designer fashion shops, and up-market department stores like Harvey Nicholls, The House of Fraser and Marks & Spencer, as well as gourmet restaurants and cinema multiplexes. "There's a much quoted image in the old book of a guy standing outside a betting shop at the Red Cow in Clondalkin which looks desolate, there's nothing there. Now the site is covered by the busiest motorway junction in Ireland. So I feel the photographs should be about change."

It's prompted him to change his camera. He used his Rollieflex with its square format on the first book. It was ideal for photographing subjects for portraits. He regarded his photographs merely as tools for painting, not as art. Although the Dublin book changed that, he never had time to develop it much further. His interest was reawakened when David Davison suggested that he might switch to a Japanese Mamiya 645 camera, which has a 64m x 45m format rather than square. "That obviously changed my vision, because you're looking into a viewfinder which is giving you a different perspective. It has two lenses. One is pretty standard and gives you a view rather like the Rollei used to do, but the other is slightly wide-angle and was a revelation to me. It just changes the way you see everything. I'm kind of still struggling with it. I've shot off seven or eight rolls, but I have to say I have very little that is publishable so far. But I'm kind of enjoying it."

The other morning he took the Mamiya up the Dublin Mountains. "It was just gorgeous up there with a fresh fall of snow. I got out and walked along the Military Road across the Featherbeds. I must have been about a half-mile from the car. Suddenly the weather changed. The sky went black and a snow storm came down. I struggled back to the car. I suddenly understood how people die on mountains. I was freezing."

He doesn't know whether he got any good pictures. "It looked lovely through the viewfinder. Let's see if I had the right settings and did the right things. The Mamiya still uses film. I didn't take the brave step into the digital world."

Betty's brother has died. He was separated from the family, but family is family. There is a funeral to arrange. Ballagh dislikes what he regards as the religious charade that accompanies death. He remembers a priest reading prayers when his mother was in the mortuary at St Vincent's Hospital. "We didn't ask for him, but he was there. He began, and then broke off mid-prayer to ask, 'What's her name?' The whole thing was like a conveyor belt. There'll be no religious ceremony when I die. I want all my organs to go to medicine and my body to be cremated."

The New Year was ushered in by spectacular fireworks displays watched around the world by millions of TV viewers, while a flick of a button away the sky over Gaza was lit up by deadly explosions and phosphorous shells as Israel forces "softened up" the civilian population in preparation for a full-scale ground invasion. With Obama about to take office and an election of their own imminent, the Israeli government decided to attempt to oust or degrade the elected Hamas government – or what they termed "the Iran-backed terrorist group" – while they still had a free hand, fully aware that such an assault on a densely populated area smaller than the Isle of Man already subjected to an 18-month blockade and desperately short of basic medical and food supplies would inevitably result in horrific civilian casualties. Bush dutifully facilitated their action – in almost his last decision in office – by ordering a US abstention on a UN Security Council resolution demanding a ceasefire which in effect left Israel free to ignore it. After 20 days and with most of Gaza in rubble including the UN headquarters, the conflict has cost 1,300 Palestinian lives – many of them women and children who had nowhere to hide – and 13 Israeli lives.

Ballagh took part in a mass protest, marching with about 3,000 other citizens from the Central Bank to the Israeli Embassy in Ballsbridge. At a press conference earlier in the week to publicise the demonstration, a reporter from the *Irish Times* asked if the organising committee was making plans to avoid "the unpleasant things" that happened outside the Dáil the previous week when

*Dublin Zoo, New Year's Day, 2010.*
Photo: Robert Ballagh

*Gaza* (2009)
*Limited edition print.*

some Palestinians had burned an Israeli flag.

"I think we have to have some sense of proportion," Ballagh replied. "Not that I support burning flags, but I was at a demonstration at the GPO on New Year's Day and I was introduced to a young Palestinian woman who lives here and who so far has lost five members of her family. I think I can understand why someone like that might make a gesture like that. But let's keep a sense of proportion. Burning a flag hardly compares with dropping phosphorous bombs on civilians."

Gaza's destruction is eerily similar to that of the Basque town of Guernica, on which German and Italian planes rained down incendiary bombs on 26 April 1937– killing 1,700 of its 5,000 inhabitants – as part of Franco's policy of wiping out resistance with a disproportionate show of force. Civilians trying to escape from the carnage were then gunned down as they were in Gaza.

Picasso's fearsome painting – a masterpiece of engaged art which was painted around the same time as Pablo Neruda wrote his chilling lines, "The blood is on the street, The blood is on the streets" – has ensured that Guernica will never be forgotten, although the war crimes that inspired it are sadly repeated again and again, most recently in Gaza. Its power is such that the famous UN replica of the painting was covered over in 2003 to avoid displeasing the US representatives when they sought approval for their 'Shock and Awe' aerial bombardment of Baghdad.

Ballagh has designed a limited edition print of a black-eyed woman, with a tear running down her cheek, to raise much-needed medical aid for Gaza. The print was supported by the Irish Congress of Trade Unions and through sales made €56,000 which will help fund in Gaza what will be called the James Connolly Operating Theatre.

Ballagh has no hesitation in taking to the streets in protest against war and oppression, or in support of the marginalised and the dispossessed. He might be powerless as an artist if, as WH Auden claimed, "poetry makes nothing happen," but as a citizen he can and does register his dissent. He feels an obligation to be an active member of the society into which he was born, what the American political theorist Benjamin Barber calls "the free space in which democratic attitudes are cultivated and democratic behaviour conditioned".

Barber argues that citizenship has been eroded by rampant consumerisim, and sees in the economic meltdown that has plunged global finances into the worst crisis since the Great Depression "the bankruptcy of the idea that we don't need to be citizens. What citizens would have done, had they involved themselves in this, would have been to insist on regulatory oversight and democratic surveillance."

Seamus Heaney reflected this year that the "writer is expected to address the violence all around you." He has done so in his poetry when the occasion demanded, particularly in *The Tolland Man* and the poem *The Strand at Lough Beg*. "You're in the 'polis' as a writer," he said, "if you like, the 'city state'." Overwhelmed by the level of bloodshed in Northern Ireland in the late 1980s he expressed a longing in his collection *Seeing Things* to get "shot of the burden of civic responsibility".

The sense of burden he felt has perhaps now been lifted by the peace process and the success of the power-sharing executive that brought Sinn Féin into government in the North with the Democratic Unionist Party. Such is the speed of change that on Good Friday this year Ballagh found himself in a café in loyalist East Belfast sharing a healthy Ulster fry with Andy Tyrie, a former leader of the Ulster Defence Association (UDA) and a key figure in the 1974 loyalist workers strike – he narrowly escaped assassination in a car bomb attack in 1988 – and with Sammy Douglas, currently a political adviser to Peter Robinson, successor to Ian Paisley as First Minister in the executive.

"As we were standing outside," says Ballagh, "everyone was saying Hi'ya Andy, Hi'ya Sammy, much as nationalists might in West Belfast to Gerry Adams." The previous Wednesday, while in Belfast with Brian O'Doherty to discuss their Falls Road sculpture commission, Ballagh was introduced to Douglas by Mairtín ÓMuilleóir at the launch of a print he did for An Cultúrlan. "Douglas said he'd love me to come and have a look at what they were doing about 're-imagining' Protestant working-class culture – the sort of thing that had been done years before in West Belfast, moving away from murals of IRA men with balaclavas and armalites."

Before breakfast Tyrie took Ballagh and O'Doherty on a walk-around to see where local people had painted over what might be considered sectarian murals and replaced them with positive images of the community. As part of this process, groups from East Belfast visited An Cultúrlan to perform Scottish dancing and Ulster Scots songs while people from West Belfast responded with Irish dancing and Irish music and poetry. "This is all a bit under the radar, but it's the best way," says Ballagh. "It's being done at a community level. It's not being imposed from above. There is this dialogue and cultural exchange going on. I've always argued that there has to be a better way than the armed struggle, and the better way is politics. In politics, as someone once said, you don't advance by talking to your friends, you must talk to your enemies. Debate and discussion and confronting our differences are all part of that."

When they were parting, Douglas gave him a book on Ulster Scots, in which he had written a dedication, 'To Robert Ballagh, Beannachtaí na Casca' (Easter blessings).

Some time before his death in 2008, the playwright Harold Pinter said, "The citizen has responsibilities to scrutinise the society in which we live quite vigorously. I still haven't stopped doing that. And I don't intend to stop either." He didn't see his political engagement as in any way compromising his art. Nor does Robert Ballagh, nor should he. Continuing in the tradition of Goya and Géricault, he too is a citizen artist.

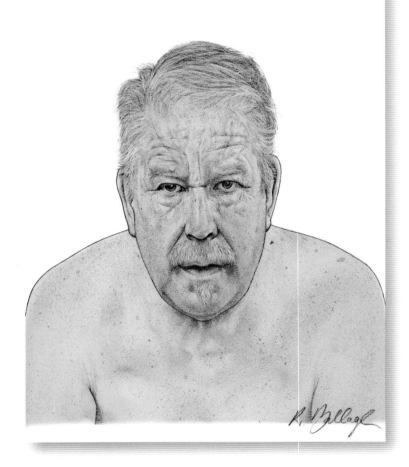

*Study - Self Portrait III (2010)*
*Pencil, water colour and gouache on paper.*


Afterword

Robert Ballagh drove slowly down an awkward hill turning into the cul-de-sac where he lives, a short, narrow terraced lane with a pavement on one side and a 12ft high stone wall on the other. His way was blocked by a parked van with a Northern registration. He got out and approached the driver. "You're parked on double yellow lines," he pointed out. "You're causing an obstruction. People can't get in or out of where they live."

The driver got out, a big man in his twenties. He gestured to a 'For Sale' sign on one of the houses. "Aw," he said, "why don't you put one of those fucking signs on your house?" With that, he unleashed a succession of punches to Ballagh's chest, knocking him to the ground. "I never saw someone lose their temper so quickly or so viciously," says Ballagh. "If he'd had a knife he'd have killed me."

We're in his Arbour Hill studio later that afternoon. Even as he talks a swelling begins to appear on his right cheek. He has problems breathing. His side hurts so bad he can't lift a portrait he's just finished of Peter McKenna, the former master of the Rotunda Hospital: he has to lower it down and shove it along the floor. "I'm the walking wounded. I've never felt threatened on the streets anywhere I've gone in the world, and now I'm beaten up on my own doorstep in Dublin."

He reluctantly agrees to see a doctor the next day. It turns out he has hairline fractures to his jaw and two of his ribs. He reported the matter to the police, nothing happened however; apparently they lost the file. It's not as if he needed any intimation of the transience of life or his own mortality. Since he completed the portrait of Castro, which shows the Cuban leader naked apart from a red flag, an old man nearing the end of his life, he has being working on a series of self-portraits, eight large drawings and eight oil paintings for which the drawings are explorations (although the drawings stand on their own as drawings, and are argueably even more compelling). Each drawing and painting is a head and shoulders close-up, without clothes or any other prop, observed with a forensic precision that lays bare the process of ageing: September 2010 marks his 67th birthday and he is already a pensioner with a travel card.

The impulse to subject himself to such scrutiny came from a suggestion by Wexford Arts Centre, who approached him about the possibility of doing a show. Was there anything he hadn't done, or that he'd like to do. Someone noticed the Castro portrait lying against the wall in his studio. "Could you do something like that?" "Well, not really. But I could possibly do a small series of self-portraits."

Out of this came the idea of approaching portraiture in a way that engaged with timelessness, avoiding anything that would associate it with any particular place or period. "I became really engaged both on an artistic level in trying to do these pictures, but also on a more philosophical level in terms of the whole nature of self-portraiture and what makes it interesting. Self-portraiture is a kind of inner thing. When people walk into a gallery, they look differently at self-portraits than at other pictures. What's that all about? Then it dawned on me that initially you think the artist is looking at you, but then you realise he's not looking at you, he's looking at his reflection in a mirror."

Until the middle of the 19th century the only way you could do a self-portrait was through using a mirror, something that can cause uneasiness. Oscar Wilde explored this ambivalence in his much-filmed (and dramatised) 1891 novel, *The Picture of Dorian Gray*, a cautionary horror tale of a gorgeous youth who wishes his painted likeness would grow old while he remains eternally young. He gets his wish but there's a twist: his portrait bears the mark not only of his age but of his sins, taunting him with the emptiness of his life. To escape its gruesome reflection, he attacks it with a knife – an act of rage and despair that causes him to age instantly, becoming the depraved figure in the portrait, decomposed and dead.

"Over-indulgence with one's reflection has been seen negatively in our culture, from Narcissus to the Queen in *Snow White and the Seven Dwarfs* who asks: 'Mirror, mirror on the wall, who is the fairest one of all?' People are suspicious of self-portraiture. Why is this guy looking at himself so much? There's a kind of sub-conscious presumption that vanity is part of it all. But with very few exceptions I don't think that is the case. Rather than self-regard, artists trying to capture their likeness represent a quest for self-knowledge - a different thing entirely."

True to the demand by Oliver Cromwell that he was to be depicted 'warts and all', and not unlike Jack Nicholson who, in his later films, almost revels in the physical manifestations of age – his flabby skin, his paunch, his balding head – there is no inclination by Ballagh to glamorise his appearance: this is how it is to be a man approaching seventy. He has stripped himself bare, confronting the physical essence of his ageing face and body. Nothing is allowed distract from this inescapable reality: even his glasses have been discarded as a distraction: "When you see old photographs of yourself with glasses, you think, Gawd, they look hopelessly old fashioned!"

This paring away of anything that might provide a clue to the subject's life other than the subject itself is a radical departure for Ballagh - although it is foreshadowed by the Castro portrait, which clearly presents the image of a man preparing to step off the stage of life: as the Bible says, naked we come into the world and naked we leave it. "Many of the portraits I painted in the past included lots of objects and references that have a symbolic purpose. These show just the figure, nothing else."

There are eight different poses in Ballagh's series of self-portraits: some are looking sideways, others are head on. Disturbingly, one shows him with his eyes shut. "Rachel, my daughter hates it. She thinks it's like a death mask. I think it's a lot of things. When you close your eyes you are shutting yourself off. So why wouldn't you have your eyes wide shut, given what has

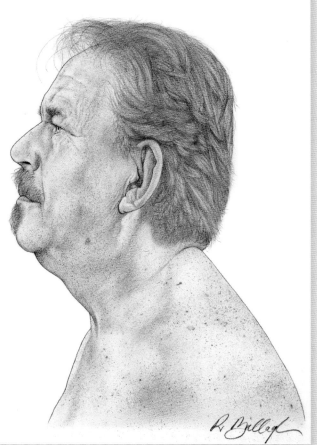

*Study - Self Portrait IV (2010)*
*Pencil and water colour on paper.*

*The Ballagh Monograph* (2010)
Limited edition.
Photo: Kip Carroll

happened to Ireland." To his own surprise, one of the side-views is eerily like his mother. "I suppose certain genetic things become evident as you age, just as when you are a baby."

Unlike Rembrandt, Goya or other classical self-portrayers who employed mirrors to pin down a likeness, Ballagh uses photographs. This raises interesting issues about the prejudice that still exists in some quarters that photography is inherently dishonest. "When you examine a self-portrait in terms of being constructed from using a reflection in a mirror, you have to consider the laws of optics. The self-portrait generated that way provides the viewer with a view of the artist that is not what a person would see looking at the artist, because the mirror image is laterally reversed. By using a photograph as a reference for a self-portrait, you're actually more truthfully presenting yourself to the world than by using a mirror. If you're using a mirror, you're seeing fleeting images of yourself and you're trying to construct a single static image from these fleeting images. If you look at the famous portrait of Van Gogh with the bandaged ear, you could be excused for saying, yeah, it's the right ear that's damaged, because as the portrait sits before you it is the right ear. But of course he must have painted it from his reflection, so in fact it's his left ear that he mutilated."

No artist has been more fascinated by his own persona than Rembrandt, painting self-portraits at every stage of his life with rigorous frankness, as if his changing face was a map to the human soul. When X-rays were made of a famous self-portrait at Kenwood House in London, showing him as an old man, it was discovered that he had changed the palette from the incorrect hand in his reflected version. "He must have realised, Oh no, I'm not left-handed, I'm right-handed. So he flipped it around."

Even though nominally people have two eyes, two nostrils, two ears, two cheeks and there's a nominal symmetry about faces, they're not symmetrical. "If you take a photograph of someone and cut it in half down the centre, then throw the right side out and flip the left side so that the two lefts form a whole, if faces were symmetrical this should produce a perfect representation of the person but in fact you will have an image that looks like someone else entirely."

Ballagh booked his regular collaborator David Davison for a photo session to create a range of shots as reference for his self-portraits. "I just pulled faces and we tried different lighting. For the first few I had a shirt on. The difference in being bare-chested is quite extraordinary. There's no such thing as neutral clothes: they're all tied to a time and a fashion. Even when we think we're wearing something neutral it's saying something. All I wanted to be there was me."

With digital photography the image pops up on the monitor immediately. "So there was a lot of control over the images we captured. From the selection of shots David produced I chose eight, trying to have eight different views of the same face, expressing different emotions and feelings. Only one could be considered in any way flattering."

The studio is stacked with cardboard boxes containing copies of the limited edition two-volume monograph combining my earlier 1986 Ballagh biography with a version of this book. An edition of 350 copies were hand-made in Amsterdam with each of

the two volumes illustrated with 12 original gyclée prints of key Ballagh works. Dermot Desmond, the collector and businessman, took up half the edition and the remaining 175 copies went on sale at the Gorry Gallery. "That level of craft costs a lot of money. You'd never design a conventional book like that, but it has surprised me by doing very well."

His work table has drawings for a theatrical set for a new Dermot Bolger play *The Parting Glass*, a one-man show to be performed by Ray Yeates at the Axis Art Centre in Ballymun. "It's a kind of sequel to Dermot's play *In High Germany*, again using football and the World Cup as a metaphor for changes in Ireland."

Apart from the McKenna portrait which, unexpectedly perhaps, provides no clue to the subject's career as a gynaecologist and hospital administrator ("it was painted with the experience of my more recent work"), Ballagh is also working on a small portrait of Captain James Kelly, a scapegoat in the 1970 Arms Trial. "His family are still fighting to clear his reputation. His daughter Sylvia, who lives in England, was over here to place flowers on his grave. She visited the National Gallery where she saw my portrait of James Connolly and thought, if only we had a picture of daddy like that. So I obliged."

Ballagh was in Washington for the unveiling on Capitol Hill of his portrait of the murdered Northern Ireland human rights lawyer Pat Finucane. "I worked on photographs provided by his son Michael and painted a head and shoulders portrait that is kind of shattered, like my Miami Showband print, to symbolise violent death." His visit to the United States coincided with the 15th-anniversary performance of *Riverdance* at Radio City which followed a 10-city Asian tour culminating in Seoul.

He is preparing a talk about his 1977 autobiographical painting *No 3* to tie in with an exhibition of Irish self-portraiture at the Hugh Lane Municipal Gallery. The painting shows Ballagh with his wife Betty and children Rachel and Bruce standing in front of their terraced home at No 3 Temple Cottages. As a joke he is hiding his face behind an open copy of a book entitled 'How To Make Your Art Commercial', an ironic comment on the fact that although he had already achieved something of a reputation, he was still on and off the dole. "*No 3* belongs to a strand of portraiture in which the artist stubbornly refuses to show his likeness. For instance, Vermeer's *The Art of Painting* shows the artist in his studio painting the portrait of a woman, but his back is to the viewer. I used this figure in *The Conversation* showing myself, glimpsed through a doorway into the same room, facing him across a table."

The idea of paintings as a means of dialogue is a recurring element in Ballagh's approach to art, whether in his early series showing people looking at modern paintings in a gallery or his series of pop art versions of Goya, Delacroix, David and Ingres, as well as several paintings such as *The Conversation* or *Winter in Ronda*, a family portrait inspired by Velazquez's *Las Meninas*. He has shown himself chatting with James Joyce and sitting in on an argument between Patrick Pearse and James Connolly. He has embraced stamps, banknotes, public art, sculpture, murals, medals, book covers, supermarket commissions and theatre design in the hope of communicating with as wide an audience as possible, using a visual language that is universally accessible.

As Ballagh immersed himself in this new series of self-portraits it became apparent to him that self-portraits are the

*Ray Yeates in Dermot Bolger's play*
*'The Parting Glass'.*

ultimate form of dialogue through art. The philosopher George Berkeley argued that you can only exist when you are perceived, much as a stone in the desert doesn't exist until someone sees it. Similarly, self-portraiture more than other forms of portraiture is something that lives in a limbo until it is observed. Laura Cumming in her recent book *A Face to the World* described how when you go into a gallery and are confronted by the gaze of an artist's self-portrait, it seems as if they have being waiting for you.

To Ballagh, a self-portrait is in the first place a monologue in which the artist is confronting his own image, whether in photos or mirrors, and "that monologue only becomes a dialogue when an observer becomes involved. In a way the creative process is only concluded when an observer becomes part of the dynamic. Whereas when an artist paints someone else, there's a dialogue already going on. In a way you – the observer – are almost an intruder in this exchange. The artist and the sitter have been talking and are engaged in their particular scenario. When you come in as an observer you're almost intruding in their ongoing dialogue."

Back in the 1980s, the Uffizi Gallery in Florence invited Ballagh to donate a work to their renowned collection of self-portraits, which includes pieces by Rembrandt and Velazquez. He declined ("I was probably foolish, a case of the head ruling the heart") because he was then chairman of the Artists Association of Ireland which was trying to encourage a policy of artists not giving their work away for nothing. On a visit to the Art Institue of Chicago some years later he came across work by the American painter Ivan Albright had been invited to donate to the Uffizi, but he had accepted. He was quite old at the time but it stimulated him to embark on a series of over twenty self-portraits which he painted over the last three years of his life.

Albright was known as "the Edgar Allan Poe of painting" because of his obsession with inexorable decay. One of his better-known works was the title painting for Albert Lewin's 1943 film version of *The Picture of Dorian Gray* portraying the utter degeneration of what had once been a man of incredible beauty. "It matters little whether I paint a squash, a striped herring, or a man," Albright once said. "The space, the light, the motion, the position have one thing in common – decay."

Ballagh's cool minimalist style has little in common with Albright's bleak expressionism and thickly laid on paint surfaces, but his self-portraits share Albright's confrontational view of the relationship between the artist and old age. "The early paintings in the series are searingly honest, warts-and-all self-portraits. And then in the middle of the series Albright had a stroke. The paintings were still honest, but the facilities were slipping. The last ones, made on his deathbed, simply feature shadowy impressions of his mouth and eyes."

Albright's dying work is a confirmation that self-portraiture is not vanity or self-regard. It is about introspection, self-examination and self-knowledge. "It's about confronting what happens in life," says Ballagh. "We all age. We all die. That's what we face."

# Gallery
## 1969-2010

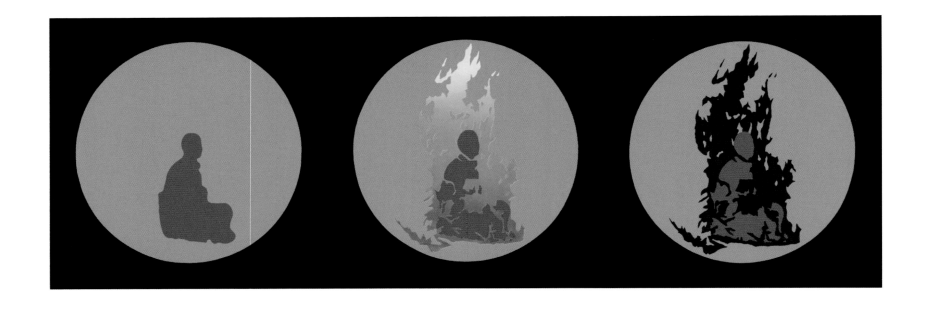

**Burning Monk** *(1969)*
*Acrylic on canvas. 71 x 213cm*
*Collection: Irish Museum of Modern Art.*

*The Rape of the Sabines after David* (1970)
Acrylic on canvas, 183 x 244cm
Collection: Crawford Art Gallery, Cork.

*Liberty on the Barricades after Delacroix* (1970)
*Acrylic on canvas. 183 x 244cm*
*Collection: Irish Museum of Modern Art.*

**The Turkish Bath after Ingres** *(1971)*
*Acrylic on canvas. 183 x 183cm*
*Private Collection.*

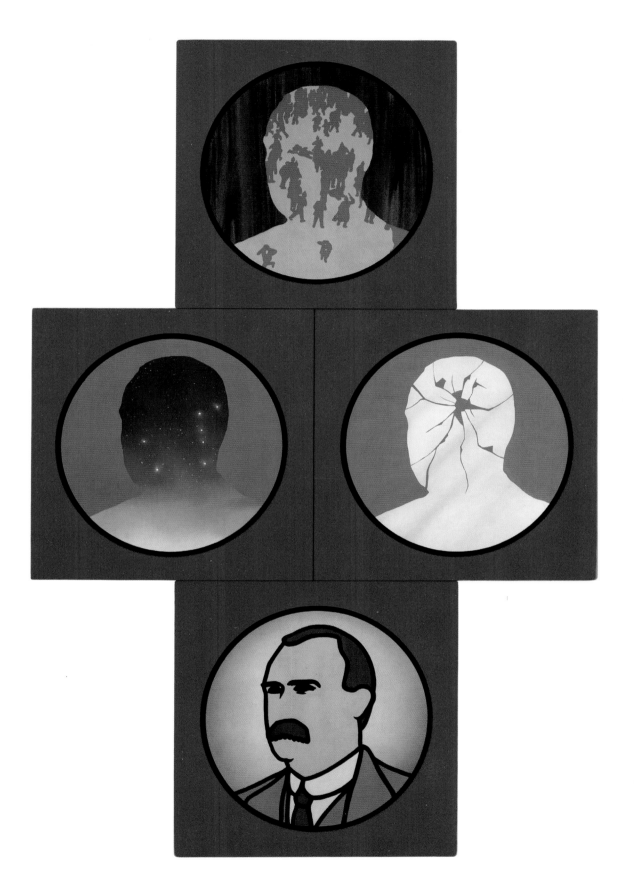

**Woman and a Pierre Soulages** *(1972)*
*Acrylic on canvas. 244 x 122cm*
*Collection: Bank of Ireland.*

*Two Men and a Picasso* (1975)
Acrylic and oil on canvas. 65 x 65cm
Private Collection.

*Laurence Sterne* (1975)
*Acrylic and oil on canvas. 91 x 180cm*
*Private Collection.*

*Rachel/Marilyn* (1976)
*Oil on canvas, 152 x 122cm*
*Collection: Crawford Art Gallery, Cork.*

*No.3* *(1977)*
*Acrylic and oil on canvas, 183 x 244cm*
*Collection: Dublin City Gallery, The Hugh Lane.*

*The Conversation* *(1977)*
*Acrylic and oil on canvas. 183 x 244cm*
*Collection: Allied Irish Bank.*

*Brendan Smith* (1978)
*Oil on canvas. 152 x 152cm*
*Collection: Olympia Theatre, Dublin.*

*James Plunkett* (1978)
Acrylic and oil on canvas. 152 x 122cm
Private Collection.

*Bernadette Greevy* (1979)
*Oil on canvas with recorded sound. 122 x 122cm*
*Collection: Irish Museum of Modern Art.*

*Inside No.3* (1979)
Acrylic and oil on canvas. 182 x 182cm
Collection: Ulster Museum.

*Winter in Ronda* (1979)
*Oil on canvas. 183 x 244cm*
*Collection: The Central Bank of Ireland.*

167

***Hugh Leonard*** *(1979)*
*Oil on canvas. 122 x 152cm*
*Collection: The Abbey Theatre, Dublin.*

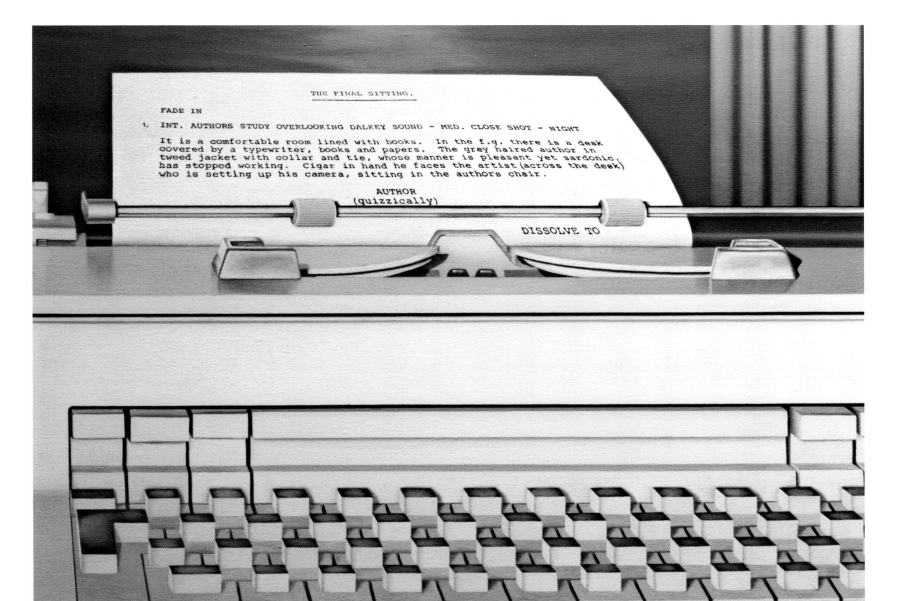

THE FINAL SITTING.

FADE IN

1. INT. AUTHORS STUDY OVERLOOKING DALKEY SOUND - MED. CLOSE SHOT - NIGHT

It is a comfortable room lined with books.  In the f.g. there is a desk
covered by a typewriter, books and papers.  The grey haired author in
tweed jacket with collar and tie, whose manner is pleasant yet sardonic,
has stopped working.  Cigar in hand he faces the artist (across the desk)
who is setting up his camera, sitting in the authors chair.

AUTHOR
(quizzically)

DISSOLVE TO

*Hugh Leonard (Detail)* (1979)
The Irish director Kieran Hickey provided Ballagh with the original script for Douglas Sirk's 'Captain Moonlight', which was
shot in Ireland, so that he could write the imagined film script for Leonard's typewriter.

***Charles J Haughey*** *(1980)*
*Oil on canvas. 122 x 152cm*
*Private Collection.*

170

*Michael Scott* (1980)
*Oil on canvas. 92 x 92cm*
*Private Collection.*

**The Downes Family at Knocktillane** *(1981)*
*Oil on canvas. 122 x 152cm*
*Private Collection.*

*Inside No.3 after Modernisation* (1982)
*Acrylic and oil on canvas. 231 x 152cm*
*Private Collection.*

**Upstairs No.3** *(1982/83)*
*Oil on canvas. 183 x 183cm*
*Private Collection.*

174

*Highfield* (1983/84)
Oil on canvas. 185 x 137cm
Private Collection.

*Homage to Dürer* (1984)
Oil on canvas. 62 x 122cm
Collection: The Albrecht Dürer House, Nuremberg.

*Noël Browne* (1985)
*Oil on canvas with books and stones. 183 x 137cm*
*Collection: The National Gallery of Ireland.*

***The Fastnet Lighthouse*** *(1986)*
*Oil on canvas. 92 x 61cm*
*Collection: Commissioners of Irish Lights.*

*In the Heart of the Hibernian Metropolis* (1988)
*Oil on canvas. 60 x 80cm*
*Private Collection.*

179

**Carmencita Hederman, Lord Mayor of Dublin** (1988)
*Oil on canvas. 92 x 92cm*
*Collection: Dublin City Council.*

*Upstairs No.4* (1989)
Oil on canvas. 198 x 152cm
Private Collection, on loan to St. James Hospital, Dublin.

**Michael O'Riordan** (1989)
Oil on canvas. 152 x 122cm
Private Collection.

**Oscar Wilde** (1990)
*Oil on canvas. 92 x 61cm*
*Collection: The Gate Theatre, Dublin.*

*Charles Stuart Parnell* (1990)
*Oil on canvas, 137 x 56cm*
*Private Collection.*

**John B Keane** *(1993)*
*Oil on canvas. 168 x 92cm*
*Private Collection.*

*Rory Rapple* (1996)
Oil on canvas. 92 x 61cm
Private Collection.

THE BOGMAN

*The Bogman* (1997)
*Oil on canvas. 200 x 122cm*
*Private Collection.*

*An Gorta Mór* (1997)
*Stained Glass Window. 183 x 183cm*
*Collection: Druid's Glen Golf Club.*

188

*Bernadette Devlin* (1998)
*Oil on canvas. 61 x 92cm*
*Collection: Druid's Glen Golf Club.*

**Neil Blaney** *(1998)*
*Oil on canvas. 78 x 155cm*
*Collection: Regional Technical College, Letterkenny, Donegal.*

*The Orchard of Nostalgia* (2000)
*Oil on canvas. 76 x 183cm*
*Private Collection.*

**Micheal Farrell** *(2001)*
*Oil and mixed media. 244 x 152cm*
*Private Collection.*

*Alex Maskey, Lord Mayor of Belfast* (2004)
*Oil on canvas. 137 x 122cm*
*Collection: Belfast City Council.*

**Seán MacReamoinn** *(2004)*
*Oil on canvas. 92 x 62cm*
*Private Collection.*

***Still Crazy After All These Years*** *(2004)*
*Oil on canvas. Diameter 122cm*
*Private Collection.*

***Maurice Cassidy*** *(2005)*
*Oil on canvas. 137 x 137cm*
*Private Collection.*

**J P Donleavy** *(2006)*
*Oil on canvas. 92 x 76cm*
*Private Collection.*

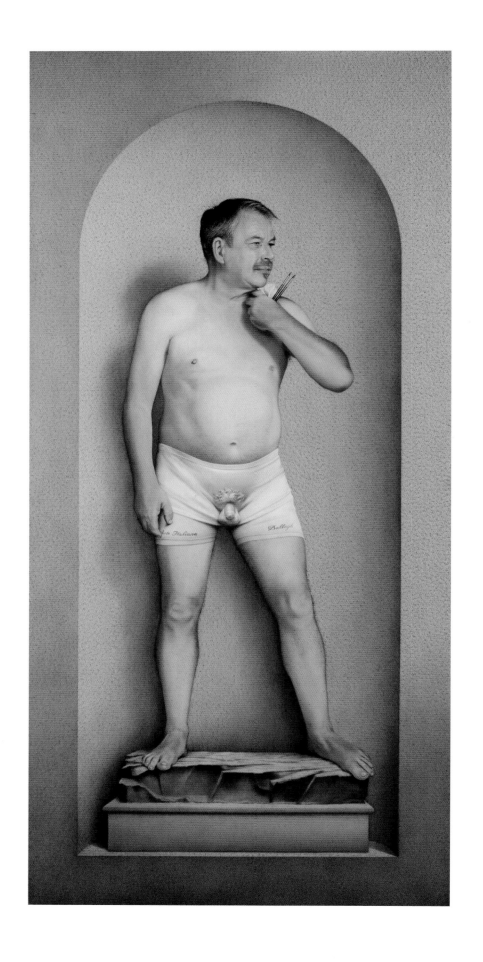

**Self-Portrait in the Italian Style** *(2006)*
*Oil on canvas. 203 x 97cm*
*Private Collection.*

*Louis le Brocquy* (2007)
*Oil on canvas. 152 x 122cm*
*Private Collection.*

**Dermot Desmond** *(2007)*
*Oil on canvas. 62 x 122cm*
*Private Collection.*

**Paul Rattigan** *(2008)*
*Oil on canvas. 122 x 92cm*
*Private Collection.*

**James D Watson** *(2008)*
*Oil on canvas with etched glass. 122 x 122cm*
*Private Collection, on loan to Trinity College, Dublin.*

**Raft of the Medusa** *(2008/09)*
*Acrylic and oil on canvas. 105 x 203cm*
*Private Collection.*

*Fidel Castro* *(2009)*
*Oil on canvas. 183 x 92cm*
*Private Collection.*

**Peter McKenna** *(2010)*
*Oil on canvas. 91 x 66cm*
*Collection: Rotunda Hospital, Dublin.*

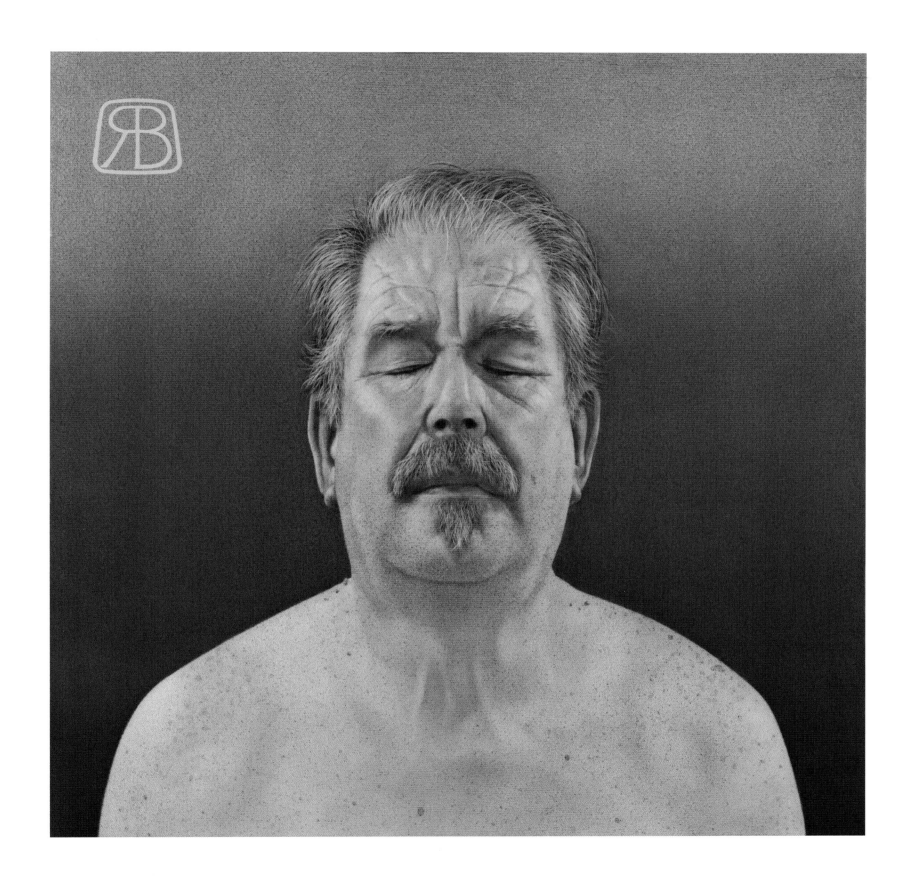

*Self Portrait 1* (2010)
*Oil on canvas. 50 x 50cm*
*Private Collection.*

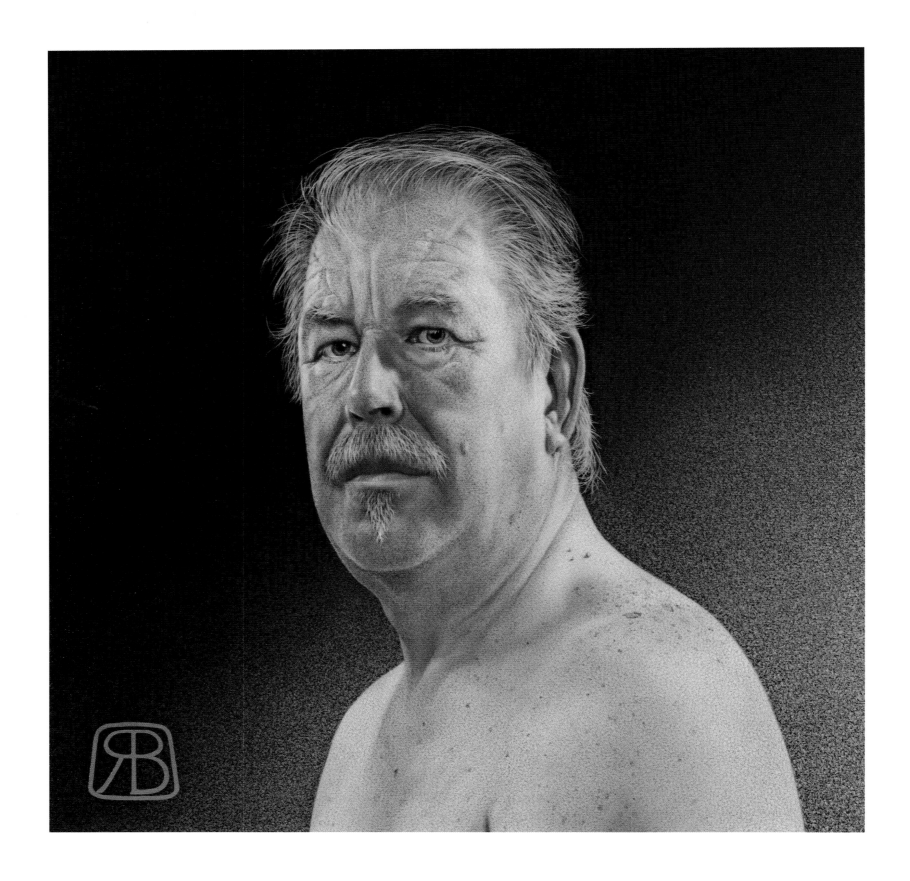

**Self Portrait VIII** *(2010)*
*Oil on canvas. 50 x 50cm*
*Private Collection.*

# Index

# Index

# Index

## Index

# Index

# Index

Artworks photographed by Davison & Associates and Robert Ballagh.